The Complete April Fools' Day RFCs

Compiled by
Thomas A. Limoncelli and Peter H. Salus

Forewords by Mike O'Dell, Scott Bradner, and Brad Templeton

February 27, 2007

The Complete April Fools' Day RFCs

Computer Classics Revisited Series
Series Editor: Peter H. Salus

Published by:
Peer-to-Peer Communications LLC
PO Box 6970
Charlottesville, VA 22906-6970 U.S.A
Website: http://www.peerllc.com
Email: info@peerllc.com

The publisher offers discounts on this book when ordered in bulk quantities.

Cover Design: Thomas A. Limoncelli
Manufactured in the United States of America
1st Edition

ISBN-13: 978-1-57398-042-5

To the Memory of Jon Postel

(1943-1998)

Contents

* indicates RFC is preceeded by commentary.

RFCs In Chronological Order

Page	RFC #	Year	Title
73	2550	1999	Y10K and Beyond
291	2551	1999	The Roman Standards Process – Revision III
373	2555	1999	30 Years of RFCs
87	2795	2000	The Infinite Monkey Protocol Suite (IMPS)
107	3091	2001	Pi Digit Generation Protocol
329	3092	2001	Etymology of "Foo"
113	3093	2001	Firewall Enhancement Protocol (FEP)
125	3251	2002	Electricity over IP
135	3252	2002	Binary Lexical Octet Ad-hoc Transport
273	3271	2002	The Internet is for Everyone
3	3514	2003	The Security Flag in the IPv4 Header (Evil Bit)
347	3751	2004	Omniscience Protocol Requirements
151	4041	2005	Requirements for Morality Sections in Routing Area Drafts
159	4042	2005	UTF-9 and UTF-18 Efficient Transformation Formats of Unicode

Foreword by Mike O'Dell

When the editors of this collection asked me to write a foreword, I was a bit puzzled about how to proceed. This is not your every-day collection of one-liners about bogus protocols and shaggy-packet stories. This is a selection from one of the most important series of technical reports ever published. This is serious stuff!

Ahem.

I had the good fortune to attend university with a Mr. George Mabry, a chap of uncommon perceptiveness and insight, who was given to producing philosophic gems at the oddest moments. My personal favorite is, "You've got to have the proper amount of disrespect for what you do." A marvelous piece of advice pertinent to most endeavors and ignored at your peril.

Luckily, the IETF community manages to abide by Mabry's advice, once a year poking fun at the ponderous officiousness which readily afflicts bodies which don the mantle of Standards Organization. The tradition of the April Fools' RFCs is one way the community manages to inject a bit of levity and "disrespect" into work which is both intellectually demanding and tends to be pedantically focused on small details. A hearty laugh is much needed every so often.

One of the more interesting things about the RFC series in general, and the April Fools' RFCs more specifically, is the overall quality of the writing. The usual engineer stereotype does not normally include facility with English nor a sparkling wit. Granted, some of the April Fools' RFCs are very much inside jokes requiring significant context to appreciate, but most of them are readily accessible and satisfying. Some of them are prose poking fun at the writing of specifications, and some of them are poems, both original and otherwise. Some of the humor is subtle, and some of it reflects a penchant for dreadful punmanship. There's even a limerick or two (in RFC 1121).

Interestingly, sometimes the author's tone and intent is ambiguous: is he making light of something, or is he making a point with a painful truth? As Mary Poppins intoned, "A spoonful of sugar helps the medicine go down."

What you will find in this collection is a real slice-of-life from the IETF community. After all, the IETF is a community of people, and connecting people is what it's all about. The evolutionary biological history of this incredible experiment called "The Internet" is recorded in the RFC series—it's our version of the fossil record. The difference is that with the RFC series, every so often there's a pair of "Groucho Glasses" there in the rock.

[Mike O'Dell received his BS and MS in Computer Science from the University of Oklahoma. In the halcyon days of the ARPAnet, he was "Liaison" for IMP-34 at Lawrence Berkeley Laboratory and spearheaded the transition from NCP to TCP/IP at Department of Energy National Laboratories. Mike served four years as Area Director for Operations and Management in the IETF, authored several IDs and RFCs, and helped birth RADIUS and SNMPv3. He was one of the two founders of UUNET.]

Foreword by Scott Bradner

The best April Fools' Day RFCs reveal truth by telling a lie.

I do not know what caused Jon Postel to decide to publish Mark Crispin's "Telnet randomly-lose option" as an RFC [748] but once he decided to publish it, I expect that Jon knew just when to publish it. Publication on any day of the year other than April 1st would have been very confusing indeed. This RFC set the model for many April 1st RFCs to come – play it straight but describe something that could not or should not be done.

But it would be more than a decade before another one would be published, this one also dealing with Telnet. Maybe everyone was too seriously working on getting this internetworking stuff right to fiddle around. I guess IETFers starting getting less uptight as the Internet boom slowly ramped up because April 1st RFCs (i.e. those where the publication date was germane, other RFCs were published on April 1st which are not thought to be jokes such as ICMP [RFC 777]) started showing up regularly since 1990. Not every year, but most.

I've been the butt of one April 1stRFC (RFC 2323), contributed to a few and authored or co-authored three (RFCs 1551, 3093 and 3751). There were other attempts that did not see the light of day, and probably should not have.

The hardest part of writing an April 1st RFC about technology is to follow Crispin's lead to make the document look "real" – play it straight . Talk about something wacko but play it straight . If no one thinks that the RFC describes something real then in some way you have failed. I take pride in the fact that about half of the many comments I received about each of the last two April 1st RFCs I've been involved in thought that I was serious. People wanted implementations of the Firewall Enhancement Protocol (RFC 3093) or wanted to chastise me for supporting Orin Hatch's desires to destroy evil doers' computers by proposing a Omniscience Protocol (RFC 3751). The latter even got slashdotted! Most often a simple return email suggesting that the reader look at the publication date was enough to cause them to go away (sometimes with a message of embarrassment or annoyance) but a few people did not understand and more explanation was needed. (Though I am told that there are implementations of RFC 3093 available.)

While not Swiftian in their importance, reading between the lines of the RFCs in this collection reveal truths behind the IETF's approach to network and device management, approach to security, the usefulness of firewalls, and of MPLS, about IPv6 addressing, email formats, XML and of transporting IP over everything. Some of the truths might sting a touch, and that is a good thing.

[Scott Bradner is University Technology Security Officer at Harvard University and writes a weekly column for *Network World*.]

Foreword by Brad Templeton

Network Working Group   B Templeton
Request for Levity: 0001   netfunny.com

                        A standard for perspective

Status of this Memo

   This memo prefaces a collection of Requests for Comment (RFCs)
   published by the Internet Engineering Task Force (IETF). This
   collection is primarily useful for amusement. These protocols are
   experimental and adoption is not recommended. Distribution of this
   memo is encouraged.

Overview and Rationale

   Let's face it, a lot of what goes on in IETF working groups,
   designing protocols and standards, is pretty dry stuff. When it's
   not dry, it's often inflammatory. Still, Internet designers and
   users have considered the transmission of comedy to be one of the
   net's primary purposes since its earliest days.

   Today, most e-mail users are all-too-familiar with how a joke can
   suddenly sweep the net, being forwarded to you multiple times by all
   your friends. (It's even scarier when people try to forward around
   funny attachments, teaching people bad virus hygiene.)

   From the earliest days of the Arpanet and USENET, "official"
   locations appeared for sharing new and not-so-new jokes. But there
   was one truly official place that satire and comedy appeared, as
   April 1st entries in the Internet standards known as RFCs.

   The term "RFC" stands for "Request for Comment." In the early days,
   it actually meant that -- somebody was publishing a proposal and

wanted people to comment on it. Today when something "becomes an RFC" it ironically means that the comment phase is effectively over.

RFCs are issued regularly by the Internet Engineering Task Force, but each April 1, one or two satirical RFCs will appear. Amazingly, each year, people forget to check the date and take even the most audacious proposals seriously.

The tradition really got going with RFC 1149, which you will find early in this collection, the standard for the transmission of IP datagrams over avian carriers. Later, my personal favourite RFC 1217 provided a more robust protocol.

I'll admit, some of the documents in this collection are only going to make sense to you if you're a dyed-in-the-wool network engineer. Others can be appreciated by anybody.

Either way, dive in.

Intellectual Property

See the copyright page of this book.

References

See table of contents

Security Considerations

If you can't laugh at these proposals, you may wish to examine your own insecurities.

Author's Address

Brad Templeton
netfunny.com

EMail: btm@templetons.com

[Brad Templeton founded ClariNet Communications Corp (the world's first "dot-com.") He also created and publishes rec.humor.funny, the most widely read USENET newsgroup and its web site, www.netfunny.com. He is currently chairman of the Electronic Frontier Foundation (EFF), the leading cyberspace civil rights foundation.]

Preface

How does the Internet work? What makes telnet, telnet? What bits are sent down the wire to make an HTTP session? How does email (SMTP) flow? What makes POP3 pop?

It's all described in a series of documents called Requests For Comment (RFCs). You can read them all on `http://www.ietf.org`

RFCs are typically written by individuals or committees of the Internet Engineering Task Force (IETF) which submits them to the RFC editor. They then flow through a well-defined process of approvals until they become standards.

Other standardization committees are serious and formal. Imagine the technical equivalent of diplomats meeting to agree to an arms reduction treaty, except instead they discuss how many bits wide a field should be.

The formality is extreme. Tuxedos are required to attend meetings of the ITU-T, the telecommunications sub-committee of ITU, the International Telecommunications Union. The ITU-T was previously known as CCITT or Comité Consultatif International Télégraphique et Téléphonique since it was the French's turn to run meetings on the date the name was picked. Competing with the Internet protocol was the Open Systems Interconnect (OSI) protocol from the ISO: the International Organization for Standardization. One would assume their acronym would be I-O-S but, alas, it is I-S-O. ISO requires all acronyms to be acceptable to speakers of English, French and Russian. I-O-S wouldn't be acceptable to Russians because if you transliterate I-O-S into the nearest Russian letters and say them out loud it sounds similar to, well, a very dirty word. It must be true; I read it on the internet once.

The ITU-T's goal is to make complicated standards that maintain a barrier to entry so-as not to threaten the international telecom oligarchy. The ISO OSI project tried to do the same for data communication.

Then came along the IETF: The long-haired hippies of the protocol world. They broke all the rules. No membership fee to keep out the riff-raff: you are a member by virtue of subscribing to a committee's email list. No exorbitant fee to get a copy of a standard: the standards are available for free on an FTP server open to everyone. And what's this? The standard documents are readable? Understandable? With clear examples? My god, if anyone will be able to implement a protocol how would companies be able to charge enough money to make back their costs? Costs such as the high fee to join the organization or request printed copies of the protocol! What? They often give the software away for free? Well that's just udder nonsense! (Can you understand why the ISO world always considered the Internet to be a passing fad?)

Why are the IETF's standard documents called Request For Comments? Crocker, who wrote the first RFC, explained the issue in RFC 1000 [August 1987] in a section called The Origins of the RFCs:

... Most of us were graduate students and we expected that a professional crew would show up eventually to take over the problems we were dealing with. Without clear definition of what the host-IMP interface would look like, or even what functions the IMP would provide, we focused on exotic ideas. We envisioned the possibility of application specific protocols, with code downloaded to user sites, and we took a crack at designing a language to support this. The first version was known as DEL, for 'Decode-Encode Language' and a later version was called NIL, for 'Network Interchange Language.' When the IMP contract was finally let and BBN provided some definite information on the host-IMP interface, all attention shifted to low-level matters and the ambitious ideas for automatic downloading of code evaporated. It was several years before ideas like remote procedure calls and typed objects reappeared.

In February of 1969 we met for the first time with BBN. I don't think any of us were prepared for that meeting. The BBN folks, led by Frank Heart, Bob Kahn, Severo Ornstein and Will Crowther, found themselves talking to a crew of graduate students they hadn't anticipated. And we found ourselves talking to people whose first concern was how to get bits to flow quickly and reliably but hadn't – of course – spent any time considering the thirty or forty layers of protocol above the link level. And while BBN didn't take over the protocol design process, we kept expecting that an official protocol design team would announce itself.

A month later, after a particularly delightful meeting in Utah, it became clear to us that we had better start writing down our discussions. We had accumulated a few notes on the design of DEL and other matters, and we decided to put them together in a set of notes. I remember having great fear that we would offend whomever the official protocol designers were, and I spent a sleepless night composing humble words for our notes. The basic ground rules were that anyone could say anything and that nothing was official. And to emphasize the point, I labeled the notes Request for Comments. I never dreamed these notes would distributed through the very medium we were discussing in these notes. Talk about Sorcerer's Apprentice!

That was it. The RFCs were ad hoc, spontaneous, useful.

As we write this, there are over 4000 RFCs (Requests for Comment). RFC 1, *Host Software*, is dated April 7, 1969. Among other things it provides for 5-bit IP addresses. We've come a long way.

By 1973, only a few years later, the first April Fools' RFC appeared. Eventually it became a yearly tradition. Some years multiple April Fools' RFCs are released. Sometimes they offer commentary on current IETF politics, sometimes on Internet culture, or even national or international politics. If anyone from the humorless world of ITU-T or ISO world knew or cared they would be shocked!

April Fools' RFCs were published every year from 1989 to 2005. None were published in 2006, though it was announced that Bert from Sesame Street had been appointed to the Internet Architecture Board.

It has been said that a joke that needs to be explained isn't funny. Therefore, we apologize. What jokes would require more explanation than a new MIME-type for transporting matter or the Hyper Text Coffee Pot Control Protocol? If one needs to explain RFC 1149, *IP over Avian Carriers*, then what's the point at explaining RFC 2549, which adds QoS?

Of course, in jokes never need to be explained to insiders. So maybe this book is really a test of your status as a part of the Internet technical community. Congratulations and welcome to the club!

Enjoy!

TAL & PHS

http://www.rfc-humor.com

Acknowledgements

We would like to thank all the authors of all the RFCs included in this book. Thanks to the IETF and The Internet Society for permission to reprint RFCs in their complete and unaltered form. We wish we had time to contact all the authors to personally thank them but most contact information contained within is no longer valid.

Thanks to Steve Bellovin for his notes about the reaction to RFC 2549.

Thanks to the authors of our three forewords. Pessimistic that anyone would have the time to write a foreword for such a foolish project we asked them all in parallel assuming they'd all reject our request. Instead we got an embarassment of riches: three excellent forewords. We choose to publish them all.

We would also like to thank our families for putting up with our long hours and stress as we brought this book to reality.

About The Compilers

Thomas A. Limoncelli:

Thomas Limoncelli is an internationally recognized author and speaker on many topics including system administration, time management, and grass-roots organizing. A system administrator since 1988, he has worked for small and large companies including Google, Cibernet, Lumeta, AT&T, Lucent / Bell Labs. He has written three books: two editions of *The Practice of System and Network Administration* from Addison-Wesley (2001, 2007) and *Time Management for System Administrators* from O'Reilly (2005). He shared SAGE's *Outstanding Achievement Award* in 2005. He holds a B.A. in C.S. from Drew University, Madison, New Jersey, USA. His web site and blog is `http://www.EverythingSysadmin.com`

Peter H. Salus:

Dr. Peter H. Salus talks too much and writes too much. He is a frequent speaker at computer events in the US, Canada, the UK, the Netherlands, Belgium, Russia, Australia, Finland, Denmark, Brazil, Chile, and the Czech Republic. He has appeared on the BBC, the Discovery Channel, PBS, PCTV, and the Dr. Dobbs webcast as computing and networking historian. Dr. Salus has written or edited over a dozen books, including *A Quarter Century of UNIX*, *Casting the Net: From ARPANET to INTERNET and Beyond*, the four-volume *Handbook of Programming Languages*, and the *Big Book of IPv6 Addressing RFCs*.

Part I

The Very Best

Introduction to RFC 3514:

Steve Bellovin's April Fools' Day RFC is so good that some readers didn't realize that it was a joke. It concerns what might be considered the "evil bit," a new flag for IP packets that would indicate that the packet was evil. Security would be made easier by simply dropping those packets.

Bellovin received email and even phone calls from many readers. Most people enjoyed the joke. The FreeBSD community responded by a funny claim that they had implemented it (see `http://www.research.att.com/~smb/3514.html`).

Bellovin has anonymized some messages and permitted us to have them. Bellovin remarks that one particular note was "a bit worrisome..."

```
Good day sir. Nice contribution for this April 1st.

But your jest, were there a reserved bit that
actually could be used, could actually have merit
to address a concern on the part of major content
providers about internet redistribution of
broadcasters' content.

So, you may see this again.... Happy April Fools' Day.
```

Bellovin notes "But some people didn't quite get it..."

```
Is Request for Comments 3514 an April Fools' day joke?
I'm trying to convince my colleague here that it is,
and I thought I'd go straight to the source for the
answer.

Thanks,

(deleted)
Senior Network Administrator
```

and

```
You've gotta be kidding me. I didn't think that
there would ever be a false RFC....Well, that just
proves what I said in the first place: I don't
know enough about the internet.
```

and this was our favorite

Good Afternoon,

What or who determines the "evilness" or "goodness"
of the packet? If a security admin or OS can
determine or flag bits as good, what keeps the
hacker from spoofing this process by setting the
bit to "good"? Does the bit change based on
behavior? Or maybe a database with signatures of
"bad" bits?

(name deleted)
Microsoft Corporation

Bellovin received an important response where RFC 2549 was concerned:

Hi,

In RFC 3514 you don't appear to discuss the
conditions that will cause the so called evil bit
to be set.

This may be considered a serious deficiency in your
proposal.

However, if we combine RFC 3514 with RFC 2549
(which updated RFC 1149), then a carrier with
suitable conditioning can be made to detect evil
intent and set the bit accordingly.

Another variation of 2549, using a K9 carrier can
be made particularly effective by biting the
attacker as well as setting the evil bit.

Network Working Group   S. Bellovin
Request for Comments: 3514   AT&T Labs Research
Category: Informational   1 April 2003

                 The Security Flag in the IPv4 Header

Status of this Memo

   This memo provides information for the Internet community. It does
   not specify an Internet standard of any kind. Distribution of this
   memo is unlimited.

Abstract

   Firewalls, packet filters, intrusion detection systems, and the like
   often have difficulty distinguishing between packets that have
   malicious intent and those that are merely unusual. We define a
   security flag in the IPv4 header as a means of distinguishing the two
   cases.

1. Introduction

   Firewalls [CBR03], packet filters, intrusion detection systems, and
   the like often have difficulty distinguishing between packets that
   have malicious intent and those that are merely unusual. The problem
   is that making such determinations is hard. To solve this problem,
   we define a security flag, known as the "evil" bit, in the IPv4
   [RFC791] header. Benign packets have this bit set to 0; those that
   are used for an attack will have the bit set to 1.

1.1. Terminology

   The keywords MUST, MUST NOT, REQUIRED, SHALL, SHALL NOT, SHOULD,
   SHOULD NOT, RECOMMENDED, MAY, and OPTIONAL, when they appear in this
   document, are to be interpreted as described in [RFC2119].

2. Syntax

   The high-order bit of the IP fragment offset field is the only unused
   bit in the IP header. Accordingly, the selection of the bit position
   is not left to IANA.

5

The bit field is laid out as follows:

```
    0
   +-+
   |E|
   +-+
```

Currently-assigned values are defined as follows:

0x0 If the bit is set to 0, the packet has no evil intent. Hosts,
     network elements, etc., SHOULD assume that the packet is
     harmless, and SHOULD NOT take any defensive measures. (We note
     that this part of the spec is already implemented by many common
     desktop operating systems.)

0x1 If the bit is set to 1, the packet has evil intent. Secure
     systems SHOULD try to defend themselves against such packets.
     Insecure systems MAY chose to crash, be penetrated, etc.

3. Setting the Evil Bit

   There are a number of ways in which the evil bit may be set. Attack
   applications may use a suitable API to request that it be set.
   Systems that do not have other mechanisms MUST provide such an API;
   attack programs MUST use it.

   Multi-level insecure operating systems may have special levels for
   attack programs; the evil bit MUST be set by default on packets
   emanating from programs running at such levels. However, the system
   MAY provide an API to allow it to be cleared for non-malicious
   activity by users who normally engage in attack behavior.

   Fragments that by themselves are dangerous MUST have the evil bit
   set. If a packet with the evil bit set is fragmented by an
   intermediate router and the fragments themselves are not dangerous,
   the evil bit MUST be cleared in the fragments, and MUST be turned
   back on in the reassembled packet.

   Intermediate systems are sometimes used to launder attack
   connections. Packets to such systems that are intended to be relayed
   to a target SHOULD have the evil bit set.

   Some applications hand-craft their own packets. If these packets are
   part of an attack, the application MUST set the evil bit by itself.

   In networks protected by firewalls, it is axiomatic that all
   attackers are on the outside of the firewall. Therefore, hosts
   inside the firewall MUST NOT set the evil bit on any packets.

Because NAT [RFC3022] boxes modify packets, they SHOULD set the evil
bit on such packets. "Transparent" http and email proxies SHOULD set
the evil bit on their reply packets to the innocent client host.

Some hosts scan other hosts in a fashion that can alert intrusion
detection systems. If the scanning is part of a benign research
project, the evil bit MUST NOT be set. If the scanning per se is
innocent, but the ultimate intent is evil and the destination site
has such an intrusion detection system, the evil bit SHOULD be set.

4. Processing of the Evil Bit

Devices such as firewalls MUST drop all inbound packets that have the
evil bit set. Packets with the evil bit off MUST NOT be dropped.
Dropped packets SHOULD be noted in the appropriate MIB variable.

Intrusion detection systems (IDSs) have a harder problem. Because of
their known propensity for false negatives and false positives, IDSs
MUST apply a probabilistic correction factor when evaluating the evil
bit. If the evil bit is set, a suitable random number generator
[RFC1750] must be consulted to determine if the attempt should be
logged. Similarly, if the bit is off, another random number
generator must be consulted to determine if it should be logged
despite the setting.

The default probabilities for these tests depends on the type of IDS.
Thus, a signature-based IDS would have a low false positive value but
a high false negative value. A suitable administrative interface
MUST be provided to permit operators to reset these values.

Routers that are not intended as as security devices SHOULD NOT
examine this bit. This will allow them to pass packets at higher
speeds.

As outlined earlier, host processing of evil packets is operating-
system dependent; however, all hosts MUST react appropriately
according to their nature.

5. Related Work

Although this document only defines the IPv4 evil bit, there are
complementary mechanisms for other forms of evil. We sketch some of
those here.

For IPv6 [RFC2460], evilness is conveyed by two options. The first,
a hop-by-hop option, is used for packets that damage the network,
such as DDoS packets. The second, an end-to-end option, is for
packets intended to damage destination hosts. In either case, the

option contains a 128-bit strength indicator, which says how evil the packet is, and a 128-bit type code that describes the particular type of attack intended.

Some link layers, notably those based on optical switching, may bypass routers (and hence firewalls) entirely. Accordingly, some link-layer scheme MUST be used to denote evil. This may involve evil lambdas, evil polarizations, etc.

DDoS attack packets are denoted by a special diffserv code point.

An application/evil MIME type is defined for Web- or email-carried mischief. Other MIME types can be embedded inside of evil sections; this permit easy encoding of word processing documents with macro viruses, etc.

6. IANA Considerations

This document defines the behavior of security elements for the 0x0 and 0x1 values of this bit. Behavior for other values of the bit may be defined only by IETF consensus [RFC2434].

7. Security Considerations

Correct functioning of security mechanisms depend critically on the evil bit being set properly. If faulty components do not set the evil bit to 1 when appropriate, firewalls will not be able to do their jobs properly. Similarly, if the bit is set to 1 when it shouldn't be, a denial of service condition may occur.

8. References

[CBR03]   W.R. Cheswick, S.M. Bellovin, and A.D. Rubin, "Firewalls and Internet Security: Repelling the Wily Hacker", Second Edition, Addison-Wesley, 2003.

[RFC791]   Postel, J., "Internet Protocol", STD 5, RFC 791, September 1981.

[RFC1750] Eastlake, D., 3rd, Crocker, S. and J. Schiller, "Randomness Recommendations for Security", RFC 1750, December 1994.

[RFC2119] Bradner, S., "Key words for use in RFCs to Indicate Requirement Levels", BCP 14, RFC 2119, March 1997.

[RFC2434] Narten, T. and H. Alvestrand, "Guidelines for Writing an IANA Considerations Section in RFCs", BCP 26, RFC 2434, October 1998.

   [RFC2460] Deering, S. and R. Hinden, "Internet Protocol, Version 6
              (IPv6) Specification", RFC 2460, December 1998.

   [RFC3022] Srisuresh, P. and K. Egevang, "Traditional IP Network
              Address Translator (Traditional NAT)", RFC 3022, January
              2001.

9. Author's Address

   Steven M. Bellovin
   AT&T Labs Research
   Shannon Laboratory
   180 Park Avenue
   Florham Park, NJ 07932

   Phone: +1 973-360-8656
   EMail: bellovin@acm.org

9

10. Full Copyright Statement

Acknowledgement

Funding for the RFC Editor function is currently provided by the
Internet Society.

Introduction to RFC 1149:

We have long assumed that packets are conveyed via copper or fiber optic cables. But is that required? Fifteen years ago, David Waitzman supplied us with an answer in RFC 1149, *Standard for the transmission of IP datagrams on Avian Carriers.*

Nine years later he refined that answer in RFC 2549, *IP over Avian Carriers with Quality of Service.*

These RFCs were successfully implemented on Saturday, April 18, 2001 by an industrious group from the BLUG (Bergen [BSD and] Linux User Group) in Norway. Information and pictures are available here:

```
http://www.blug.linux.no/rfc1149
```

The pinglog of the session is quite revealing:

```
Script started on Sat Apr 28 11:24:09 2001
vegard@gyversalen:~$ /sbin/ifconfig tun0
tun0      Link encap:Point-to-Point Protocol
          inet addr:10.0.3.2  P-t-P:10.0.3.1  Mask:255.255.255.255
          UP POINTOPOINT RUNNING NOARP MULTICAST  MTU:150  Metric:1
          RX packets:1 errors:0 dropped:0 overruns:0 frame:0
          TX packets:2 errors:0 dropped:0 overruns:0 carrier:0
          collisions:0
          RX bytes:88 (88.0 b)  TX bytes:168 (168.0 b)

vegard@gyversalen:~$ ping -i 900 10.0.3.1
PING 10.0.3.1 (10.0.3.1): 56 data bytes
64 bytes from 10.0.3.1: icmp_seq=0 ttl=255 time=6165731.1 ms
64 bytes from 10.0.3.1: icmp_seq=4 ttl=255 time=3211900.8 ms
64 bytes from 10.0.3.1: icmp_seq=2 ttl=255 time=5124922.8 ms
64 bytes from 10.0.3.1: icmp_seq=1 ttl=255 time=6388671.9 ms

--- 10.0.3.1 ping statistics ---
9 packets transmitted, 4 packets received, 55% packet loss
round-trip min/avg/max = 3211900.8/5222806.6/6388671.9 ms
vegard@gyversalen:~$ exit

Script done on Sat Apr 28 14:14:28 2001
```

Network Working Group   D. Waitzman
Request for Comments: 1149   BBN STC
                                                              1 April 1990

       A Standard for the Transmission of IP Datagrams on Avian Carriers

Status of this Memo

   This memo describes an experimental method for the encapsulation of
   IP datagrams in avian carriers. This specification is primarily
   useful in Metropolitan Area Networks. This is an experimental, not
   recommended standard. Distribution of this memo is unlimited.

Overview and Rational

   Avian carriers can provide high delay, low throughput, and low
   altitude service. The connection topology is limited to a single
   point-to-point path for each carrier, used with standard carriers,
   but many carriers can be used without significant interference with
   each other, outside of early spring. This is because of the 3D ether
   space available to the carriers, in contrast to the 1D ether used by
   IEEE802.3. The carriers have an intrinsic collision avoidance
   system, which increases availability. Unlike some network
   technologies, such as packet radio, communication is not limited to
   line-of-sight distance. Connection oriented service is available in
   some cities, usually based upon a central hub topology.

Frame Format

   The IP datagram is printed, on a small scroll of paper, in
   hexadecimal, with each octet separated by whitestuff and blackstuff.
   The scroll of paper is wrapped around one leg of the avian carrier.
   A band of duct tape is used to secure the datagram's edges. The
   bandwidth is limited to the leg length. The MTU is variable, and
   paradoxically, generally increases with increased carrier age. A
   typical MTU is 256 milligrams. Some datagram padding may be needed.

   Upon receipt, the duct tape is removed and the paper copy of the
   datagram is optically scanned into a electronically transmittable
   form.

Discussion

   Multiple types of service can be provided with a prioritized pecking
   order. An additional property is built-in worm detection and
   eradication. Because IP only guarantees best effort delivery, loss
   of a carrier can be tolerated. With time, the carriers are self-

regenerating. While broadcasting is not specified, storms can cause
data loss. There is persistent delivery retry, until the carrier
drops. Audit trails are automatically generated, and can often be
found on logs and cable trays.

Security Considerations

    Security is not generally a problem in normal operation, but special
    measures must be taken (such as data encryption) when avian carriers
    are used in a tactical environment.

Author's Address

    David Waitzman
    BBN Systems and Technologies Corporation
    BBN Labs Division
    10 Moulton Street
    Cambridge, MA 02238

    Phone: (617) 873-4323

    EMail: dwaitzman@BBN.COM

Network Working Group   D. Waitzman
Request for Comments: 2549   IronBridge Networks
Updates: 1149   1 April 1999
Category: Experimental

            IP over Avian Carriers with Quality of Service

Status of this Memo

    This memo defines an Experimental Protocol for the Internet
    community. It does not specify an Internet standard of any kind.
    Discussion and suggestions for improvement are requested.
    Distribution of this memo is unlimited.

Abstract

    This memo amends RFC 1149, "A Standard for the Transmission of IP
    Datagrams on Avian Carriers", with Quality of Service information.
    This is an experimental, not recommended standard.

Overview and Rational

    The following quality of service levels are available: Concorde,
    First, Business, and Coach. Concorde class offers expedited data
    delivery. One major benefit to using Avian Carriers is that this is
    the only networking technology that earns frequent flyer miles, plus
    the Concorde and First classes of service earn 50% bonus miles per
    packet. Ostriches are an alternate carrier that have much greater
    bulk transfer capability but provide slower delivery, and require the
    use of bridges between domains.

    The service level is indicated on a per-carrier basis by bar-code
    markings on the wing. One implementation strategy is for a bar-code
    reader to scan each carrier as it enters the router and then enqueue
    it in the proper queue, gated to prevent exit until the proper time.
    The carriers may sleep while enqueued.

    For secure networks, carriers may have classes Prime or Choice.
    Prime carriers are self-keying when using public key encryption.
    Some distributors have been known to falsely classify Choice carriers
    as Prime.

    Packets MAY be marked for deletion using RED paint while enqueued.

Weighted fair queueing (WFQ) MAY be implemented using scales, as
shown:

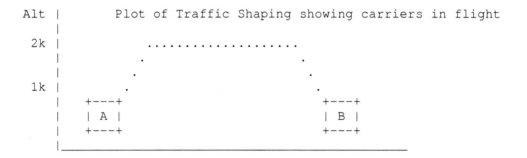

Carriers in the queue too long may leave log entries, as shown on the
scale.

The following is a plot of traffic shaping, from coop-erative host
sites.

```
   Alt |            Plot of Traffic Shaping showing carriers in flight
       |
    2k |              ....................
       |          .                        .
       |        .                            .
    1k |      .                            .
       |    +---+                        +---+
       |    | A |                        | B |
       |    +---+                        +---+
       |_____
```

Avian carriers normally bypass bridges and tunnels but will seek out
worm hole tunnels. When carrying web traffic, the carriers may
digest the spiders, leaving behind a more compact representation.
The carriers may be confused by mirrors.

Round-robin queueing is not recommended. Robins make for well-tuned
networks but do not support the necessary auto-homing feature.

A BOF was held at the last IETF but only Avian Carriers were allowed
entry, so we don't know the results other than we're sure they think
MPLS is great. Our attempts at attaching labels to the carriers have
been met with resistance.

NATs are not recommended either -- as with many protocols, modifying the brain-embedded IP addresses is difficult, plus Avian Carriers MAY eat the NATs.

Encapsulation may be done with saran wrappers. Unintentional encapsulation in hawks has been known to occur, with decapsulation being messy and the packets mangled.

Loose source routes are a viable evolutionary alternative enhanced standards-based MSWindows-compliant technology, but strict source routes MUST NOT be used, as they are a choke-point.

The ITU has offered the IETF formal alignment with its corresponding technology, Penguins, but that won't fly.

Multicasting is supported, but requires the implementation of a clone device. Carriers may be lost if they are based on a tree as it is being pruned. The carriers propagate via an inheritance tree. The carriers have an average TTL of 15 years, so their use in expanding ring searches is limited.

Additional quality of service discussion can be found in a Michelin's guide.

MIB and Management issues

```
AvCarrier2 OBJECT-TYPE
   SYNTAX      SEQUENCE OF DNA
   MAX-ACCESS can't-read
   STATUS     living
   DESCRIPTION "Definition of an avian carrier"
   ::= { life eukaryotes mitochondrial_eukaryotes crown_eukaryotes
       metazoa chordata craniata vertebrata gnathostomata
       sarcopterygii terrestrial_vertebrates amniota diapsida
       archosauromorpha archosauria dinosauria aves neornithes
       columbiformes columbidae columba livia }

AvCarrier OBJECT-TYPE
   SYNTAX      SET OF Cells
   MAX-ACCESS not-accessible
   STATUS     obsolete
   DESCRIPTION "Definition of an avian carrier"
   ::= { life animalia chordata vertebrata aves
       columbiformes columbidae columba livia }

PulseRate OBJECT-TYPE
   SYNTAX      Gauge(0..300)
   MAX-ACCESS read-only
```

17

```
        STATUS       current
        DESCRIPTION "Pulse rate of carrier, as measured in neck.
                     Frequent sampling is disruptive to operations."
        ::= { AvCarrier 1}
```

The carriers will not line up in lexigraphic order but will
naturally order in a large V shape. Bulk retrieval is possible
using the Powerful Get-Net operator.

Specification of Requirements

In this document, several words are used to signify the requirements
of the specification. These words are often capitalized.

MUST   Usually.

MUST NOT   Usually not.

SHOULD   Only when Marketing insists.

MAY   Only if it doesn't cost extra.

Security Considerations

There are privacy issues with stool pigeons.

Agoraphobic carriers are very insecure in operation.

Patent Considerations

There is ongoing litigation about which is the prior art: carrier or
egg.

References

Waitzman, D., "A Standard for the Transmission of IP Datagrams on
Avian Carriers", RFC 1149, 1 April 1990.

ACKnowledgments

Jim.Carlson.Ibnets.com > Jon.Saperia . ack 32 win 123 (DF)
Ross Callon, Scott Bradner, Charlie Lynn ...

Author's Address

    David Waitzman
    IronBridge Networks
    55 Hayden Ave
    Lexington, MA 02421
    Phone: (781) 372-8161

    EMail: djw@vineyard.net

Full Copyright Statement

20

Network Working Group   R. Callon, Editor
Request for Comments: 1925   IOOF
Category: Informational   1 April 1996

The Twelve Networking Truths

Status of this Memo

Abstract

   This memo documents the fundamental truths of networking for the
   Internet community. This memo does not specify a standard, except in
   the sense that all standards must implicitly follow the fundamental
   truths.

Acknowledgements

   The truths described in this memo result from extensive study over an
   extended period of time by many people, some of whom did not intend
   to contribute to this work. The editor merely has collected these
   truths, and would like to thank the networking community for
   originally illuminating these truths.

1. Introduction

   This Request for Comments (RFC) provides information about the
   fundamental truths underlying all networking. These truths apply to
   networking in general, and are not limited to TCP/IP, the Internet,
   or any other subset of the networking community.

2. The Fundamental Truths

   (1) It Has To Work.

   (2) No matter how hard you push and no matter what the priority,
        you can't increase the speed of light.

        (2a) (corollary). No matter how hard you try, you can't make a
             baby in much less than 9 months. Trying to speed this up
             might make it slower, but it won't make it happen any
             quicker.

21

(3) With sufficient thrust, pigs fly just fine. However, this is
     not necessarily a good idea. It is hard to be sure where they
     are going to land, and it could be dangerous sitting under them
     as they fly overhead.

(4) Some things in life can never be fully appreciated nor
     understood unless experienced firsthand. Some things in
     networking can never be fully understood by someone who neither
     builds commercial networking equipment nor runs an operational
     network.

(5) It is always possible to aglutenate multiple separate problems
     into a single complex interdependent solution. In most cases
     this is a bad idea.

(6) It is easier to move a problem around (for example, by moving
     the problem to a different part of the overall network
     architecture) than it is to solve it.

     (6a) (corollary). It is always possible to add another level of
          indirection.

(7) It is always something

     (7a) (corollary). Good, Fast, Cheap: Pick any two (you can't
          have all three).

(8) It is more complicated than you think.

(9) For all resources, whatever it is, you need more.

     (9a) (corollary) Every networking problem always takes longer to
          solve than it seems like it should.

(10) One size never fits all.

(11) Every old idea will be proposed again with a different name and
     a different presentation, regardless of whether it works.

     (11a) (corollary). See rule 6a.

(12) In protocol design, perfection has been reached not when there
     is nothing left to add, but when there is nothing left to take
     away.

Security Considerations

   This RFC raises no security issues. However, security protocols are
   subject to the fundamental networking truths.

References

   The references have been deleted in order to protect the guilty and
   avoid enriching the lawyers.

Author's Address

   Ross Callon
   Internet Order of Old Farts
   c/o Bay Networks
   3 Federal Street
   Billerica, MA 01821

   Phone: 508-436-3936
   EMail: rcallon@baynetworks.com

Network Working Group   A. Bressen
Request for Comments: 2321   Cohesive Network Systems
Category: Informational   1 April 1998

RITA -- The Reliable Internetwork Troubleshooting Agent

Status of this Memo

Copyright Notice

Abstract

   A Description of the usage of Nondeterministic Troubleshooting and
   Diagnostic Methodologies as applied to today's complex
   nondeterministic networks and environments.

1. Introduction

   Increasingly, IETF efforts have been devoted to aiding network
   management, troubleshooting, and diagnosis. Results have included
   SNMP, cflowd, and RMON, and ongoing projects at the time of this
   writing include Universal Logging Protocol and Distributed
   Management. These tools work well within the horizon of
   deterministic situations in which the configuration of the network or
   relevant components is known or can be relatively easily determined.
   They do not well address many problems that are related to the
   complex internetworks we have today, such as:

     o Networks where the root bridge for a world-wide bridged
        network is suboptimally located, such as under the desk of a
        secretary who kicks off her shoes when she arrives in the
        morning.
     o Networks where a hub is located adjacent to a monitor that
        emits disruptive RF when displaying certain graphics.
     o Networks where an ISP and several of their customers use
        network 10.0.0.0 internally and do not hide RIP broadcasts from
        one another.
     o Networks where gateways are data-sensitive
     o Networks where vendors inadvertently ship units with
        duplicate MAC addresses to the same end-user or where all users
        have a tool for changing MAC addresses.

In this document we introduce a new hardware-based tool for diagnosis
and repair of network related hardware and software problems. This
tool is best suited to addressing nondeterministic problems such as
those described above. This tool has broad areas of application at
all levels of the OSI model; in addition to uses in the physical,
network, transport and application layers, it has been used to
successfully address problems at the political and religious layers
as well. RITA, the Reliable Internet Troubleshooting Agent, was
developed initially at The Leftbank Operation (now known as Cohesive
Network Systems, New England Division) based on a hardware platform
supplied by Archie McPhee (Reference [1]). A typical RITA unit is
depicted in Figure 1.

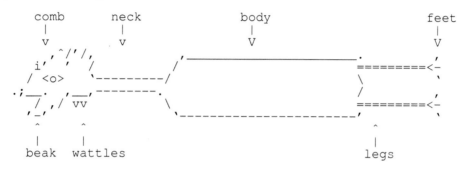

```
        comb          neck                body                       feet
         |             |                   |                          |
         v             v                   V                          V
          ,'/''/,           ,————————————————————————.              ,
       i'  '  /          / ————————————————————————.              =========<-
      / <o>    '————————/                           \             `
    .,___., ,__,————————.                            /            =========<-
     / ,,/ vv                 \                     /              ,
     ,'_,'                      '————————————————————/              `
       ^       ^                                      ^
       |       |                                      |
     beak   wattles                                  legs
```

Figure 1.

2. Specification

A typical RITA is 51.25 cm long and yellow-orange in color. Either
natural or artificial substances may be used for construction. RITA
has very flexible characteristics, and thus can interoperate within
fairly broad parameters. Unlike most other tools described in
forthcoming RFC's, RITA does not require any IANA namespace
management. It is not anticipated that versions will be
incompatible, thus no versioning field is present. Interoperability
testing may be conducted at a future meeting of the IETF.

3. Diagnostic Usage:

RITA may be applied in two diagnostic fashions, however only one of
these methods, described below in 3.1, has been refined to a state
such that we feel comfortable publishing the methodology.

3.1   The first method provides a broad-spectrum evaluation of quality of the entity tested, and is thus known as the BS eval test. This method can be used with great success on both deterministic and non-deterministic problems. Testing is performed by placing the RITA unit on top of a suspect piece of hardware, or, in the case of software, placing the unit on a packaged copy of the program, or hard copy of the source code.

If the RITA does not get up and fly away, the hardware or software being tested is misconfigured, fubar, or broken as designed. While this method does identify all equipment and software as sub-optimal, Sturgeon's Law (see reference [5]) indicates that at least 90% of these results are accurate, and it is felt that a maximum 10% false positive result is within acceptable parameters.

3.2 The second method involves applications of traditional techniques of haruspication (see reference [3]) and to date has been practiced with much greater success using implements other than RITA. The absence of entrails in the RITA unit may contribute to this; future design enhancements may address this issue by the addition of artificial giblets.

An alternative approach that has been discarded involved cleromantic principles (see reference [3]), and was known as "flipping the bird".

4. Corrective Usage:

Corrective usage of RITA is most successful in dealing with the most difficult class of networking problems: those that seem to exhibit sporadic, non-deterministic behavior.

RITA units enhance normal corrective measures of these problems, methods such as rebooting, reseating of components and connectors, changing tabs to spaces or vice-versa in configuration files, blaming third-party vendors, and use of ballistic implements to effect wholesale displacement of systems and software, to at least 100% of their normal efficacy.

Specific Problem Methodologies:

  o Physical Layer: Wave RITA unit towards malfunctioning
     components.
  o Network Layer: Wave RITA unit towards malfunctioning
     components.
  o Transport Layer: Wave RITA unit towards malfunctioning
     components.

o Application Layer: Strike product vendor representative
   (or programmer, if available) with RITA, preferably on the top
   of the skull, while shouting, "Read The Fine RFC's comma darn
   it!"
o Political Layer: Strike advocates of disruptive or
   obstructive policies with RITA, preferably on the top of the
   skull. In extreme cases insertion of RITA into bodily apertures
   may become necessary. WARNING: subsequent failure to remove RITA
   may cause further problems.
o Religious Layer: Strike advocates of disruptive or
   obstructive religions, and their vendor representatives, with
   RITA, preferably on the top of the skull. In extreme cases, the
   RITA may be used as a phlactory, funerary urn, or endcap for
   bus-and-tag cables.

5. Further Work

   A RITA MIB is under development. This may require adding interface
   technology and hardware to RITA; a prototype is depicted in Figure 2.

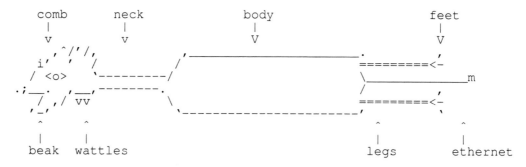

Figure 2.

There has been to date no investigation of the possible use of RITA
to implement RFC 1149.

Additionally, this tool has been used with some success for dealing
with non-network problems, particularly in the debugging of SCSI bus
malfunctions.

28

6. Security Considerations

   The RITA will only have serious impact on system security facilities
   if it is filled with lead shot. It does however, increase the
   personal security of system administrators; few network toughs are
   willing to face down a sysadmin armed with a RITA and a confident
   demeanor.

7. Citations and References

   [1] Postel, J., and J. Reynolds, "Instructions to RFC Authors", RFC
   2223, October 1997.

   [2] McPhee, A., http://www.mcphee.com

   [3] http://www.clix.net/5thworld/no-osphere/3e/manteia.html

   [4] Waitzman, D., "Transmission of IP Datagrams on Avian Carriers"
   RFC 1149, April 1990.

   [5] Raymond, E. (editor), "The New Hacker's Dictionary" 2nd ed., MIT
   Press, September 1993. ISBN 0-262-18154-1

8. Acknowledgments

   Initial Development of RITA, Editing, and excellent leather jacket
   provided by Bob Antia, first reading by John "cgull" Hood,
   illustrations done using equipment provided by Elizabeth Goodman and
   Gerry Goodnough.

9. Author's Address

   Andrew K. Bressen
   72 Endicott Street
   Somerville, MA

   Phone: 617-776-2373
   EMail: bressen@leftbank.com, bressen@cohesive.com, bressen@mirror.to

29

10. Full Copyright Statement

Part II

New Protocols: Rube Goldberg would be proud

In 1969 when the ARPAnet was born there were programs. There were no protocols. You could move files from one location to another (what we'd now think of as ftp – and guess what that p stands for) and login to a remote machine (what we'd now think of as rlogin or telnet).

By 1993 there was a protocol glut and making up more elaborate protocols was fun. Considering that many programmers were (and still are) science fiction fans, the effect of programs like Star Trek is unsurprising. RFC 1437 is a result.

RFC 1926 combines this with a play on the name ATM (Asynchronous Transfer Mode), which came from the telecom world, more known for their Acoustical Transmission Media than data communication.

RFC 1927 elaborates on MIME (Multipurpose Internet Mail Extension), allowing for associating documents through the use of electronic paper clips and staples. Very important if we want the paperless office to become a reality.

RFC 2322 describes some brilliant work of a Dutch group in solving the problem of assigning unique IP numbers to field networks.

Early on, students at the University of Waterloo in Canada and at the Massachusetts Institute of Technology enabled reportage of their soda vending machines via the Internet. RFC 2324 enables a yet-more-vital substance, coffee, to be monitored and controlled. RFC 2325 takes us a step further, giving the user managed objects for the beverage via a Coffee Pot Managed Information Base.

RFC 2550 offers a solution for another problem: following the year 2000 (Y2K), we need to be suitably prepared for Y10K, when four-digit dates will be insufficient.

RFC 2795 introduces long-needed protocols for an old problem: if an infinite number of monkeys at an infinite number of typewriters can type the works of William Shakespeare, what are the appropriate communications and control protocols? Here they are.

RFC 3093 provides us with data for the ultimate firewall: one with provides security and transparency.

Realization of just how antiquated our electrical distribution system is gave rise to RFC 3251, which provides for an elaborate system of routers and controls to replace our legacy distribution system.

In a day when everyone seems to be rewriting standards just to format them in XML, RFC 3252 provides a brilliant rewriting of UDP and of TCP in XML, offering a suitable display of BLOAT to every transmission.

Network Working Group   N. Borenstein
Request for Comments: 1437   Bellcore
                                                            M. Linimon
                                        Lonesome Dove Computing Services
                                                         1 April 1993

          The Extension of MIME Content-Types to a New Medium

Status of this Memo

   This memo provides information for the Internet community. It does
   not specify an Internet standard. Distribution of this memo is
   unlimited.

Abstract

   A previous document, RFC 1341, defines a format and general framework
   for the representation of a wide variety of data types in Internet
   mail. This document defines one particular type of MIME data, the
   matter-transport/sentient-life-form type. The matter-
   transport/sentient-life-form MIME type is intended to facilitate the
   wider interoperation of electronic mail messages that include entire
   sentient life forms, such as human beings.

   Other informally proposed subtypes, such as "non-sentient-life-form",
   "non-sentient-non-life-form", and the orthogonally necessary but
   nevertheless puzzling "sentient-non-life-form", are not described in
   this memo.

The matter-transport/sentient-life-form MIME type

   In order to promote the wider interoperability of life-bearing email,
   this document defines a new MIME content-type, "matter-transport",
   and for an initial subtype, "sentient-life-form". This subtype was
   designed to meet the following criteria:

      1. The syntax must be extremely simple to parse, to minimize the
      risk of accidental death due to misinterpretation of the standard.

      2. The data format must be extremely robust, with redundancy to
      ensure that individual life forms will survive and be
      reconstituted in such a form as to be nearly indistinguishable
      from their initial state, no matter how many bizarre email
      gateways are encountered in transit.

      3. The syntax must be extensible to allow for the description of
      all yet-undiscovered aspects of life forms which will be required

Borenstein & Linimon   [Page 1] for the transport of non-human species (e.g. dolphins, Klingons, or politicians).

4. The syntax must be compatible with SGML, so that with an appropriate DTD (Document Type Definition -- the standard mechanism for defining a document type using SGML), a general SGML parser could be written to parse the data structure and produce directives to a lifeform-reconstitution mechanism. However, despite this compatibility, the syntax will most likely be far simpler than that of full SGML (so that no SGML knowledge is required in order to implement it), since it is anticipated that the full complexities of SGML will not be necessary for the description of even arbitrarily complex organic life forms.

The syntax of the new content-type is very simple, and indeed makes considerable sacrifice of efficiency in the interest of simplicity. It is assumed to describe a three-dimensional rectangular solid, with the height, width, and depth (calibrated in centimeters) specified as parameters on the content-type line. (In general, this should be a cube that completely contains the life form being transported; but, where high bandwidth is not available, a somewhat smaller cube can be used, provided that facilities are known to be available at the recipient's end to administer the medical first aid that could be necessary if an individual is reconstituted sans some of its extremities.) A fourth parameter gives the resolution of the matter scan, calibrated in Angstroms. Thus, the following Content-type value:

    Content-type: matter-transport/sentient-life-form;
            height = 200; width = 60; depth=60; resolution=10

implies that the cube being described is 60 cm by 60 cm by 200 cm, and is described to a resolution of 10 Angstroms. The resolution gives the quantization unit, and therefore determines the quality of the reproduction. The data stream itself then consists of a readout of the molecule found at each location, using the given resolution. If the resolution is high enough that more than one molecule is found in a given location, the molecule whose nucleus is closest to the center of the cube is used. Each molecule is described by its molecular formula, rendered in ASCII for maximum readability if matter-transport mail is inadvertently delivered to a human recipient and displayed on a terminal screen. Each molecule is followed by a space (ASCII 32) to separate it from the subsequent molecule description. Extremely long molecules may require the use of a content-transfer-encoding such as quoted-printable, to ensure that line-wrapping mail systems do not, for example, cause the unintended breakdown of complex proteins into their constituent elements.

The following is a message that gives a somewhat simplified rendition
of a well-known American politician, starting from the top:

```
From:  "Nathaniel S. Borenstein" <nsb@bellcore.com>
To: Mark Linimon <linimon@lonesome.com>
Subject: Think hard before reconstructing
Content-description:  Dan Quayle, low-res version
Content-type: matter-transport/sentient-life-form
        height = 200; width = 60; depth=60; resolution=100000

Fe Fe Fe Fe Fe  Fe Fe Fe Fe Fe  Fe Fe Fe Fe Fe  Fe Fe Fe Fe Fe Fe   Fe
Fe Fe Fe Fe Fe  Fe Fe Fe Fe Fe  Fe Fe Fe Fe Fe  Fe Fe Fe Fe Fe Fe   Fe
Fe NO2 NO2 NO2 NO2 NO2 NO2 NO2 NO2 NO2 NO2 NO2 NO2 NO2 NO2 NO2 NO2 Fe
Fe NO2 NO2 NO2 NO2 NO2 NO2 NO2 NO2 NO2 NO2 NO2 NO2 NO2 NO2 NO2 NO2 Fe
Fe NO2 NO2 NO2 NO2 NO2 NO2 NO2 NO2 NO2 NO2 NO2 NO2 NO2 NO2 NO2 NO2 Fe
Fe NO2 NO2 NO2 NO2 NO2 NO2 NO2 NO2 NO2 NO2 NO2 NO2 NO2 NO2 NO2 NO2 Fe
Fe NO2 NO2 NO2 NO2 NO2 NO2 NO2 NO2 NO2 NO2 NO2 NO2 NO2 NO2 NO2 NO2 Fe
Fe NO2 NO2 NO2 NO2 NO2 NO2 NO2 NO2 NO2 NO2 NO2 NO2 NO2 NO2 NO2 NO2 Fe
Fe NO2 NO2 NO2 NO2 NO2 NO2 NO2 NO2 NO2 NO2 NO2 NO2 NO2 NO2 NO2 NO2 Fe
Fe NO2 NO2 NO2 NO2 NO2 NO2 NO2 NO2 NO2 NO2 NO2 NO2 NO2 NO2 NO2 NO2 Fe
Fe NO2 NO2 NO2 NO2 NO2 NO2 NO2 NO2 NO2 NO2 NO2 NO2 NO2 NO2 NO2 NO2 Fe
Fe NO2 NO2 NO2 NO2 NO2 NO2 NO2 NO2 NO2 NO2 NO2 NO2 NO2 NO2 NO2 NO2 Fe
Fe NO2 NO2 NO2 NO2 NO2 NO2 NO2 NO2 NO2 NO2 NO2 NO2 NO2 NO2 NO2 NO2 Fe
Fe NO2 NO2 NO2 NO2 NO2 NO2 NO2 NO2 NO2 NO2 NO2 NO2 NO2 NO2 NO2 NO2 Fe
Fe Fe Fe Fe Fe  Fe Fe Fe Fe Fe  Fe Fe Fe Fe Fe  Fe Fe Fe Fe Fe Fe   Fe
Fe Fe Fe Fe Fe  Fe Fe Fe Fe Fe  Fe Fe Fe Fe Fe  Fe Fe Fe Fe Fe Fe   Fe
```

Obviously, a real politician's skull is more complex than pure iron,
as is its interior, but this simplified example should give the
general flavor of the protocol.

(A caveat, however, in the reconstitution of Vice-Presidents of the
United States: allegedly, some of the matter-reconstitution schemes
currently under development are reputed to perform less than
optimally while trying to reconstitute areas of relatively high
vacuum; for instance, their skulls. A recommended acceptance test
might be to experiment with subjects whose skulls are only at partial
vacuum, such as Vice-Presidents of Marketing.)

MHS (X.400) Gateway Considerations

The proper behavior of a MIME/MHS gateway with regard to the
transmission of complex multimedia messages is a topic of ongoing
investigation under the auspices of the IETF. The addition of matter
transport should not significantly complicate that effort, as it is
already necessary to specify gateway behavior for MIME types that
have no X.400 equivalents, and matter transport is simply another

such untranslatable type.

However, real-world X.400 gateways might be considered to
significantly increase the hazard that mail containing a human being
will be rejected with a message so cryptic that the recipient deletes
it without ever realizing that an embedded human being is enclosed.
For this reason, it is recommended that the subject of matter
transport be explicitly marked "for further study" in the next
generation of the X.400 specification, X.400-1996. This will give
the community ample time to define a more complete specification for
matter transport as part of X.400-2000, and possibly even a readily-
implementable specification as part of X.400-2004, although some will
no doubt argue that this would be too strong a break with tradition.

Implementation Considerations

The user is cautioned against passing MIME transporter messages
through computers equipped with the NFS file system. A no-file space
error caused one of the laboratory rats on our prototype system to be
truncated to a zero-length file. Unfortunately we had neglected to
mount a scratch rat. (We have decided to permanently retain the
empty filename in his honor).

Byte swapping problems on other storage systems can be similarly
annoying, but should not be a problem if network byte order is always
maintained ocrrcelty.

Despite the authors' belief in the robustness of the protocol,
passage of email through certain systems seems to result in the
sentient-life-form arriving at its destination upside down, resulting
in an annoying "thud". The cause is still under investigation.

Interoperation with matter-transporters using polar coordinate
systems is discouraged, due to round-off and other algorithmic errors
in certain ubiquitous floating-point implementations, leading to
results which are best discreetly described as "disappointing."

Similarly, off-by-one errors should be avoided.

Widespread adoption of this protocol may lead to an increase in user
demand for reliable backup systems. More importantly, for the first
time management may be motivated to adequately fund such systems when
they discover the possibility that proper email backup may confer
upon them virtual immortality. (On the other hand, implementors
should seriously consider the desirability of making their managers
immortal.)

An additional concern reflects the fact that, prior to the
introduction of this content-type, duplicate mail delivery was a
relatively minor nuisance. With the mail extensions described in
this document, however, comes the possibility that duplicate mail
delivery will leave a user with, for example, multiple spouses or
mothers-in-law. The relative weights of the desire to avoid
duplicate delivery and the desire to avoid lost mail may change
accordingly.

Security Considerations

Security considerations are not discussed in this memo. However, law
enforcement officials might wish to consider the possibility that
this mechanism could be used by criminals, either to escape
extradition by mailing themselves outside of a legal jurisdiction, or
to outwait the statute of limitations by mailing themselves through
complex mail routes with long delays. (One supposes that they could
also look on the bright side, and consider MIME as a possible
approach to solving the long-standing problem of prison
overcrowding.)

Authors

The authors of this document may be reconstituted by feeding the
following data to an Internet-connected MIME reader:

Content-type: multipart/mixed; boundary=NextAuthor

--NextAuthor
Content-type: message/external-body; access-type=anon-ftp;
      site=thumper.bellcore.com; directory=pub/nsb; name=nsb.flesh
Content-Description: Nathaniel Borenstein

Content-type: matter-transport/sentient-life-form
      height = 200; width = 60; depth=60; resolution=100000
--NextAuthor
Content-type: message/external-body; access-type=anon-ftp;
      site=thumper.bellcore.com; directory=pub/nsb; name=linimon.flesh
Content-Description: Mark Linimon

Content-type: matter-transport/sentient-life-form
      height = 200; width = 60; depth=60; resolution=100000
--NextAuthor--

Authors' Addresses

    Nathaniel Borenstein
    Bellcore Room MRE 2D-296
    445 South Street
    Morristown, NJ 07962-1910

    Phone: (201) 829-4270
    EMail: nsb@bellcore.com

    Mark Linimon
    Lonesome Dove Computing Services
    P.O. Box 20291
    Roanoke, VA 24018

    Phone: (703) 776-1004
    EMail: linimon@LONESOME.COM

Network Working Group   J. Eriksson
Request for Comments: 1926   KTH NOC
Category: Informational   1 April 1996

         An Experimental Encapsulation of IP Datagrams on Top of ATM

Status of this Memo

Abstract

   This RFC describes a method of encapsulating IP datagrams on top of
   Acoustical Transmission Media (ATM). This is a non-recommended
   standard. Distribution of this memo is unnecessary.

Overview

   The modern laptop computer of today often contains the hardware
   needed to perform wireless communications by using Acoustical
   Transmission Media, i.e. sound waves. Until this moment there has
   been no standard on how to run IP on such media. This document is an
   attempt to fill this silence.

Frame transmission

   The IP datagram is divided into four-bit chunks, in network beep
   order, and converted to characters according to the table below. A
   single "b" character is prepended as a frame start signal, the
   characters are then transmitted in ordinary morse code by modulating
   a steady tone on and off. The frequency of this tone is also known
   as the Acoustical Signature (AS number) of the sender.

        Bits   Character   Bits   Character

        0000   "i"   1000   "u"
        0001   "t"   1001   "m"
        0010   "s"   1010   "v"
        0011   "a"   1011   "f"
        0100   "n"   1100   "w"
        0101   "h"   1101   "l"
        0110   "d"   1110   "k"
        0111   "r"   1111   "g"

To allow more than one Local Acoustical Network (LAN) to coexist the
use of different AS numbers for different LANs is suggested. This
document proposes seven standard AS numbers to be used, see the table
below for details.

```
    Name    Frequency

    "a"     440 Hz
    "b"     494 Hz
    "c"     523 Hz
    "d"     587 Hz
    "e"     659 Hz
    "f"     698 Hz
    "g"     784 Hz
```

It is assumed that for normal operation AS number "a", 440 Hz will be
used.

Frame reception

The above process is simply performed backwards.

Security Considerations

The author assumes that the users take whatever precautions that are
necessary before attempting to use this protocol in any crowded area.

Author's Address

    Johnny Eriksson
    KTH NOC
    EMail: bygg@sunet.se

    or

    -... -.-- --. --. @ ... ..- .- . - .-.-.- ... .

Network Working Group   C. Rogers
Request for Comments: 1927   ISI
Category: Informational   1 April 1996

Suggested Additional MIME Types for Associating Documents

Status of this Memo

1)   New MIME Types: Staple and "Paper" Clip

        1) indicates the degree of binding of multipart documents:
           stapled documents should stay together on the desktop,
           while paper clipped ones should be easily spreadable

        2) big paper clips vs small ones; heirarchical assembly

        3) big vs small for large documents vs. small ones?

        4) warning! the presence of electronic staples or paper clips
           may break some programs, particularly those designed to do
           high-speed copying!

2)   patents on the electronic staple and paper clip

        1) use First Virtual to record a charge each time new staples
           or paper clips are made.

        2) to reduce transmission charges, electronic staples should be
           bought in boxes of 5000. Reference: Apple's "bento"
           technology?

        3) electonic staples should have a standard "size and shape"
           so a supply of staples could be used be used by several
           programs.

3)   recycling electronic staples and paper clips

        1) to assure proper accounting, and to detect patent violations
           (people making their own electronic staples), it may be
           necessary to attach a certificate to each staple or paper
           clip.

2) When a file or folder is deleted, a "recycler" program could
   look inside for staples or paper clips that could be reused
   or recycled.

   1) staples could be reycled for a small credit

   2) paper clips could be reused.

4)   custom-look electronic staples and paper clips

   1) when stabled or clipped documents are displayed on the
      desktop, there should be some icon or visual indicator to
      show the presence of the (possibly removable) staple
      or paper clip

   2) "color=" and "shape=" attributes in the MIME line should
      allow senders to customize the appearance of individual
      staples or paper clips.

      1) this could have some significance for office filing
         systems, for instance: a silver paper clip could
         trigger one workflow component, while
         a gold paper clip could trigger another.

   3) "src=" would allow the specification of a URL of the image to
      be shown, for even greater control of appearance.

   4) it should be possible to specify 3D modelling of your custom
      paper clip, for electronic desktops being viewed through
      virtual reality headsets

5)   electronic paper clip sculpture

   1) instead of discarding or reusing paper clips, it should be
      possible to "bend" them and display the resulting sculpture
      on the desktop

      1) a morphing interface would be suitable

   2) linked chains of paper clips

   3) each paper clip should keep track of how many times it has
      been bent. Above a certain limit, the clip should fail.

6)   electronic paper clips as page flags

   1) in addition to using electronic paper clips to group related
      documents, it should be possible to attach an electronic
      paper clip to a single page of a multipage document or
      collection of documents. This highlights or draws
      attention to the page.

   2) it should be possible to include positioning information
      with the electronic paper clip, to mark specific paragraphs
      or sentences

   3) combinations of color, shape, size, position, orientation,
      etc. could have special meaning

7)   additional safety hazards of electronic paper clips

   1) they should not be used on data flines which might end up in
      the hands of very small children

      1) thus, one should consider keeping them in a locked
         drawer of the electonic desk on home PCs

   2) they should not be attached to documents on floppy disks, as
      they may erase portions of the floppy

Security Considerations

   Security issues are not discussed in this memo.

Author's Address

   Craig Milo Rogers
   USC/Information Sciences Institute
   4676 Admiralty Way
   Marina del Rey, CA 90292

   Phone: 310-822-1511
   EMail: rogers@isi.edu

Network Working Group   K. van den Hout
Request for Comments: 2322   HvU/HIP-networkteam
Category: Informational   A. Koopal
                                                 UUnet NL/HIP-networkteam
                                                          R. van Mook
                                    University of Twente/HIP-networkteam
                                                         1 April 1998

Management of IP numbers by peg-dhcp

Status of this Memo

Copyright Notice

Introduction

   This RFC describes a protocol to dynamically hand out ip-numbers on
   field networks and small events that don't necessarily have a clear
   organisational body.

   It can also provide some fixed additional fields global for all
   clients like netmask and even autoproxyconfigs. It does not depend on
   a particular ip-stack.

History of the protocol.

   The practice of using pegs for assigning IP-numbers was first used at
   the HIP event (http://www.hip97.nl/). HIP stands for Hacking In
   Progress, a large three-day event where more then a thousand hackers
   from all over the world gathered. This event needed to have a TCP/IP
   lan with an Internet connection. Visitors and participants of the
   HIP could bring along computers and hook them up to the HIP network.

   During preparations for the HIP event we ran into the problem of how
   to assign IP-numbers on such a large scale as was predicted for the
   event without running into troubles like assigning duplicate numbers
   or skipping numbers. Due to the variety of expected computers with
   associated IP stacks a software solution like a Unix DHCP server
   would probably not function for all cases and create unexpected
   technical problems.

van den Hout, et. al.   Informational   [Page 1]

                                  47

So a way of centrally administrating IP-numbers and giving them out
to people to use on their computers had to be devised. After some
discussion, the idea came up of using wooden clothes-pegs. Using pegs
has the following advantages in respect to other methods:

    - cheap
    - a peg is a 'token' and represents one IP-number, therefore
      making the status of the IP-number (allocated or not allocated)
      visible.
    - a peg can be clipped to a network cable giving a very clear
      view of where a given IP-number is in use.

Credits for the original idea of using wooden pegs go to Daniel
Ockeloen.

The server.

The server can have many appearances. At HIP it was a large tent
situated at the central field where all the activities were. It can
also be a small table in the corner of a terminalroom.

The server can hand out two parts to the client, the peg and a paper
with additional fields fixed for the site the server is running for.
We will describe both here.

The peg.

On the peg the IP-number is mentioned. The text on the peg can be
described according to the following BNF:

Total ::== IP | Net

IP ::== num.num.num.num | num.num | num

Net ::== num.num.num/mask | num.num/mask | num/mask

num ::== {1..255}

mask ::== {8..31}

The Net-method of writing larger nets is an optional part of the
protocol, it doesn't have to be implemented. If it is implemented, it
requires more administration at the server (see below).

The short versions of the IP-number with only 1 or 2 chunks are meant
for large servers where writing the whole number on the peg is just
boring and time-consuming. It requires the prefix to be mentioned on
the additional field paper, but that can be produced in more

48

convenient ways. It is not recommended to work with more prefixes. It
is better to write more numbers on the peg and use a smaller prefix.

If the network to be numbered is rather large and some kind of
subnetting has to be implemented it is possible to give the pegs from
the different subnets different colors. This has proven to be a very
convenient way at HIP.

The additional vendorfield paper.

    This part is meant for information that is fixed for the whole site.
    It can either be implemented as small printed notes handed out with
    the peg or as a large paper billboard hung at a convenient place
    where everybody can read it.

    The information can be described with the following BNF:

    Network ::== num.num.num.num

    Netmask ::== num.num.num.num | num

    Gateway ::== num.num.num.num | num.num | num

    Proxy ::== num.num.num.num:port | num.num:port | num:port

    Paper ::== Network Netmask Gateway Proxy | Network Netmask Gateway

    num ::== {0..255}

    port ::== {1..65535}

    The paper and the peg are of course one part, if two numbers are used
    on the peg, two numbers are used on the paper.

    Because it is fixed information, it can be produced with means of
    mass-production (printing, copying).

The IP-repository

    Due to the nature of the peg, the repository can be quite simple.
    Just a clothes-line with all the pegs that are ready to be handed out
    attached to it. If you work with different subnets, it is convenient
    to group the pegs for the different subnets (colors).

    At large networks where it is not really known how many IP-numbers
    are needed, a first set of pegs can be made in advance, and the
    administration of produced pegs kept on paper so it is known for
    which numbers pegs have already been made. If use is made of the

49

net-extension on the pegs, numbers given out that way can be
administrated this way too.

Issuing IP-numbers.

   The pegs and the IP-numbers are issued at the server to the client.
   Normally the client has to visit the server personally. Depending on
   how secure and controlled you want the process, the client has to ask
   for a peg to a responsible person, or he or she can just get a peg
   from store himself.

   If someone could apply for a networkrange, and he net-extension isn't
   used, coat-hangers can be prepared with sets of pegs attached to
   them.

   The vendorfields paper doesn't have to be issued with every peg, it
   is only needed when wanted.

Reclaiming and reusing IP-numbers.

   It is not easy to implement a TTL in this protocol. One obvious TTL
   is the duration of the event after which the IP-numbers are not valid
   anymore.

   However, if a client decides that it doesn't need an IP-number
   anymore it can bring the peg back to the server.

   The server should at that point decide what to do, if desired, it can
   bring the peg back into the pool (attach it to the clothes-line
   again).

   If the server is not manned (the client has to help themselves), the
   only thing possible is that the client just places the peg back into
   the pool.

The client side.

   The optimum location for the peg is clipped to the network cable near
   the NIC of the device needing an IP-number allocated. This ensures a
   clear visual connection between the device and the IP-number
   allocated and makes it an easy task to see which IP-number is
   allocated.

   Transfer of the IP information from the peg and the additional
   vendorfield paper note to the settings in the IP stack is done by
   human transfer. A person reads the information from the peg and from
   the additional information and enters this in the configuration of
   the used IP stack. This transfer is not completely free of

corruption of the information or loss of the information contained on
the peg.

A certain amount of knowledge of the logic of IP settings is also
assumed on the part of the person transferring the information.

Other information on the vendorfield paper note has to be transferred
to the settings within specific application programs.

Use with other protocols

This protocol could be combined with avian carriers as described in
RFC 1149 to hand out IP-numbers remote.

At the first avian carrier, the peg is clipped to the leg of the
carrier after rolling the additional vendorfield paper around it.

The remote site can take the peg on arrival of the avian carrier and
use the information on it.

This part of the protocol is still experimental and requires some
additional research on topics like the weight of the peg and loss of
the peg/whole carrier.

Security Considerations

Some remarks about security can be made.

Pegs are small devices and can be lost. At that time, the IP-number
which was lost can't be used anymore because someone else can find
the peg and use the information stored on it. But, once the peg is
attached to a network cable, the chance to loose the peg is
minimized.

All the information on both the peg and on the additional 'fixed'
fields on the paper record are plain text and readable for everyone.
Private information should not be exchanged through this protocol.

On the client side all sorts of clients exist and cooperate freely.
Due to the human factor of the clients transferring information from
peg to IP stack, the information can be misinterpreted, which could
cause network troubles. In the field test at HIP this became
perfectly clear when someone mixed up the numbers and used the
address from the default router as his IP-number, rendering the
network useless for a period of time.

Authors' Addresses

    Koos van den Hout
    Hogeschool van Utrecht / Expertisecentrum Cetis
    P.O. box 85029
    3508 AA Utrecht
    The Netherlands

    Phone: +31-30-2586287
    Fax: +31-30-2586292
    EMail: koos@cetis.hvu.nl

    Andre Koopal
    UUnet Netherlands
    P.O. box 12954
    1100 AZ   AMSTERDAM
    The Netherlands

    Phone: +31-20-4952727
    Fax: +31-20-4952737
    EMail: andre@NL.net

    Remco van Mook
    Van Mook Consulting
    Calslaan 10-31
    7522 MA Enschede
    The Netherlands

    Phone: +31-53-4895267
    EMail: remco@sateh.com

Full Copyright Statement

   Copyright (C) The Internet Society (1998). All Rights Reserved.

53

Network Working Group   L. Masinter
Request for Comments: 2324   1 April 1998
Category: Informational

Hyper Text Coffee Pot Control Protocol (HTCPCP/1.0)

Status of this Memo

Copyright Notice

Abstract

   This document describes HTCPCP, a protocol for controlling,
   monitoring, and diagnosing coffee pots.

1. Rationale and Scope

   There is coffee all over the world. Increasingly, in a world in which
   computing is ubiquitous, the computists want to make coffee. Coffee
   brewing is an art, but the distributed intelligence of the web-
   connected world transcends art. Thus, there is a strong, dark, rich
   requirement for a protocol designed espressoly for the brewing of
   coffee. Coffee is brewed using coffee pots. Networked coffee pots
   require a control protocol if they are to be controlled.

   Increasingly, home and consumer devices are being connected to the
   Internet. Early networking experiments demonstrated vending devices
   connected to the Internet for status monitoring [COKE]. One of the
   first remotely _operated_ machine to be hooked up to the Internet,
   the Internet Toaster, (controlled via SNMP) was debuted in 1990
   [RFC2235].

   The demand for ubiquitous appliance connectivity that is causing the
   consumption of the IPv4 address space. Consumers want remote control
   of devices such as coffee pots so that they may wake up to freshly
   brewed coffee, or cause coffee to be prepared at a precise time after
   the completion of dinner preparations.

This document specifies a Hyper Text Coffee Pot Control Protocol
(HTCPCP), which permits the full request and responses necessary to
control all devices capable of making the popular caffeinated hot
beverages.

HTTP 1.1 ([RFC2068]) permits the transfer of web objects from origin
servers to clients. The web is world-wide. HTCPCP is based on HTTP.
This is because HTTP is everywhere. It could not be so pervasive
without being good. Therefore, HTTP is good. If you want good coffee,
HTCPCP needs to be good. To make HTCPCP good, it is good to base
HTCPCP on HTTP.

Future versions of this protocol may include extensions for espresso
machines and similar devices.

2. HTCPCP Protocol

The HTCPCP protocol is built on top of HTTP, with the addition of a
few new methods, header fields and return codes. All HTCPCP servers
should be referred to with the "coffee:" URI scheme (Section 4).

2.1 HTCPCP Added Methods

2.1.1 The BREW method, and the use of POST

Commands to control a coffee pot are sent from client to coffee
server using either the BREW or POST method, and a message body with
Content-Type set to "application/coffee-pot-command".

A coffee pot server MUST accept both the BREW and POST method
equivalently. However, the use of POST for causing actions to happen
is deprecated.

Coffee pots heat water using electronic mechanisms, so there is no
fire. Thus, no firewalls are necessary, and firewall control policy
is irrelevant. However, POST may be a trademark for coffee, and so
the BREW method has been added. The BREW method may be used with
other HTTP-based protocols (e.g., the Hyper Text Brewery Control
Protocol).

2.1.2 GET method

In HTTP, the GET method is used to mean "retrieve whatever
information (in the form of an entity) identified by the Request-
URI." If the Request-URI refers to a data-producing process, it is
the produced data which shall be returned as the entity in the
response and not the source text of the process, unless that text
happens to be the output of the process.

In HTCPCP, the resources associated with a coffee pot are physical, and not information resources. The "data" for most coffee URIs contain no caffeine.

2.1.3 PROPFIND method

If a cup of coffee is data, metadata about the brewed resource is discovered using the PROPFIND method [WEBDAV].

2.1.4 WHEN method

When coffee is poured, and milk is offered, it is necessary for the holder of the recipient of milk to say "when" at the time when sufficient milk has been introduced into the coffee. For this purpose, the "WHEN" method has been added to HTCPCP. Enough? Say WHEN.

2.2 Coffee Pot Header fields

HTCPCP recommends several HTTP header fields and defines some new ones.

2.2.1 Recommended header fields

2.2.1.1 The "safe" response header field.

[SAFE] defines a HTTP response header field, "Safe", which can be used to indicate that repeating a HTTP request is safe. The inclusion of a "Safe: Yes" header field allows a client to repeat a previous request if the result of the request might be repeated.

The actual safety of devices for brewing coffee varies widely, and may depend, in fact, on conditions in the client rather than just in the server. Thus, this protocol includes an extension to the "Safe" response header:

```
        Safe                 = "Safe" ":" safe-nature
        safe-nature          = "yes" | "no" | conditionally-safe
        conditionally-safe   = "if-" safe-condition
        safe-condition       = "user-awake" | token
```

indication will allow user agents to handle retries of some safe requests, in particular safe POST requests, in a more user-friendly way.

57

2.2.2 New header fields

2.2.2.1 The Accept-Additions header field

   In HTTP, the "Accept" request-header field is used to specify media
   types which are acceptable for the response. However, in HTCPCP, the
   response may result in additional actions on the part of the
   automated pot. For this reason, HTCPCP adds a new header field,
   "Accept-Additions":

```
     Accept-Additions = "Accept-Additions" ":"
                         #( addition-range [ accept-params ] )

     addition-type    = ( "*"
                        | milk-type
                        | syrup-type
                        | sweetener-type
                        | spice-type
                        | alcohol-type
                        ) *( ";" parameter )
     milk-type        = ( "Cream" | "Half-and-half" | "Whole-milk"
                        | "Part-Skim" | "Skim" | "Non-Dairy" )
     syrup-type       = ( "Vanilla" | "Almond" | "Raspberry"
                        | "Chocolate" )
     alcohol-type     = ( "Whisky" | "Rum" | "Kahlua" | "Aquavit" )
```

2.2.3 Omitted Header Fields

   No options were given for decaffeinated coffee. What's the point?

2.3 HTCPCP return codes

   Normal HTTP return codes are used to indicate difficulties of the
   HTCPCP server. This section identifies special interpretations and
   new return codes.

2.3.1 406 Not Acceptable

   This return code is normally interpreted as "The resource identified
   by the request is only capable of generating response entities which
   have content characteristics not acceptable according to the accept
   headers sent in the request. In HTCPCP, this response code MAY be
   returned if the operator of the coffee pot cannot comply with the
   Accept-Addition request. Unless the request was a HEAD request, the
   response SHOULD include an entity containing a list of available
   coffee additions.

In practice, most automated coffee pots cannot currently provide
additions.

2.3.2 418 I'm a teapot

Any attempt to brew coffee with a teapot should result in the error
code "418 I'm a teapot". The resulting entity body MAY be short and
stout.

3. The "coffee" URI scheme

Because coffee is international, there are international coffee URI
schemes. All coffee URL schemes are written with URL encoding of the
UTF-8 encoding of the characters that spell the word for "coffee" in
any of 29 languages, following the conventions for
internationalization in URIs [URLI18N].

```
coffee-url  =  coffee-scheme ":" [ "//" host ]
               ["/" pot-designator ] ["?" additions-list ]

coffee-scheme = ( "koffie"                     ; Afrikaans, Dutch
                | "q%C3%A6hv%C3%A6"            ; Azerbaijani
                | "%D9%82%D9%87%D9%88%D8%A9" ; Arabic
              | "akeita"                       ; Basque
              | "koffee"                       ; Bengali
              | "kahva"                        ; Bosnian
              | "kafe"                         ; Bulgarian, Czech
              | "caf%C3%E8"                    ; Catalan, French, Galician
                | "%E5%92%96%E5%95%A1"         ; Chinese
                | "kava"                       ; Croatian
              | "k%C3%A1va"                    ; Czech
              | "kaffe"                        ; Danish, Norwegian, Swedish
              | "coffee"                       ; English
              | "kafo"                         ; Esperanto
                | "kohv"                        ; Estonian
              | "kahvi"                        ; Finnish
              | "%4Baffee"                     ; German
              | "%CE%BA%CE%B1%CF%86%CE%AD" ; Greek
              | "%E0%A4%95%E0%A5%8C%E0%A4%AB%E0%A5%80" ; Hindi
              | "%E3%82%B3%E3%83%BC%E3%83%92%E3%83%BC" ; Japanese
              | "%EC%BB%A4%ED%94%BC"          ; Korean
              | "%D0%BA%D0%BE%D1%84%D0%B5" ; Russian
              | "%E0%B8%81%E0%B8%B2%E0%B9%81%E0%B8%9F" ; Thai
                )

pot-designator = "pot-" integer  ; for machines with multiple pots
additions-list = #( addition )
```

All alternative coffee-scheme forms are equivalent. However, the use
of coffee-scheme in various languages MAY be interpreted as an
indication of the kind of coffee produced by the coffee pot. Note
that while URL scheme names are case-independent, capitalization is
important for German and thus the initial "K" must be encoded.

4. The "message/coffeepot" media type

The entity body of a POST or BREW request MUST be of Content-Type
"message/coffeepot". Since most of the information for controlling
the coffee pot is conveyed by the additional headers, the content of
"message/coffeepot" contains only a coffee-message-body:

coffee-message-body = "start" | "stop"

5. Operational constraints

This section lays out some of the operational issues with deployment
of HTCPCP ubiquitously.

5.1 Timing Considerations

A robust quality of service is required between the coffee pot user
and the coffee pot service. Coffee pots SHOULD use the Network Time
Protocol [NTP] to synchronize their clocks to a globally accurate
time standard.

Telerobotics has been an expensive technology. However, with the
advent of the Cambridge Coffee Pot [CAM], the use of the web (rather
than SNMP) for remote system monitoring and management has been
proven. Additional coffee pot maintenance tasks might be
accomplished by remote robotics.

Web data is normally static. Therefore to save data transmission and
time, Web browser programs store each Web page retrieved by a user on
the user's computer. Thus, if the user wants to return to that page,
it is now stored locally and does not need to be requested again from
the server. An image used for robot control or for monitoring a
changing scene is dynamic. A fresh version needs to be retrieved from
the server each time it is accessed.

5.2 Crossing firewalls

In most organizations HTTP traffic crosses firewalls fairly easily.
Modern coffee pots do not use fire. However, a "firewall" is useful
for protection of any source from any manner of heat, and not just
fire. Every home computer network SHOULD be protected by a firewall
from sources of heat. However, remote control of coffee pots is

important from outside the home. Thus, it is important that HTCPCP cross firewalls easily.

By basing HTCPCP on HTTP and using port 80, it will get all of HTTP's firewall-crossing virtues. Of course, the home firewalls will require reconfiguration or new versions in order to accommodate HTCPCP-specific methods, headers and trailers, but such upgrades will be easily accommodated. Most home network system administrators drink coffee, and are willing to accommodate the needs of tunnelling HTCPCP.

6. System management considerations

Coffee pot monitoring using HTTP protocols has been an early application of the web. In the earliest instance, coffee pot monitoring was an early (and appropriate) use of ATM networks [CAM].

The traditional technique [CAM] was to attach a frame-grabber to a video camera, and feed the images to a web server. This was an appropriate application of ATM networks. In this coffee pot installation, the Trojan Room of Cambridge University laboratories was used to give a web interface to monitor a common coffee pot. of us involved in related research and, being poor, impoverished academics, we only had one coffee filter machine between us, which lived in the corridor just outside the Trojan Room. However, being highly dedicated and hard-working academics, we got through a lot of coffee, and when a fresh pot was brewed, it often didn't last long.

This service was created as the first application to use a new RPC mechanism designed in the Cambridge Computer Laboratory - MSRPC2. It runs over MSNL (Multi-Service Network Layer) - a network layer protocol designed for ATM networks.

Coffee pots on the Internet may be managed using the Coffee Pot MIB [CPMIB].

7. Security Considerations

Anyone who gets in between me and my morning coffee should be insecure.

Unmoderated access to unprotected coffee pots from Internet users might lead to several kinds of "denial of coffee service" attacks. The improper use of filtration devices might admit trojan grounds. Filtration is not a good virus protection method.

61

Putting coffee grounds into Internet plumbing may result in clogged plumbing, which would entail the services of an Internet Plumber [PLUMB], who would, in turn, require an Internet Plumber's Helper.

Access authentication will be discussed in a separate memo.

8. Acknowledgements

Many thanks to the many contributors to this standard, including Roy Fielding, Mark Day, Keith Moore, Carl Uno-Manros, Michael Slavitch, and Martin Duerst. The inspiration of the Prancing Pony, the CMU Coke Machine, the Cambridge Coffee Pot, the Internet Toaster, and other computer controlled remote devices have led to this valuable creation.

9. References

[RFC2068] Fielding, R., Gettys, J., Mogul, J., Frystyk, H., and T. Berners-Lee, "Hypertext Transfer Protocol -- HTTP/1.1", RFC 2068, January 1997.

[RFC2186] Wessels, D., and K. Claffy, "Internet Cache Protocol (ICP), version 2," RFC 2186, September 1997

[CPMIB] Slavitch, M., "Definitions of Managed Objects for Drip-Type Heated Beverage Hardware Devices using SMIv2", RFC 2325, 1 April 1998.

[HTSVMP] Q. Stafford-Fraser, "Hyper Text Sandwich Van Monitoring Protocol, Version 3.2". In preparation.

[RFC2295] Holtman, K., and A. Mutz, "Transparent Content Negotiation in HTTP", RFC 2295, March 1998.

[SAFE] K. Holtman. "The Safe Response Header Field", September 1997.

[CAM] "The Trojan Room Coffee Machine", D. Gordon and M. Johnson, University of Cambridge Computer Lab, <http://www.cl.cam.ac.uk/coffee/coffee.html>

[CBIO] "The Trojan Room Coffee Pot, a (non-technical) biography", Q. Stafford-Fraser, University of Cambridge Computer Lab, <http://www.cl.cam.ac.uk/coffee/qsf/coffee.html>.

[RFC2235] Zakon, R., "Hobbes' Internet Timeline", FYI 32, RFC 2230, November 1997. See also <http://www.internode.com.au/images/toaster2.jpg>

[NTP] Mills, D., "Network Time Protocol (Version 3) Specification, Implementation and Analysis", RFC 1305, March 1992.

[URLI18N] Masinter, L., "Using UTF8 for non-ASCII Characters in Extended URIs" Work in Progress.

[PLUMB] B. Metcalfe, "Internet Plumber of the Year: Jim Gettys", Infoworld, February 2, 1998.

[COKE] D. Nichols, "Coke machine history", C. Everhart, "Interesting uses of networking", <http://www-cse.ucsd.edu/users/bsy/coke.history.txt>.

10. Author's Address

Larry Masinter
Xerox Palo Alto Research Center
3333 Coyote Hill Road
Palo Alto, CA 94304

EMail: masinter@parc.xerox.com

11. Full Copyright Statement

   Copyright (C) The Internet Society (1998). All Rights Reserved.

   This document and translations of it may be copied and furnished to
   others, and derivative works that comment on or otherwise explain it
   or assist in its implementation may be prepared, copied, published
   and distributed, in whole or in part, without restriction of any
   kind, provided that the above copyright notice and this paragraph are
   included on all such copies and derivative works. However, this
   document itself may not be modified in any way, such as by removing
   the copyright notice or references to the Internet Society or other
   Internet organizations, except as needed for the purpose of
   developing Internet standards in which case the procedures for
   copyrights defined in the Internet Standards process must be
   followed, or as required to translate it into languages other than
   English.

   The limited permissions granted above are perpetual and will not be
   revoked by the Internet Society or its successors or assigns.

   This document and the information contained herein is provided on an
   "AS IS" basis and THE INTERNET SOCIETY AND THE INTERNET ENGINEERING
   TASK FORCE DISCLAIMS ALL WARRANTIES, EXPRESS OR IMPLIED, INCLUDING
   BUT NOT LIMITED TO ANY WARRANTY THAT THE USE OF THE INFORMATION
   HEREIN WILL NOT INFRINGE ANY RIGHTS OR ANY IMPLIED WARRANTIES OF
   MERCHANTABILITY OR FITNESS FOR A PARTICULAR PURPOSE.

Network Working Group   M. Slavitch
Request for Comments: 2325   Loran Technologies Inc.
Category: Informational   1 April 1998

            Definitions of Managed Objects for Drip-Type Heated Beverage
                        Hardware Devices using SMIv2

Status of this Memo

   This memo provides information for the Internet community. It does
   not specify an Internet standard of any kind. Distribution of this
   memo is unlimited.

Table of Contents

1. Introduction

   This memo defines an extension to the Management Information Base
   (MIB) for use with network management protocols in the Internet
   community. In particular, it defines objects for the management of
   coffee-brewing and maintenance devices.

2. The SNMPv2 Network Management Framework

   The SNMPv2 Network Management Framework consists of four major
   components. They are:

       o   RFC 1442 [1] which defines the SMI, the mechanisms used for
            describing and naming objects for the purpose of management.

                                    65

o   STD 17, RFC 1213 [2] defines MIB-II, the core set of managed
     objects for the Internet suite of protocols.

o   RFC 1445 [3] which defines the administrative and other
     architectural aspects of the framework.

o   RFC 1448 [4] which defines the protocol used for network
     access to managed objects.

The Framework permits new objects to be defined for the purpose of
experimentation and evaluation.

2.1. Object Definitions

Managed objects are accessed via a virtual information store, termed
the Management Information Base or MIB. Objects in the MIB are
defined using the subset of Abstract Syntax Notation One (ASN.1)
defined in the SMI. In particular, each object object type is named
by an OBJECT IDENTIFIER, an administratively assigned name. The
object type together with an object instance serves to uniquely
identify a specific instantiation of the object. For human
convenience, we often use a textual string, termed the descriptor, to
refer to the object type.

3. Overview

The COFFEE POT MIB applies to managed devices that brew, store, and
deliver heated coffee beverages. The COFFEE POT MIB is mandatory for
all systems that have such a hardware port supporting services
managed through some other MIB.

The MIB contains objects that relate to physical connections,
configuration, storage levels, availabilty, quality of service, and
availability.

3.1. Relationship to Interface MIB

The COFFEE-POT-MIB is one of many MIBs designed for layered use as
described in the Interface MIB [5]. In most implementations where it
is present, it will be in the lowest interface sublayer, that is, the
COFFEE-POT-MIB represents the physical layer, providing service to
higher layers such as the Character MIB [6].

Although it is unlikely that a coffee port will actually be used as a
network interface, which is the intent of the Interface MIB, the
COFFEE-POT-MIB is closely connected to the Character MIB, which can
share hardware interfaces with network operation, and relate to the
RS-232 MIB [7].

The Interface MIB's ifTestTable and ifRcvAddressTable are not
relevant to the COFFEE-POT-MIB.

The COFFEE-POT-MIB is relevant for ifType values sip(31), and perhaps
others.

The COFFEE-POT-MIB requires the conformance groups ifGeneralGroup,
and ifFixedLengthGroup.

Usefulness of error counters in this MIB depends on the octet
counters in ifFixedLengthGroup.

4. Definitions

    COFFEE-POT-MIB DEFINITIONS ::= BEGIN

    IMPORTS
        MODULE-IDENTITY, OBJECT-TYPE, NOTIFICATION-TYPE,
        TimeStamp, TimeInterval,
        Counter32, Integer32
            FROM SNMPv2-SMI
        InterfaceIndex
            FROM IF-MIB
        transmission
            FROM RFC1213-MIB
        MODULE-COMPLIANCE, OBJECT-GROUP
            FROM SNMPv2-CONF;

    coffee MODULE-IDENTITY
        LAST-UPDATED "9803231700Z"
        ORGANIZATION "Networked Appliance Management Working Group"

        CONTACT-INFO
                "   Michael Slavitch
                     Loran Technologies,
                     955 Green Valley Crescent
                     Ottawa, Ontario Canada K2A 0B6

                 Tel: 613-723-7505
                 Fax: 613-723-7209
             E-mail: slavitch@loran.com"
        DESCRIPTION
               "The MIB Module for coffee vending devices."
        ::= { transmission 132 }

    potName OBJECT-TYPE
        SYNTAX   DisplayString (SIZE (0..255))
        MAX-ACCESS read-only

67

```
        STATUS current
        DESCRIPTION
                "The vendor description of the pot under management"
        ::= { coffee 1 }


    potCapacity OBJECT-TYPE
        SYNTAX Integer32
        MAX-ACCESS read-only
        STATUS current
        DESCRIPTION
            "The number of units of beverage supported by this device
             (regardless of its current state) ."
        ::= { coffee 2 }


    potType OBJECT-TYPE
        SYNTAX       INTEGER {
            automatic-drip(1),
            percolator(2),
            french-press(3),
            espresso(4),
            }
        MAX-ACCESS read-write
        STATUS current
        DESCRIPTION
                "The brew type of the coffee pot."
        ::= { coffee 3 }

    potLocation OBJECT-TYPE {
        SYNTAX       DisplayString (SIZE (0..255))
        MAX-ACCESS read-write
        STATUS current
        DESCRIPTION
                "The physical location of the pot in question"
        ::= { coffee 4 }


    potMonitor               OBJECT IDENTIFIER ::= { coffee 6 }


    potOperStatus
        SYNTAX       Integer {
                    off(1),
                    brewing(2),
                    holding(3),
                    other(4),
                    waiting(5)
```

```
                              }
           MAX-ACCESS read-only
           STATUS current
           DESCRIPTION
                   "The operating status of the pot in question. Note
                   that this is a read-only feature. Current hardware
                   prevents us from changing the port state via SNMP."
           ::= { potMonitor 1 }

      potLevel OBJECT-TYPE
           SYNTAX      Integer32
           MAX-ACCESS read-only
           STATUS current
           DESCRIPTION
                   "The number of units of coffee under management. The
                   units of level are defined in potMetric below."
           ::= { potMonitor 2 }

      potMetric  OBJECT-TYPE
           SYNTAX      Integer {
                   espresso(1),
                   demi-tasse(2),
                   cup(3),
                   mug(4),
                   bucket(5)
                   }
           MAX-ACCESS read-only
           STATUS current
           DESCRIPTION
                   "The vendor description of the pot under management"
           ::= { potMonitor 3 }


      potStartTime OBJECT-TYPE
           SYNTAX      Integer64
           MAX-ACCESS read-write
           STATUS      current
           DESCRIPTION
                   "The time in seconds since Jan 1 1970 to start the pot
                   if and only if potOperStatus is waiting(5)"
           ::= { potMonitor 4 }


      lastStartTime OBJECT-TYPE
           SYNTAX      TimeInterval
           MAX-ACCESS read-only
           STATUS      current
           DESCRIPTION
```

```
                "The amount of time, in TimeTicks, since the coffee
                making process was initiated."
            ::= { potMonitor 5 }


        potTemperature OBJECT-TYPE
            SYNTAX     Integer32
            UNITS      "degrees Centigrade"
            MAX-ACCESS read-only
            STATUS     current
            DESCRIPTION
                "The ambient temperature of the coffee within the pot"

            ::= { potMonitor 6 }

        END
```

5. Acknowledgements

    Networked Appliance Management Working Group (not) of the IETF.

6. References

    [1] Case, J., McCloghrie, K., Rose, M., and S. Waldbusser, "Structure
        of Management Information for version 2 of the Simple Network
        Management Protocol (SNMPv2)", RFC 1442, April 1993.

    [2] McCloghrie, K., and M. Rose, Editors, "Management Information
        Base for Network Management of TCP/IP-based internets: MIB-II",
        STD 17, RFC 1213, March 1991.

    [3] Galvin, J., and K. McCloghrie, "Administrative Model for version
        2 of the Simple Network Management Protocol (SNMPv2)", RFC 1445,
        April 1993.

    [4] Case, J., McCloghrie, K., Rose, M., and S. Waldbusser, "Protocol
        Operations for version 2 of the Simple Network Management
        Protocol (SNMPv2)", RFC 1448, April 1993.

    [5] McCloghrie, K., and F. Kastenholz, "Evolution of the Interfaces
        Group of MIB-II", RFC 1573, January 1994.

    [6] Valdez, Juan, "Definitions of Columbian Objects for Coffee Pot
        Devices using SMIv2", Columbia, Inc., March 1998.

7. Security Considerations

    Security issues are not discussed in this memo.

8. Author's Address

Michael Slavitch
Loran Technologies
955 Green Valley Crescent
Ottawa, Ontario Canada K2C 3V4

Phone: 613 723 7505
EMail: slavitch@loran.com

9. Full Copyright Statement

72

Network Working Group   S. Glassman
Request for Comments: 2550   M. Manasse
Category: Stinkards Track   J. Mogul
                                         Compaq Computer Corporation
                                                       1 April 1999

                          Y10K and Beyond

Status of this Memo

Copyright Notice

Abstract

   As we approach the end of the millennium, much attention has been
   paid to the so-called "Y2K" problem. Nearly everyone now regrets the
   short-sightedness of the programmers of yore who wrote programs
   designed to fail in the year 2000. Unfortunately, the current fixes
   for Y2K lead inevitably to a crisis in the year 10,000 when the
   programs are again designed to fail.

   This specification provides a solution to the "Y10K" problem which
   has also been called the "YAK" problem (hex) and the "YXK" problem
   (Roman numerals).

1. Introduction, Discussion, and Related Work

   Many programs and standards contain, manipulate and maintain dates.
   Comparing and sorting dates is a common activity. Many different
   formats and standards for dates have been developed and all have been
   found wanting.

   Early date formats reserved only two digits to represent the year
   portion of a date. Programs that use this format make mistakes when
   dealing with dates after the year 2000. This is the so-called Y2K
   problem.

Glassman, et. al.   Informational   [Page 1]

73

The most common fix for the Y2K problem has been to switch to 4-digit
years. This fix covers roughly the next 8,000 years (until the year
9999) by which time, everyone seems convinced that all current
programs will have been retired. This is exactly the faulty logic
and lazy programming practice that led to the current Y2K problem!
Programmers and designers always assume that their code will
eventually disappear, but history suggests that code and programs are
often used well past their intended circumstances.

The 4-digit year leads directly to programs that will fail in the
year 10,000. This proposal addresses the Y10K problem in a general
way that covers the full range of date and time format issues.

1.1 Current approaches

A large number of approaches exist for formatting dates and times.
All of them have limitations. The 2-digit year runs into trouble
next year. The 4-digit year hits the wall in the year 10,000. A
16-bit year runs out in the year 65,536. A 32-bit counter for the
number of seconds since 1970 [UNIX] wraps in 2038. A 32-bit counter
for the number of milli-seconds since booting crashes a Windows (TM)
PC in 49.7 days [Microsoft].

In this specification, we focus on the Y10K problems since they are
most common and a large number of existing standards and protocols
are susceptible to them (section 7). These standards, and new
proposals on their way, will lead to a serious world-wide problem
unless efforts are made now to correct the computing, government, and
business communities.

Already, a small cottage industry is popping up to deal with the Y10K
problem [YUCK]. We encourage these efforts and, in the coming years,
this effort can only grow in size and importance.

1.2 A Fixed Format Y10K Fix

At the time of this writing, only one proposal [Wilborne] directly
deals with the Y10K problem. In that proposal, dates are represented
as decimal numbers with the dates compared numerically. The proposed
format is simply YYYYYMMDD - i.e. 5-digit years.

To allow numerical comparison of dates, this representation requires
a completely fixed representation for the date. There can be no
optional fields, the date resolution is limited to the granularity of
one day, and this solution fails in the year 100,000 (Y100K).

1.2.2 Limitations of Numerical Comparison

   While sufficient for the specific Y10K problem, this solution is
   limited. Even if extended for 6-digit years, it fails on 32-bit
   systems (and future 32-bit system emulators) after the date
   represented by the number 2147481231 (December 31, 214748) leading to
   a Y214749 problem. Similarly, 64-bit and 128-bit systems also will
   fail, although somewhat later (after December 31, 922,337,203,685,477
   and December 31, 17,014,118,346,046,923,173,168,730,371,588,410
   respectively).

1.2.3 Granularity Issues

   The granularity problems of a fixed format date can be improved by
   extending the date format to include greater precision in the date.
   However, since numerical comparison of dates requires a fixed
   representation date, an extended format can not provide sufficient
   resolution for all foreseeable needs.

   For instance, if the precision were extended to the femto-second
   range the date format would become YYYYYMMDDHHMMSSmmmuuunnnpppfff
   (year, month, day, hour, minute, second, milli-second, micro-second,
   nano-second, pico-second, and femto-second). The additional 21
   digits of this format limit the set of representable dates. Compared
   to 1.2.2, the 32-bit and 64-bit forms of the date are instantly
   exceeded, while the 128-bit version would be viable - expiring on
   December 31, 17,014,118,346,046.

1.2.3.1 Extrapolation of Future Granularity Issues

   However, a simple extrapolation of Moore's law shows that even
   femto-second resolution will soon be inadequate. Projecting current
   CPU clock speeds forward, a femto-second clock speed will be achieved
   in only 30 years. And, by the year 10,000 the projected clock speed
   of the Intel Pentium MMDCLXVI (TM) will be approximately 10 ** (-
   1609) seconds.

   This discussion clearly shows that any fixed-format, integer
   representation of a date is likely to be insufficiently precise for
   future uses.

1.2.3.2 Floating Point Is No Solution

   The temptation to use floating point numbers to represent dates
   should be avoided. Like the longer fixed-format, integer
   representations of the date, floating point representations merely
   delay the inevitable time when their range is exceeded. In addition,

the well known problems of real numbers - rounding, de-normalization, non-uniform distribution, etc. - just add to the problems of dealing with dates.

2 Structure of Y10K Solution

   Any Y10K solution should have the following characteristics.

2.1 Compatibility

   The format must be compatible with existing 4-digit date formats. Y2K compliant programs and standards must continue to work with Y10K dates before the year 10,000. Y10K compliant programs can gradually be developed over time and coexist with non-Y10K compliant programs.

2.2 Simplicity and Efficiency

   Y10K dates must allow dates after 10,000 to be easily identified. Within a program, there must be a simple procedure for recognizing the Y10K dates and distinguishing them from legacy dates.

2.3 Lexical Sorting

   Y10K dates must be sortable lexically based on their ASCII representation. The dates must not require specialized libraries or procedures.

2.4 Future Extensibility

   Y10K dates must support arbitrary precision dates, and should support dates extending arbitrarily far into the future and past. Y10K dates from different eras and with different precisions must be directly comparable and sortable.

2.4.1 Environmental Considerations

   The known universe has a finite past and future. The current age of the universe is estimated in [Zebu] as between $10 ** 10$ and $2 * 10 ** 10$ years. The death of the universe is estimated in [Nigel] to occur in $10 ** 11$ - years and in [Drake] as occurring either in $10 ** 12$ years for a closed universe (the big crunch) or $10 ** 14$ years for an open universe (the heat death of the universe).

   In any case, the prevailing belief is that the life of the universe (and thus the range of possible dates) is finite.

2.4.2 Transcending Environmental Considerations

   However, we might get lucky. So, Y10K dates are able to represent
   any possible time without any limits to their range either in the
   past or future.

   Y10K compliant programs MAY choose to limit the range of dates they
   support to those consistent with the expected life of the universe.
   Y10K compliant systems MUST accept Y10K dates from 10 ** 12 years in
   the past to 10 ** 20 years into the future. Y10K compliant systems
   SHOULD accept dates for at least 10 ** 29 years in the past and
   future.

3 Syntax Overview

   The syntax of Y10K dates consists of simple, printable ASCII
   characters. The syntax and the characters are chosen to support a
   simple lexical sort order for dates represented in Y10K format. All
   Y10K dates MUST conform to these rules.

   Every Y10K date MUST begin with a Y10K year. Following the year,
   there MAY be an arbitrary sequence of digits. The digits are
   interpreted as MMDDHHMMSSmmmuuunnnpppfff... (month, day, hour,
   minute, second, milli-second, micro-second, nano-second pico-second,
   femto-second, etc. - moving left to right in the date, digits always
   decrease in significance).

   All dates and times MUST be relative to International Atomic Time
   (TAI) [NRAO].

   When comparing dates, a date precedes every other date for which it
   is a prefix. So, the date "19990401000000" precedes the date
   "199904010000000000". In particular, dates with the format YYYYMMDD
   are interpreted to represent the exact instant that the day begins
   and precede any other date contained in that day.

3.1 Years 1 - 9999

   The current 4-digit year syntax covers all years from 1000 - 9999.
   These years are represented as 4 decimal digits. Leading 0's MUST be
   added to the years before 1000 to bring the year to 4 digits. Files
   containing legacy pre-Y1K [Mike] dates will have to be converted.

3.2 Years 10,000 through 99,999

   Four digits are not sufficient to represent dates beyond the year
   9999. So, all years from 10,000 - 99,999 are represented by 5 digits
   preceded by the letter 'A'. So, 10,000 becomes "A10000" and 99,999

becomes "A99999". Since 'A' follows '9' in the ASCII ordering, all
dates with 5-digit years will follow all dates with 4-digit years
(for example, "A10000" will sort after "9999"). This gives us the
sort and comparison behaviour we want.

3.3 Years 100,000 up to 10 ** 30

By a simple generalization of 3.2, 6-digit years are preceded by the
letter 'B', 7-digit years by 'C', etc. Using just the 26 upper-case
ASCII characters, we can cover all years up to 10**30 (the last year
representable is "Z999999999999999999999999999999"). Again, since
the ASCII characters are sorted alphabetically, all dates sort
appropriately.

3.4 Years 10 ** 30 and beyond (Y10**30)

As discussed in 2.4.1, the end of the universe is predicted to occur
well before the year 10 ** 30. However, if there is one single
lesson to be learned from the current Y2K problems, it is that
specifications and conventions have a way of out living their
expected environment. Therefore we feel it is imperative to
completely solve the date representation problem once and for all.

3.4.1 Naive Approach for Y10**30 Problem

The naive solution is to prepend a single '^' (caret) - caret sorts
after all letters in the ASCII order) before all years from 10 ** 30
to 10 ** 56. Thus the year "Z999999999999999999999999999999" is
followed by the year "^A1000000000000000000000000000000". Similarly,
all years from 10 ** 56 to 10 ** 82 get one more caret. So, the year
"^Z9999999999999999999999999999999999999999999999999999999999" is
followed by the year
"^^A10000000000000000000000000000000000000000000000000000000000". This
scheme can be extended indefinitely by prepending one addition caret
for each additional factor of 10 ** 26 in the range of the year.

In this approach, the number of digits in a date that are used to
represent the year is simply:

    26 * <number of '^'> + ASCII(<prefix letter>) - ASCII('A') + 5

Note: this algorithm is provided for informational purposes only and
to show the path leading to the true solution. Y10K dates MUST NOT
use this format. They MUST use the format in the next section.

3.4.2 Space Efficient Approach for Y10**30 Problem

   The solution in 3.4.1 is not a space efficient format for giving the
   number of digits in the year. The length of the prefix grows
   linearly in the length of the year (which, itself, grows
   logarithmically over time). Therefore, Y10K format dates use an
   improved, more compact encoding of the number of digits in the year.

3.4.2.1 Years 10 ** 30 to 10 ** 56

   As in 3.4.1, a single 'ˆ' and letter precede the year.

3.4.2.2 Years 10 ** 56 to 10 ** 732

   The year is preceded by two carets ("ˆˆ") and two letters. The
   letters create a two digit, base 26 number which is the number of
   digits in the year minus 57. So, the year
   "ˆZ99999999999999999999999999999999999999999999999999999999" is
   followed by the year
   "ˆˆAA100000000000000000000000000000000000000000000000000000000". The
   last representable year with two carets is the year (10 ** 732) - 1
   and is "ˆˆZZ999..999" (i.e. two carets and two Z's, followed by 732
   consecutive 9's).

   The formula for the number of digits in the year is, based on the two
   digit prefix is:

     26 * (ASCII(<prefix letter1>) - ASCII('A')) +
          ASCII(<prefix letter2>) - ASCII('A') + 57

3.4.2.3 Years 10 ** 732 to 10 ** 18308

   The next block of years has the number of digits given by three
   carets ("ˆˆˆ") followed by three letters forming a three-digit, base
   26 number. The number of digits in the year is given by the formula:

     676 * (ASCII(<prefix letter1>) - ASCII('A')) +
      26 * (ASCII(<prefix letter2>) - ASCII('A')) +
           ASCII(<prefix letter3>) - ASCII('A') + 733

3.4.2.4 General Format for Y10K Dates

   In general, if there is at least one letter in a Y10K year, the
   number of the digits in the year portion of the date is given by the
   formula:

       base26(fib(n) letters) + y10k(n)

Where "n" is the number of leading carets and the fig, base26 and
y10k functions are defined with the following recurrence relations:

    fib(n) is the standard Fibonacci sequence with:

    fib(0) = 1

    fib(1) = 1

    fib(n+2) = fib(n) + fib(n+1)

    base26(m letters) is the base 26 number represented by m letters
    A-Z:

    base26(letter) = ASCII(<letter>) - ASCII('A')
    base26(string letter) = 26 * base26(string) + base26(letter)

    y10k(n) is the necessary fudge factor to align the sequences

    properly:

    y10k(0) = 5
    y10k(n+1) = 26 ** fib(n) + y10k(n)

If the year does not have at least one letter in the year, then the
number of digits in the year is:

    4

This year format is space-efficient. The length of the prefix giving
number of digits in the year only grows logarithmically with the
number of digits in the year. And, the number of carets preceding
the prefix only grows logarithmically with the number of digits in
the prefix.

3.5 B.C.E. (Before Common Era) Years

Now that have a format for all of the years in the future, we'll take
on the "negative" years. A negative year is represented in "Y10K-
complement" form. A Y10K-complement year is computed as follows:

  1) Calculate the non-negative Y10K year string as in 3.4.2.4.
  2) Replace all letters by their base 26 complement. I.E. A -> Z, B
     -> Y, ... Z -> A.
  3) Replace all digits in the year portion of the date by their base
     10 complement. I.E. 0 -> 9, 1 -> 8, ... 9 -> 0.
  4) Replace carets by exclamation points ('!').
  5) Four-digit years are pre-pended with a slash ('/')

6) Years that don't now begin with an exclamation point or slash are pre-pended with a star ('*'). (This rule covers the negative 5-31 digit years).

For example, the year 1 BCE is represented by "/9998". The conversion is accomplished by applying rules:

1) Calculate the non-negative Y10K year ("1" -> "0001")
2) Complement the digits ("0001" -> "9998")
3) Four-digit numbers get a leading slash.

The earliest four-digit BCE year (9999 BCE) becomes "/0000" and the year before that (10000 BCE) becomes "*Z89999". The earliest 5-digit BCE year (99999 BCE) is "*Z00000". And the year before that (100000 BCE) is "*Y899999". And so on.

These rules give the desired sort order for BCE dates. For example, the following dates get translated and sorted as:

```
Jun 6, 200 BCE           /97990606
199 BCE                  /9800
Jan 1, 199 BCE           /98000101
```

3.6 Restrictions on Y10K Dates

There are no restrictions on legal values for Y10K dates. Y10K compliant programs MUST accept any syntactically legal Y10K date as a valid date. A '0' can be appended to the end of any Y10K date, yielding an equivalent date that sorts immediately after the original date and represents the instant after the original date.

The following are all valid representations (in sorted order) of the first instant of A10000:

```
A1
A10000
A1000001
A100000101000000
A100000101000000000000000000000000
```

Similarly, the following are all valid Y10K dates (in sorted order) for the time after the last instant of the A99999 and before the first instant of B100000:

```
A999991231250000
A999991232
A999992
A9999999999
A9999999999990000000000000
```

4 ABNF

The following ABNF [Crocker] gives the formal syntax for Y10K years.

The initial characters definitions are given in their lexical collation (ASCII) order.

```
exclamation = '!'
star        = '*'
slash       = '/'
digit       = 0 | 1 | 2 | 3 | 4 | 5 | 6 | 7 | 8 | 9
letter      = A | B | C | D | E | F | G | H | I | J | K | L | M |

              N | O | P | Q | R | S | T | U | V | W | X | Y | Z
caret       = '^'


year     = [*(caret | exclamation) | star | slash ] [ *letter ]
           *digit
month    = 2digit
day      = 2digit
hour     = 2digit
minute   = 2digit
second   = 2digit
fraction = *digit
date     = year [ month [ day [ hour [ minute [ second [ fraction
           ]]]]]]
```

5 Open Issues

There are a number date comparison problems that are beyond the scope of this specification.

1) Dates from different calendar systems can not be directly compared. For instance, dates from the Aztec, Bhuddist, Jewish, Muslim, and Hittite calendars must be converted to a common calendar before comparisons are possible.

2) Future re-numberings of years are not covered. If, and when, a new "Year 0" occurs and comes into general use, old dates will have to be adjusted.

3) Continued existence of Earth-centric time periods (year, day, etc.) are problematical past the up-coming destruction of the solar system (5-10 billion years or so). The use of atomic-time helps some since leap seconds are no longer an issue.

   4) Future standards and methods of synchronization for inter-
      planetary and inter-galactic time have not been agreed to.

   5) Survivability of dates past the end of the universe is uncertain.

6 Affected Standards

   A number of standards currently and RFCs use 4-digit years and are
   affected by this proposal:

      rfc2459: Internet X.509 Public Key Infrastructure
               Certificate and CRL Profile
      rfc2326: Real Time Streaming Protocol (RTSP)
      rfc2311: ODETTE File Transfer Protocol
      rfc2280: Routing Policy Specification Language (RPSL)
      rfc2259: Simple Nomenclator Query Protocol (SNQP)
      rfc2244: ACAP -- Application Configuration Access Protocol
      rfc2167: Referral Whois (RWhois) Protocol V1.5
      rfc2065: Domain Name System Security Extensions
      rfc2060: Internet Message Access Protocol - Version 4rev1
      rfc1922: Chinese Character Encoding for Internet Messages
      rfc1912: Common DNS Operational and Configuration Errors
      rfc1903: Textual Conventions for Version 2 of the
               Simple Network Management Protocol (SNMPv2)
      rfc1521: MIME (Multipurpose Internet Mail Extensions) Part One:

      rfc1123: Requirements for Internet hosts - application and support

   The following standards internally represent years as 16-bit numbers
   (0..65536) and are affected by this proposal:

      rfc2021: Remote Network Monitoring Management Information Base
               Version 2 using SMIv2
      rfc1514: Host Resources MIB

   The following ISO standard is affected:
      ISO8601: International Date Format

8 Security Considerations

   Y10K dates will improve the security of all programs where they are
   used. Many errors in programs have been tracked to overflow while
   parsing illegal input. Programs allocating fixed size storage for
   dates will exhibit errors when presented with larger dates. These
   errors can be exploited by wily hackers to compromise the security of
   systems running these programs. Since Y10K dates are arbitrary
   length strings, there is no way to make them overflow.

In addition, positive Y10K dates are easy to compare and less error-prone for humans. It is easier to compare the three projected end of the universe dates - "H100000000000", "I1000000000000" and "K100000000000000" - by looking at the leading letter than by counting the 0's. This will reduce inadvertent errors by people. This advantage will become more noticeable when large dates are more common.

Unfortunately, negative Y10K dates are a bit more difficult to decipher. However, by comparing the current age of the universe to its projected end, it is obvious that there will be many more positive dates than negative dates. And, while the number of negative dates for human history is currently greater than the number of positive dates, the number of negative dates is fixed and the number of positive dates is unbounded.

9 Conclusion

It is not too early to aggressively pursue solutions for the Y10K problem. This specification presents a simple, elegant, and efficient solution to this problem.

10 References

[Crocker]   Crocker, D. and P. Overell, "Augmented BNF for Syntax
             Specifications: ABNF", RFC 2234, November 1997.

[Drake]   Review for the Drake Equation
             http://www.umsl.edu/~bwilking/assign/drake.html

[Microsoft] SNMP SysUpTime Counter Resets After 49.7 Days
             http://support.microsoft.com/support/kb/articles/Q169/
             8/47.asp

[Mike]   Y1K http://lonestar.texas.net/~mdlvas/y1k.htm

[Nigel]   Nigel's (en)lighening tour of Thermodynamics for
             Economists ;-) http://www.santafe.edu/~nigel/thermo-
             primer.html

[NRAO]   Astronomical Times
             http://sadira.gb.nrao.edu/~rfisher/Ephemerides/times.html

[RFC]   Here are all the online RFCs. Note: this is a LONG menu.
             http://info.internet.isi.edu/1s/in-notes/rfc/files

[UNIX]   Year 2000 Issues http://www.rdrop.com/users/caf/y2k.html

    [Wilborne]   PktCDateLig
                 http://www3.gamewood.net/mew3/pilot/pocketc/pktcdate/
                 index.html

    [YUCK]   Y10K Unlimited Consulting Knowledgebase
                 http://www.loyd.net/y10k/index.html

    [Zebu]   The Search for H0
                 http://zebu.uoregon.edu/1997/ph410/16.html

11 Authors' Addresses

    Steve Glassman
    Compaq Systems Research Center
    130 Lytton Avenue
    Palo Alto, CA 94301 USA

    Phone: +1 650-853-2166
    EMail: steveg@pa.dec.com

    Mark Manasse
    Compaq Systems Research Center
    130 Lytton Avenue
    Palo Alto, CA 94301 USA

    Phone: +1 650-853-2221
    EMail: msm@pa.dec.com

    Jeff Mogul
    Compaq Western Resarch Lab
    250 University Avenue
    Palo Alto, CA 94301 USA

    Phone: +1 650-617-3300
    EMail: mogul@pa.dec.com

12. Full Copyright Statement

Network Working Group   S. Christey
Request for Comments: 2795   MonkeySeeDoo, Inc.
Category: Informational   1 April 2000

The Infinite Monkey Protocol Suite (IMPS)

Status of this Memo

Copyright Notice

Abstract

   This memo describes a protocol suite which supports an infinite
   number of monkeys that sit at an infinite number of typewriters in
   order to determine when they have either produced the entire works of
   William Shakespeare or a good television show. The suite includes
   communications and control protocols for monkeys and the
   organizations that interact with them.

Table of Contents

1. Introduction

   It has been posited that if an infinite number of monkeys sit at an
   infinite number of typewriters and randomly press keys, they will
   eventually produce the complete works of Shakespeare [1] [2]. But if
   such a feat is accomplished, how would anybody be able to know? And
   what if the monkey has flawlessly translated Shakespeare's works into
   Esperanto? How could one build a system that obtains these works
   while addressing the basic needs of monkeys, such as sleep and food?
   Nobody has addressed the practical implications of these important
   questions [3].

   In addition, it would be a waste of resources if such a sizable
   effort only focused on Shakespeare. With an infinite number of
   monkeys at work, it is also equally likely that a monkey could
   produce a document that describes how to end world poverty, cure
   disease, or most importantly, write a good situation comedy for
   television [4]. Such an environment would be ripe for innovation
   and, with the proper technical design, could be effectively utilized
   to "make the world a whole lot brighter" [5].

   The Infinite Monkey Protocol Suite (IMPS) is an experimental set of
   protocols that specifies how monkey transcripts may be collected,
   transferred, and reviewed for either historical accuracy (in the case
   of Shakespearean works) or innovation (in the case of new works). It
   also provides a basic communications framework for performing normal
   monkey maintenance.

2. Objects in the Suite

   There are four primary entities that communicate within an IMPS
   network. Groups of monkeys are physically located in Zone Operations
   Organizations (ZOOs). The ZOOs maintain the monkeys and their
   equipment, obtain transcripts from the monkeys' typewriters, and
   interact with other entities who evaluate the transcripts.

   A SIMIAN (Semi-Integrated, Monkey-Interfacing Anthropomorphic Node)
   is a device that is physically attached to the monkey. It provides
   the communications interface between a monkey and its ZOO. It is

effectively a translator for the monkey. It sends status reports and resource requests to the ZOO using human language phrases, and responds to ZOO requests on behalf of the monkey.

The SIMIAN uses the Cross-Habitat Idiomatic Message Protocol (CHIMP) to communicate with the ZOO. The ZOO uses the Knowledgeable and Efficient Emulation Protocol for Ecosystem Resources (KEEPER) to interact with the SIMIAN.

The ZOO obtains typewriter transcripts from the SIMIAN, which is responsible for converting the monkey's typed text into an electronic format if non-digital typewriters are used. The ZOO may then forward the transcripts to one or more entities who review the transcript's contents. IMPS defines two such reviewer protocols, although others could be added.

For Shakespearean works, as well as any other classic literature that has already been published, the ZOO forwards the transcript to a BARD (Big Annex of Reference Documents). The BARD determines if a transcript matches one or more documents in its annex. The ZOO sends the transcript to a BARD using the Inter-Annex Message Broadcasting Protocol for Evaluating Neoclassical Transcripts (IAMB-PENT). The transcripts are considered Neoclassical because (a) they are transferred in electronic media instead of the original paper medium, and (b) the word "classical" does not begin with the letter N.

For new and potentially innovative works, the ZOO submits a transcript to a CRITIC (Collective Reviewer's Innovative Transcript Integration Center). The CRITIC determines if a transcript is sufficiently innovative to be published. The ZOO uses the Protocol for Assessment of Novelty (PAN) to communicate with the CRITIC. The process of using PAN to send a transcript to a CRITIC is sometimes referred to as foreshadowing.

A diagram of IMPS concepts is provided below. Non-technical readers such as mid-level managers, marketing personnel, and liberal arts majors are encouraged to skip the next two sections. The rest of this document assumes that senior management has already stopped reading.

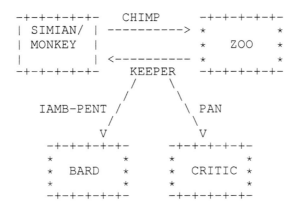

```
       -+-+-+-+-+-    CHIMP     -+-+-+-+-+-
       | SIMIAN/ | ----------> *            *
       | MONKEY  |             *    ZOO    *
       |         | <----------  *            *
       -+-+-+-+-+-    KEEPER    -+-+-+-+-+-
                     /     \
                    /       \
       IAMB-PENT  /          \ PAN
                 /            \
                V              V
       -+-+-+-+-+-    -+-+-+-+-+-
       *          *   *            *
       *  BARD  *   *  CRITIC  *
       *          *   *            *
       -+-+-+-+-+-    -+-+-+-+-+-
```

3. IMPS Packet Structure

    All IMPS protocols must utilize the following packet structure.

```
|-+-+-+-+-+-+-+-+-+-+-+-+-+-+-+-+-+-+-+-+-+-+-+-+--|
|Version | Seq  # | Protocol # | Reserved  | Size  |
|-+-+-+-+-+-+-+-+-+-+-+-+-+-+-+-+-+-+-+-+-+-+-+-+--|
|        Source         |        Destination        |
|-+-+-+-+-+-+-+-+-+-+-+-+-+-+-+-+-+-+-+-+-+-+-+-+--|
|        Data                            | Padding |
|-+-+-+-+-+-+-+-+-+-+-+-+-+-+-+-+-+-+-+-+-+-+-+-+--|
```

    The Version, Sequence Number, Protocol Number, and Reserved fields
    are 32 bit unsigned integers. For IMPS version 1.0, the Version must
    be 1. Reserved must be 0 and will always be 0 in future uses. It is
    included because every other protocol specification includes a
    "future use" reserved field which never, ever changes and is
    therefore a waste of bandwidth and memory. [6] [7] [8].

    The Source and Destination are identifiers for the IMPS objects that
    are communicating. They are represented using Infinite TAGs (see
    next section).

    The Data section contains data which is of arbitrary length.

    The Size field records the size of the entire packet using Infinite
    TAG encoding.

    The end of the packet may contain extra padding, between 0 and 7
    bits, to ensure that the size of packet is rounded out to the next
    byte.

4. Infinite Threshold Accounting Gadget (I-TAG) Encoding

   Each SIMIAN requires a unique identifier within IMPS. This section
   describes design considerations for the IMPS identifier, referred to
   as an Infinite Threshold Accounting Gadget (I-TAG). The I-TAG can
   represent numbers of any size.

   To uniquely identify each SIMIAN, a system is required that is
   capable of representing an infinite number of identifiers. The set
   of all integers can be used as a compact representation. However,
   all existing protocols inherently limit the number of available
   integers by specifying a maximum number of bytes to be used for an
   integer. This approach cannot work well in an IMPS network with an
   infinite number of monkeys to manage.

   Practically speaking, one could select a byte size which could
   represent an integer that is greater than the number of atoms in the
   known universe. There are several limitations to this approach,
   however: (a) it would needlessly exclude IMPS implementations that
   may utilize sub-atomic monkeys and/or multiple universes; (b) there
   is not a consensus as to how many atoms there are in this universe;
   and (c) while the number is extremely large, it still falls pitifully
   short of infinity. Since any entity that fully implements IMPS is
   probably very, very good at handling infinite numbers, IMPS must
   ensure that it can represent them.

   Netstrings, i.e. strings which encode their own size, were
   considered. However, netstrings have not been accepted as a
   standard, and they do not scale to infinity. As stated in [9],
   "[Greater than] 999999999 bytes is bad." Well put.

   A scheme for identifying arbitrary dates was also considered for
   implementation [10]. While it solves the Y10K problem and does scale
   to infinity, its ASCII representation wastes memory by a factor
   greater than 8. While this may not seem important in an environment
   that has enough resources to support an infinite number of monkeys,
   it is inelegant for the purpose of monkey identification. It is also
   CPU intensive to convert such a representation to a binary number (at
   least based on the author's implementation, which was written in a
   combination of LISP, Perl, and Java). The algorithm is complicated
   and could lead to incorrect implementations. Finally, the author of
   this document sort of forgot about that RFC until it was too late to
   include it properly, and was already emotionally attached to the I-
   TAG idea anyway. It should be noted, however, that if a monkey had
   typed this particular section and it was submitted to a CRITIC, it
   would probably receive a PAN rejection code signifying the
   reinvention of the wheel.

Since there is no acceptable representation for I-TAGs available, one
is defined below.

An I-TAG is divided into three sections:

```
|-+-+-+-+-+-+-+-+-+-|-+-+-+-+-+-+-|-+-+-+-+-+-+|
|    META-SIZE      |    SIZE     |    ID     |
|-+-+-+-+-+-+-+-+-+-|-+-+-+-+-+-+-|-+-+-+-+-+-+|
```

SIZE specifies how many bytes are used to represent the ID, which is
an arbitrary integer. META-SIZE specifies an upper limit on how many
bits are used to represent SIZE.

META-SIZE is an arbitrary length sequence of N '1' bits terminated by
a '0' bit, i.e. it has the form:

    11111...1110

where N is the smallest number such that 2^N exceeds the number of
bits required to represent the number of bytes that are necessary to
store the ID (i.e., SIZE).

The SIZE is then encoded using N bits, ordered from the most
significant bit to the least significant bit.

Finally, the ID is encoded using SIZE bytes.

This representation, while clunky, makes efficient use of memory and
is scalable to infinity. For any number X which is less than 2^N
(for any N), a maximum of $(N + \log(N) + \log(\log(N)))/8$ bytes is
necessary to represent X. The math could be slightly incorrect, but
it sounds right.

A remarkable, elegant little C function was written to implement I-
TAG processing, but it has too many lines of code to include in this
margin [11].

5. KEEPER Specification

Following is a description of the Knowledgeable and Efficient
Emulation Protocol for Ecosystem Resources (KEEPER), which the ZOO
uses to communicate with the SIMIAN. The IMPS protocol number for
KEEPER is 1.

KEEPER is a connectionless protocol. The ZOO sends a request to the
SIMIAN using a single IMPS packet. The SIMIAN sends a response back
to the ZOO with another IMPS packet. The data portion of the packet
is of the following form:

92

```
+-+-+-+-+-+-+-+-+-+-+-+-+-+-+-+-+-+-+-+-+-+-+-+-+
|   Version   | Type | Message ID   | Message Code  |
+-+-+-+-+-+-+-+-+-+-+-+-+-+-+-+-+-+-+-+-+-+-+-+-+
```

Version, Type, Message ID, and Message are all 16-bit integers.

Version = the version of KEEPER being used (in this document, the
          version is 1)

Type = the type of message being sent. '0' is a request; '1' is a
       response

Message ID = a unique identifier to distinguish different messages

Message Code = the specific message being sent

When a ZOO sends a KEEPER request, the SIMIAN must send a KEEPER
response which uses the same Message ID as the original request.

5.1 KEEPER Message Request Codes (ZOO-to-SIMIAN)

```
    CODE     NAME       DESCRIPTION
    +---------------------------------------------------------------+
    | 0     | RESERVED | Reserved                                   |
    +---------------------------------------------------------------+
    | 1     | STATUS   | Determine status of monkey                 |
    +---------------------------------------------------------------+
    | 2     | HEARTBEAT| Check to see if monkey has a heartbeat     |
    +---------------------------------------------------------------+
    | 3     | WAKEUP   | Wake up monkey                             |
    +---------------------------------------------------------------+
    | 4     | TYPE     | Make sure monkey is typing                 |
    +---------------------------------------------------------------+
    | 5     | FASTER   | Monkey must type faster                    |
    +---------------------------------------------------------------+
    | 6     |TRANSCRIPT| Send transcript                            |
    +---------------------------------------------------------------+
    | 7     | STOP     | Stop all monkey business                   |
    +---------------------------------------------------------------+
    |8-512  | FUTURE   | Reserved for future use                    |
    +---------------------------------------------------------------+
    | 513+  | USER     | User defined                               |
    +---------------------------------------------------------------+
```

93

5.2 KEEPER Message Response Codes (SIMIAN-to-ZOO)

```
  CODE    NAME      DESCRIPTION
  +-------------------------------------------------------------+
  | 0     | RESERVED | Reserved                                 |
  +-------------------------------------------------------------+
  | 1     | ASLEEP   | Status: Monkey is asleep                 |
  +-------------------------------------------------------------+
  | 2     | GONE     | Status: Monkey is not at typewriter      |
  +-------------------------------------------------------------+
  | 3     |DISTRACTED| Status: Monkey is distracted (not typing)|
  +-------------------------------------------------------------+
  | 4     |NORESPONSE| Status: Monkey is not responding         |
  +-------------------------------------------------------------+
  | 5     | ALIVE    | Status: Monkey is alive                  |
  +-------------------------------------------------------------+
  | 6     | DEAD     | Status: Monkey is dead                   |
  +-------------------------------------------------------------+
  | 7     | ACCEPT   | Monkey accepts request                   |
  +-------------------------------------------------------------+
  | 8     | REFUSE   | Monkey refuses request                   |
  +-------------------------------------------------------------+
  | 9-512 | FUTURE   | Reserved for future use                  |
  +-------------------------------------------------------------+
  | 513+  | USER     | User defined                             |
  +-------------------------------------------------------------+
```

5.3 Requirements for KEEPER Request and Response Codes

Below are the requirements for request and response codes within KEEPER.

1. A SIMIAN must respond to a STATUS request with an ALIVE, DEAD, ASLEEP, GONE, DISTRACTED, or NORESPONSE code.

2. A SIMIAN must respond to a HEARTBEAT request with an ALIVE or DEAD code. SIMIAN implementors must be careful when checking the heartbeat of very relaxed monkeys who practice transcendental meditation or yoga, as they may appear DEAD even if they are still alive.

3. A SIMIAN must respond to a STOP request with a NORESPONSE, ALIVE, DEAD, or GONE code. How a SIMIAN stops the monkey is implementation-specific. However, the SIMIAN should preserve the monkey's ALIVE status to protect the ZOO from being shut down by authorities or animal rights groups. If the monkey is present but the SIMIAN interface is unable to verify whether the monkey is ALIVE or DEAD, then it must use a NORESPONSE.

4. A SIMIAN should respond to a TYPE or FASTER request with an ACCEPT code, especially if there are deadlines. The only other allowed responses are REFUSE, ASLEEP, GONE, NORESPONSE, or DEAD. This protocol does not define what actions should be taken if a SIMIAN responds with REFUSE, although a BRIBE_BANANA command may be added in future versions.

5. A SIMIAN must respond to a WAKEUP request with ACCEPT, REFUSE, GONE, NORESPONSE, or DEAD.

6. A SIMIAN must respond to a TRANSCRIPT request by establishing a CHIMP session to send the transcript to the ZOO.

5.4 Example ZOO-to-SIMIAN Exchanges using KEEPER

Assume a ZOO (SanDiego) must interact with a monkey named BoBo. Using KEEPER, SanDiego would interface with BoBo's SIMIAN (BoBoSIM). The following exchange might take place if BoBo begins to evolve self-awareness and independence.

```
SanDiego> STATUS
BoBoSIM>  DISTRACTED
SanDiego> TYPE
BoBoSIM>  REFUSE
SanDiego> TYPE
BoBoSIM>  REFUSE
SanDiego> TYPE
BoBoSIM>  GONE
```

The following exchange might take place early in the morning, if BoBo was being poorly maintained and was working at its typewriter very late the night before.

```
SanDiego> WAKEUP
BoBoSIM>  NORESPONSE
SanDiego> WAKEUP
BoBoSIM>  NORESPONSE
SanDiego> WAKEUP
BoBoSIM>  NORESPONSE
SanDiego> HEARTBEAT
BoBoSIM>  DEAD
SanDiego> TRANSCRIPT
```

6. CHIMP Specification

Following is a description of the Cross-Habitat Idiomatic Message Protocol (CHIMP), which the SIMIAN uses to communicate with the ZOO. The IMPS protocol number for CHIMP is 2.

CHIMP is a connection-oriented protocol. A SIMIAN (the "client")
sends a series of requests to the ZOO (the "server"), which sends
replies back to the SIMIAN.

6.1. SIMIAN Client Requests

SEND <resource>

   The SIMIAN is requesting a specific resource. The resource
   may be FOOD, WATER, MEDICINE, VETERINARIAN, or TECHNICIAN.
   The SIMIAN makes requests for FOOD or WATER by interpreting
   the monkey's behavior and environment, e.g. its food dish. It
   requests MEDICINE or VETERINARIAN if it observes that the
   monkey's health is declining in any way, e.g. carpal tunnel
   syndrome or sore buttocks. How the SIMIAN determines health
   is implementation-specific. In cases where the SIMIAN itself
   may be malfunctioning, it may request a TECHNICIAN.

REPLACE <item>

   The ZOO must replace an item that is used by the monkey during
   typing activities. The item to be replaced may be TYPEWRITER,
   PAPER, RIBBON, CHAIR, TABLE, or MONKEY.

CLEAN <item>

   The SIMIAN is requesting that the ZOO must clean an item. The
   item may be CHAIR, TABLE, or MONKEY. How the ZOO cleans the
   item is implementation-specific. This command is identified
   in the protocol because it has been theorized that if an
   infinite number of monkeys sit at an infinite number of
   typewriters, the smell would be unbearable [12]. If this
   theory is proven true, then CLEAN may become the most critical
   command in the entire protocol suite.

NOTIFY <status>

   The SIMIAN notifies the ZOO of the monkey's status. The status
   may be any status as defined in the KEEPER protocol,
   i.e. ASLEEP, GONE, DISTRACTED, NORESPONSE, ALIVE, or DEAD.

TRANSCRIPT <size>

   The SIMIAN notifies the ZOO of a new transcript from the monkey.
   The number of characters in the transcript is specified in the
   size parameter.

BYE

   The SIMIAN is terminating the connection.

6.2. ZOO Server Responses

   HELO <free text>

   Upon initial connection, the ZOO must send a HELO reply.

   ACCEPT

   The ZOO will fulfill the SIMIAN's request.

   DELAY

   The ZOO will fulfill the SIMIAN's request at a later time.

   REFUSE

   The ZOO refuses to fulfill the SIMIAN's request.

   RECEIVED

   The ZOO has received the full text of a transcript that has been
   submitted by the SIMIAN.

6.3 Example SIMIAN-to-ZOO Session using CHIMP

   Assume a monkey BoBo with a SIMIAN interface named BoBoSIM, and a ZOO
   named SanDiego. Once the BoBoSIM client has established a connection
   to the SanDiego server, the following session might take place.

```
SanDiego> HELO CHIMP version 1.0 4/1/2000
BoBoSIM> REPLACE PAPER
SanDiego> ACCEPT
BoBoSIM>  TRANSCRIPT 87
SanDiego> ACCEPT
BoBoSIM>  xvkxvn i hate Binky xFnk , feEL hungry and sIck sbNf
BoBoSIM>  so so sad sDNfkodgv .,n.,   ,HELP MEEEEEEEE cv.Cvn l
SanDiego> RECEIVED
BoBoSIM>  SEND FOOD
SanDiego> ACCEPT
BoBoSIM>  SEND MEDICINE
SanDiego> DELAY
BoBoSIM>  SEND VETERINARIAN
SanDiego> REFUSE
BoBoSIM>  SEND VETERINARIAN
```

97

```
         SanDiego> REFUSE
         BoBoSIM>  NOTIFY NORESPONSE
         SanDiego> ACCEPT
         BoBoSIM>  NOTIFY DEAD
         SanDiego> ACCEPT
         BoBoSIM>  REPLACE MONKEY
         SanDiego> ACCEPT
```

7. IAMB-PENT Specification

   Following is a description of the Inter-Annex Message Broadcasting
   Protocol for Evaluating Neoclassical Transcripts (IAMB-PENT), which a
   ZOO uses to send transcripts to a BARD. The IMPS protocol number is
   5.

   IAMB-PENT is a connection-oriented protocol. A ZOO (the "client")
   sends a transcript phrases to the BARD (the "server"), which
   evaluates the transcript and notifies the ZOO if the transcript
   matches all of a classical work or a portion thereof.

7.1. ZOO Client Requests

   RECEIVETH <transcript name>

      The ZOO notifies the BARD of a new transcript to be evaluated.
      The name of the transcript is provided.

   ANON <size>

      The ZOO notifies the BARD that a transcript of the given size is
      to be provided soon. The text of the transcript is then sent.

   ABORTETH <A2> <U3> <A3> <U4> <A4> <U5> <A5>

      The ZOO notifies the BARD that it is about to close the
      connection. The ZOO must specify a closing message. A2, A3,
      A4, and A5 must be accented syllables. U3, U4, and U5 must not
      be accented.

7.2 BARD Responses

   HARK <U1> <A2> <U3> <A3> <U4> <A4> <U5> <A5>

      When the ZOO establishes a connection, the BARD must send a HARK
      command. A2, A3, A4, and A5 must be accented syllables. U1,
      U2, U3, U4, and U5 must not be accented.

PRITHEE <A2> <U3> <A3> <U4> <A4> <U5> <A5>

When a ZOO uses a RECEIVETH command to specify a forthcoming transcript, the BARD must respond with a PRITHEE. A2, A3, A4, and A5 must be accented syllables. U3, U4, and U5 must not be accented.

REGRETTETH <A2> <U3> <A3> <U4> <A4> <U5> <A5>

If the BARD does not have the transcript in its Annex, it uses the REGRETTETH command to notify the ZOO. A2, A3, A4, and A5 must be accented syllables. U3, U4, and U5 must not be accented.

ACCEPTETH <A2> <U3> <A3> <U4> <A4> <U5> <A5>

If the BARD has located the transcript in its Annex, it uses the ACCEPTETH command to notify the ZOO. A2, A3, A4, and A5 must be accented syllables. U3, U4, and U5 must not be accented.

7.3 Example ZOO-to-BARD Session using IAMB-PENT

This is a sample IAMB-PENT session in which a ZOO (SanDiego) sends a transcript to a BARD (William).

```
William> HARK now, what light through yonder window breaks?
SanDiego> RECEIVETH TRANSCRIPT SanDiego.BoBo.17
William> PRITHEE thy monkey's wisdom poureth forth!
SanDiego> ANON 96
SanDiego> I must be cruel, only to be kind.  Thus bad begins,
          and worse remains in front.
William> REGRETTETH none hath writ thy words before
SanDiego> ABORTETH Fate may one day bless my zone
```

8. PAN Specification

Following is a description of the Protocol for Assessment of Novelty (PAN). A ZOO uses PAN to send monkey transcripts for review by a CRITIC. The IMPS protocol number for PAN is 10 [13].

PAN is a connection-oriented protocol. A ZOO (the "unwashed masses") sends a request to the CRITIC (the "all-powerful"), which sends a response back to the ZOO.

8.1. ZOO Requests

COMPLIMENT <text>

The ZOO may say something nice to the CRITIC using the given
text. The CRITIC does not respond to the compliment within the
protocol. However, it is generally believed that the CRITIC is
more likely to accept a new transcript when a ZOO uses many
compliments.

TRANSCRIPT <name> <size>

The ZOO notifies the CRITIC of a new transcript for review.
The name of the transcript, plus the number of characters, are
specified as parameters to this request. The text of the
transcript is then sent.

THANKS

This is an indicator that a ZOO is about to terminate the
connection.

8.2. CRITIC Responses

SIGH <insult>

When the ZOO establishes a connection, the CRITIC must respond
with a SIGH and an optional insult.

IMPRESS_ME

A CRITIC must respond with an IMPRESS_ME once a ZOO has made a
TRANSCRIPT request.

REJECT <code> REJECT 0 <text>

When a transcript has been received, the CRITIC must respond
with a REJECT and a code that indicates the reason for
rejection. A table of rejection codes is provided below. When
the code is 0, the CRITIC may respond using free text. A CRITIC
may send a REJECT before it has received or processed the full
text of the transcript.

DONT_CALL_US_WE'LL_CALL_YOU

The CRITIC makes this statement before terminating the
connection.

GRUDGING_ACCEPTANCE

THIS RESPONSE IS NOT SUPPORTED IN THIS VERSION OF PAN. The
Working group for the Infinite Monkey Protocol Suite (WIMPS)
agreed that it is highly unlikely that a CRITIC will ever use
this response when a REJECT is available. It is only included
as an explanation to implementors who do not fully understand
how CRITICs work. In time, it is possible that a CRITIC may
evolve (in much the same way that a monkey might). Should such
a time ever come, the WIMPS may decide to support this response
in later versions of PAN.

8.3. Table of CRITIC Reject Codes

CODE DESCRIPTION

| 0 | <Encrypted response following; see below>

| 1 | "You're reinventing the wheel."

| 2 | "This will never, ever sell."

| 3 | "Huh? I don't understand this at all."

| 4 | "You forgot one little obscure reference from twenty years
| | ago that renders your whole idea null and void."

| 5 | "Due to the number of submissions, we could not accept every
| | transcript."

| 6 | "There aren't enough charts and graphs. Where is the color?"

| 7 | "I'm cranky and decided to take it out on you."

| 8 | "This is not in within the scope of what we are looking for."

| 9 | "This is too derivative."

|10 | "Your submission was received after the deadline. Try again
| | next year."

If the CRITIC uses a reject code of 0, then the textual response
must use an encryption scheme that is selected by the CRITIC.
Since the PAN protocol does not specify how a ZOO may determine
what scheme is being used, the ZOO might not be able to understand
the CRITIC's response.

8.4. Example ZOO-to-CRITIC Session using PAN

   Below is a sample session from a ZOO (SanDiego) to a CRITIC
   (NoBrainer).

      NoBrainer> SIGH Abandon hope all who enter here
      SanDiego> COMPLIMENT We love your work. Your words are like
      SanDiego> COMPLIMENT jewels and you are always correct.
      SanDiego> TRANSCRIPT RomeoAndJuliet.BoBo.763 251
      NoBrainer> IMPRESS_ME
      SanDiego> Two households, both alike in dignity,
      SanDiego> In fair Verona, where we lay our scene,
      SanDiego> From ancient grudge break to new mutiny,
      SanDiego> Where civil blood makes civil hands unclean.
      SanDiego> From forth the fatal loins of these two foes
      SanDiego> A pair of star-cross'd lovers take their life;
      NoBrainer> REJECT 2   ("This will never, ever sell.")
      SanDiego> THANKS
      NoBrainer> DONT_CALL_US_WE'LL_CALL_YOU

9. Security Considerations

   In accordance with the principles of the humane treatment of
   animals, the design of IMPS specifically prohibits the CRITIC from
   contacting the SIMIAN directly and hurting its feelings. BARDs
   and CRITICs are also separated because of fundamental
   incompatibilities and design flaws.

   The security considerations for the rest of IMPS are similar to
   those for the original Internet protocols. Specifically, IMPS
   refuses to learn from the mistakes of the past and blithely
   repeats the same errors without batting an eye. Spoofing and
   denial of service attacks abound if untrusted entities gain access
   to an IMPS network. Since all transmissions occur in cleartext
   without encryption, innovative works are subject to theft, which
   is not a significant problem unless the network contains entities
   other than CRITICs. The open nature of BARDs with respect to
   IAMB-PENT messages allows a BARD to borrow heavily from
   transmitted works, but by design BARDs are incapable of stealing
   transcripts outright.

   The ZOO may be left open to exploitation by pseudo-SIMIANs from
   around the world. A third party could interrupt communications
   between a ZOO and a SIMIAN by flooding the SIMIAN with packets,
   incrementing the message ID by 1 for each packet. More heinously,
   the party could exploit the KEEPER protocol by sending a single
   STOP request to each SIMIAN, thus causing a massive denial of
   service throughout the ZOO. The party could also spoof a CHIMP

request or send false information such as a DEAD status, which
could cause a ZOO to attempt to replace a monkey that is still
functioning properly.

In addition, if a ZOO repeatedly rejects a SIMIAN's requests
(especially those for FOOD, WATER, and VETERINARIAN), then the ZOO
may inadvertently cause its own denial of service with respect to
that particular SIMIAN. However, both KEEPER and CHIMP allow the
ZOO to detect this condition in a timely fashion via the
NORESPONSE or DEAD status codes.

All BARDs are inherently insecure because they face insurmountable
financial problems and low prioritization, which prevents them
from working reliably. In the rare cases when a BARD
implementation overcomes these obstacles, it is only successful
for 15 minutes, and reverts to being insecure immediately
thereafter [14]. Since a CRITIC could significantly reduce the
success of a BARD with an appropriate PAN response, this is one
more reason why BARDs and CRITICs should always be kept separate
from each other.

It is expected that very few people will care about most
implementations of CRITIC, and CRITICs themselves are inherently
insecure. Therefore, security is not a priority for CRITICs. The
CRITIC may become the victim of a denial of service attack if too
many SIMIANs submit transcripts at the same time. In addition,
one SIMIAN may submit a non-innovative work by spoofing another
SIMIAN (this is referred to as the Plagiarism Problem). A CRITIC
response can also be spoofed, but since the only response
supported in PAN version 1 is REJECT, this is of little
consequence. Care must be taken in future versions if a
GRUDGING_ACCEPTANCE response is allowed. Finally, a transcript
may be lost in transmission, and PAN does not provide a mechanism
for a ZOO to determine if this has happened. Future versions of
IMPS may be better suited to answer this fundamental design
problem: if an innovative work is lost in transmission, can a
CRITIC still PAN it?

Based on the number of packet-level vulnerabilities discovered in
recent years, it is a foregone conclusion that some
implementations will behave extremely poorly when processing
malformed IMPS packets with incorrect padding or reserved bits
[15] [16] [17].

Finally, no security considerations are made with respect to the
fact that over the course of infinite time, monkeys may evolve and
discover how to control their own SIMIAN interfaces and send false
requests, or to compose and submit their own transcripts. There
are indications that this may already be happening [18].

10. Acknowledgements

The author wishes to thank Andre Frech for technical comments that
tripled the size of this document, Kean Kaufmann and Amanda
Vizedom for lectures on Shakespearean grammar, Rohn Blake for
clarifying the nature of the entire universe, William Shakespeare
for accents, the number 16, and the color yellow.

11. References

[1]   The Famous Brett Watson, "The Mathematics of Monkeys and
      Shakespeare." http://www.nutters.org/monkeys.html

[2]   Dr. Math. "Monkeys Typing Shakespeare: Infinity Theory."
      http://forum.swarthmore.edu/dr.math/problems/bridge8.5.98.html

[3]   K. Clark, Stark Mill Brewery, Manchester, NH, USA. Feb 18,
      2000. (personal communication). "Good question! I never thought
      of that! I bet nobody else has, either. Please pass the french
      fries."

[4]   The author was unable to find a reference in any issue of TV
      Guide published between 1956 and the date of this document.

[5]   "Dough Re Mi," The Brady Bunch. Original air date January 14,
      1972.

[6]   Postel, J., " Internet Protocol", STD 5, RFC 791, September 1981.

[7]   Postel, J., "Transmission Control Protocol", STD 7, RFC 793,
      September 1981.

[8]   Brown, C. and A. Malis, "Multiprotocol Interconnect over Frame
      Relay", STD 55, RFC 2427, September 1998.

[9]   Internet-Draft, bernstein-netstrings-06 (expired Work in
      Progress). D.J. Bernstein. Inclusion of this reference is a
      violation of RFC 2026 section 2.2.

[10] Glassman, S., Manasse, M. and J. Mogul, "Y10K and Beyond", RFC
      2550, 1 April 1999.

   [11] "My Last Theorem: A Prankster's Guide to Ageless Mathematical
         Jokes That are Funny Because They're True and People Can't Prove
         Them for Centuries." P. Fermat. Circa 1630.

   [12] .signature in various USENET postings, circa 1994. Author
         unknown.

   [13] "Recognizing Irony, or How Not to be Duped When Reading."
         Faye Halpern. 1998.
         http://www.brown.edu/Student_Services/Writing_Center/halpern1.htm

   [14] Andy Warhol. Circa 1964.

   [15] CERT Advisory CA-98-13. CERT. December 1998.
         http://www.cert.org/advisories/

   [16] CERT Advisory CA-97.28. CERT. December 1997.
         http://www.cert.org/advisories/

   [17] CERT Advisory CA-96.26. CERT. December 1996.
         http://www.cert.org/advisories/

   [18] All issues of TV Guide published between 1956 and the date of
         this document.

12. Author's Address

   SteQven M. Christey
   EMail: steqve@shore.net

13. Full Copyright Statement

Acknowledgement

Funding for the RFC Editor function is currently provided by the
Internet Society.

106

Network Working Group   H. Kennedy
Request for Comments: 3091   University of Michigan
Category: Informational   1 April 2001

Pi Digit Generation Protocol

Status of this Memo

Copyright Notice

Abstract

   This memo defines a protocol to provide the Pi digit generation
   service (PIgen) used between clients and servers on host computers.

Introduction

   This protocol is intended to provide the Pi digit generation service
   (PIgen), and be used between clients and servers on host computers.
   Typically the clients are on workstation hosts lacking local Pi
   support, and the servers are more capable machines with greater Pi
   calculation capabilities. The essential tradeoff is the use of
   network resources and time instead of local computational cycles.

   The key words "MUST", "MUST NOT", "REQUIRED", "SHALL", "SHALL NOT",
   "SHOULD", "SHOULD NOT", "RECOMMENDED", "MAY", and "OPTIONAL" in this
   document are to be interpreted as described in RFC 2119 [RFC2119].

Note

   All digits supplied by implementations of this service are ASCII
   [US-ASCII] representations of decimal (base 10) numbers following the
   decimal point in values or approximations of Pi. There MUST be an
   implied decimal value of 3 (three) preceding the values provided by
   the service defined by this protocol.

1.   TCP Based Digit Generator Service

   One REQUIRED PIgen service is defined as a stateless TCP service. A
   server listens on TCP port 314159. Once a connection is established
   the server sends a stream of data, one digit of Pi at at time,

starting with the most significant digit following the decimal point.
Any incoming data MUST be discarded. This continues until the client
closes the connection.

The data flow over the connection is limited by the normal TCP flow
control mechanisms, so there is no concern about the server sending
data faster than the client can process it.

Servers MAY use any appropriate method of Pi digit generation to
provide this service, including (but not limited to) table lookup
[DIGITS], numerical calculation [FIBPI,PIFFT] and statistical
sampling [MCM]. However, the method chosen SHOULD provide a precise
value for the digits of Pi generated.

Implementors of PIgen MUST provide this service to be conditionally
compliant with this RFC.

1.1.   Approximate Service

An OPTIONAL PIgen service is defined as a stateless TCP service. A
server listens on TCP port 220007. Once a connection is established
the server sends a stream of data, one digit of the rational number
22/7 at a time, starting with the most significant digit following
the decimal point. Any incoming data MUST be discarded. This
continues until the client closes the connection.

2.   UDP Based Digit Generator Service

An OPTIONAL PIgen service is defined as a stateless UDP service. A
server listens on UDP port 314159. When a datagram requesting a
specific digit of Pi is received, an answering datagram is sent
containing the value of the requested digit of Pi according to the
format defined in sections 2.1.1. and 2.1.2.

The requested digit value MAY be determined by any appropriate method
of Pi digit generation. RECOMMENDED methods include table lookup
[DIGITS], or numerical calculation [BBPPA].

2.1.   Packet Format

The datagram-based components of the PIgen protocol suite all share
the following UDP data payload formats (defined in the ABNF of RFC
2234 [RFC2234]).

2.1.1. Request Payload Format

```
request   = nth_digit

nth_digit = 1*DIGIT  ; specifying the n-th digit following the
                     ; decimal point
```

2.1.2. Reply Payload Format

```
reply  = nth_digit ":" DIGIT ; where DIGIT is the value of the n-th
                             ; digit following the decimal
                             ; point
```

2.2.   Approximate Service

An OPTIONAL PIgen service is defined as a stateless UDP service. A
server listens on UDP port 220007. When a datagram requesting a
specific digit of the rational number 22/7 is received, an answering
datagram is sent containing the value of the requested digit of 22/7
according to the format defined in sections 2.1.1. and 2.1.2.

3.   IP Multicast Based Digit Generator Service

An OPTIONAL PIgen service is defined as a stateless UDP service. A
random distribution of digits of Pi are sent using the payload format
described in section 2.1.2. to the IP multicast group
314.159.265.359.

There is no request structure. If a server implementing this
component of the protocol suite joins the PIgen multicast group and
does not detect a server providing digits within 30 seconds, it MAY
elect to become the PIgen multicast provider.

The PIgen multicast provider generates a random distribution of the
digits of Pi and sends them out to the multicast group. PIgen
multicast clients build up a coherent value of Pi by listening to the
multicast group over time.

The randomly selected digit value MAY be determined by any
appropriate method of Pi digit generation. RECOMMENDED methods
include table lookup [DIGITS], or numerical calculation [BBPPA]. To
ensure an adequately random distribution, a proper random number
generator should be used, see [RANDOM] for some examples.

4.   Service Discovery

     Clients SHOULD discover PIgen servers via the DNS SRV algorithm
     [RFC2782]. The service used is "pigen" and the protocols used are
     "tcp" and "udp". Approximate services (sections 1.1. and 2.2.)
     should be discovered using a service of "pigem". This allows for
     central administration of addressing, fallback for failed relays and
     collectors, and static load balancing.

5.   Security Considerations

     As almost every secure Internet protocol requires a highly accurate
     value of Pi in order to function correctly, it is imperative that
     clients only use a trusted PIgen server. The imminent collapse of
     the Internet is assured if this guideline is not strictly followed.

6. References

     [RFC2119]   Bradner, S., "Key words for use in RFCs to Indicate
                 Requirement Levels", BCP 14, RFC 2119, March 1997.

     [US-ASCII] Coded Character Set--7-Bit American Standard Code for
                 Information Interchange, ANSI X3.4-1986.

     [DIGITS]   ftp://pi.super-computing.org/pub/pi

     [FIBPI]   Pi and the Fibonacci Numbers
                 http://www.mcs.surrey.ac.uk/Personal/R.Knott/Fibonacci/
                 fibpi.html

     [PIFFT]   Pi Calculation based on FFT and AGM http://momonga.t.u-
                 tokyo.ac.jp/~ooura/pi_fft.html

     [MCM]   The Monte Carlo Method
                 http://www.daimi.aau.dk/~u951581/pi/MonteCarlo/pimc.html

     [BBPPA]   Bailey-Borwien-Plouffe Pi Algorithm
                 http://www.mathsoft.com/asolve/plouffe/plouffe.html

     [RFC2234]   Crocker, D. and P. Overell, "Augmented BNF for Syntax
                 Specifications: ABNF", RFC 2234, November 1997.

     [RANDOM]   Randomness for Crypto http://www.cs.berkeley.edu/~daw/rnd/

     [RFC2782]   Gulbrandsen, A., Vixie, P. and L. Esibov, "A DNS RR for
                 specifying the location of services (DNS SRV)", RFC 2782,
                 February 2000.

   [CHARGEN]   Postel, J., "Character Generation Protocol", STD 22, RFC
               864, May 1983.

7. Author's Address

   Hugh Kennedy
   University of Michigan
   2281 Bonisteel Blvd.
   Ann Arbor, MI 48109-2099
   USA

   EMail: kennedyh@engin.umich.edu

111

Full Copyright Statement

Acknowledgement

Funding for the RFC Editor function is currently provided by the
Internet Society.

Network Working Group   M. Gaynor
Request for Comments: 3093   S. Bradner
Category: Informational   Harvard University
                                                          1 April 2001

Firewall Enhancement Protocol (FEP)

Status of this Memo

Copyright Notice

Abstract

   Internet Transparency via the end-to-end architecture of the Internet
   has allowed vast innovation of new technologies and services [1].
   However, recent developments in Firewall technology have altered this
   model and have been shown to inhibit innovation. We propose the
   Firewall Enhancement Protocol (FEP) to allow innovation, without
   violating the security model of a Firewall. With no cooperation from
   a firewall operator, the FEP allows ANY application to traverse a
   Firewall. Our methodology is to layer any application layer
   Transmission Control Protocol/User Datagram Protocol (TCP/UDP)
   packets over the HyperText Transfer Protocol (HTTP) protocol, since
   HTTP packets are typically able to transit Firewalls. This scheme
   does not violate the actual security usefulness of a Firewall, since
   Firewalls are designed to thwart attacks from the outside and to
   ignore threats from within. The use of FEP is compatible with the
   current Firewall security model because it requires cooperation from
   a host inside the Firewall. FEP allows the best of both worlds: the
   security of a firewall, and transparent tunneling thought the
   firewall.

1.0 Terminology

   The key words "MUST", "MUST NOT", "REQUIRED", "SHALL", "SHALL NOT",
   "SHOULD", "SHOULD NOT", "RECOMMENDED", "MAY", and "OPTIONAL" in this
   document are to be interpreted as described in RFC 2119.

2.0 Introduction

   The Internet has done well, considering that less than 10 years ago
   the telco's were claiming it could not ever work for the corporate
   environment. There are many reasons for this; a particularly strong
   one is the end-to-end argument discussed by Reed, Seltzer, and Clark
   [2]. Innovation at the ends has proven to be a very powerful
   methodology creating more value than ever conceived of. But, the
   world is changing as Clark notes in [6]. With the connection of the
   corporate world to the Internet, security concerns have become
   paramount, even at the expense of breaking the end-to-end paradigm.
   One example of this is the Firewall - a device to prevent outsiders
   from unauthorized access into a corporation. Our new protocol, the
   Firewall Enhancement Protocol (FEP), is designed to restore the end-
   to-end model while maintaining the level of security created by
   Firewalls.

   To see how powerful the end-to-end model is consider the following
   example. If Scott and Mark have a good idea and some implementation
   talent, they can create an artifact, use it, and send it to their
   friends. If it turns out to be a good idea these friends can adopt
   it and maybe make it better. Now enter the Firewall: if Mark happens
   to work at a company that installs a Firewall, he can't experiment
   with his friend Scott. Innovation is more difficult, maybe
   impossible. What business is it of an IT manager if Scott and Mark
   want to do some experiments to enable them to better serve their
   users? This is how the web was created: one guy with talent, a few
   good ideas, and the ability to innovate.

   Firewalls are important, and we do respect the right of anybody to
   protecting themselves any way they want (as long as others are not
   inconvenienced). Firewalls work, and have a place in the Internet.
   However, Firewalls are built to protect from external threats, not
   internal ones. Our proposed protocol does not break the security
   model of the Firewall; it still protects against all external risks
   that a particular Firewall can protect against. For our protocol to
   work someone inside the Firewall must run an application level
   protocol that can access TCP port 80. Our concept allows a
   consistent level of security while bypassing the IT manager in charge
   of the Firewall. We offer freedom to innovate without additionally
   compromising external security, and the best part, no need to waste
   time involving any managers for approval.

   We got this idea from the increasing number of applications that use
   HTTP specifically because it can bypass Firewall barriers. This
   piecemeal deployment of specific applications is not an efficient way
   to meet the challenge to innovation created by Firewalls. We decided
   to develop a process by which TCP/IP itself is carried over HTTP.

114

With this innovation anyone can use any new TCP/IP application
immediately without having to go through the laborious process of
dealing with Firewall access for the particular application. An
unintended byproduct of this proposal is that existing TCP/IP
applications can also be supported to better serve the users. With
FEP, the users can decide what applications they can run.

Our protocol is simple and is partly based on the Eastlake [3]
proposal for MIME encoding of IP packets. We use the ubiquitous HTTP
protocol format. The IP datagram is carried in the message body of
the HTTP message and the TCP packet header information is encoded
into HTTP headers of the message. This ASCII encoding of the header
fields has many advantages, including human readability, increasing
the debuggability of new applications, and easy logging of packet
information. If this becomes widely adopted, tools like tcpdump will
become obsolete.

3.0 FEP Protocol

Figure 1 shows a high level view of our protocol. The application
(1) in host A (outside the Firewall) sends a TCP/IP datagram to host
B (within the firewall). Using a tunnel interface the TCP/IP
datagram is routed to our FEP software (2), which encodes the
datagram within a HTTP message. Then this message is sent via a
HTTP/TCP/IP tunnel (3) to host B on the normal HTTP port (4). When
it arrives at host B, this packet is routed via the tunnel to the FEP
software (5), which decodes the packet and creates a TCP/IP datagram
to insert into host's B protocol stack (6). This packet is routed to
the application on host B (7), as if the Firewall (8) never existed.

```
        host A                                    host B
      ----------                                ----------
     |   App    | (1)                          |   App    | (7)
     |----------|                              |----------|
     |   TCP    |                              |   TCP    |
     |----------|                              |----------|
     |   IP     |                              |   IP     | (6)
     |----------|                              |----------|
     | FEP dvr  | (2)                          | FEP dvr  | (5)
     |----------|                              |----------|
     |   TCP    |                              |   TCP    |
     |----------|                              |----------|
     |   IP     |         Firewall (8)         |   IP     |
      ----------             ---                ----------
         |       (3)        | |                    ^  (4)
         +---------------->|  |----------------------+
                           |  |
                           |  |
                            ---
                         Figure 1
```

3.1 HTTP Method

   FEP allows either side to look like a client or server. Each TCP/IP
   packet is sent as either a HTTP GET request or a response to a GET
   request. This flexibility work well with firewalls that try to
   verify valid HTTP commands crossing the Firewall stopping the
   unwanted intercepting of FEP packets.

3.2 TCP Header Encapsulation:

   The TCP/IP packet is encoded into the HTTP command in two (or
   optionally three) steps. First, the IP packet is encoded as the
   message body in MIME format, as specified in [3]. Next, the TCP [4]
   packet header is parsed and encoded into new HTTP headers. Finally,
   as an option, the IP header can also be encoded into new optional
   HTTP headers. Encoding the TCP and optionally the IP header is
   strictly for human readability, since the entire IP datagram is
   encoded in the body part of the HTTP command.

   This proposal defines the following new HTTP headers for representing
   TCP header information.

   TCP_value_opt - This ASCII string represents the encoding type for
      the TCP fields where a mandatory encoding type is not specified.
      The legitimate values are:

TCP_binary - ASCII representation of the binary representation of the
   value of the field.

TCP_hexed - ASCII representation of the hex representation of the
   value of the field.

TCP_Sport - The 16-bit TCP Source Port number, encoded as an ASCII
   string representing the value of port number.

TCP_Dport - The 16-bit TCP Destination Port number, encoded as an
   ASCII string representing the value of the port number.

TCP_SeqNum - The 32-bit Sequence Number, encoded as an ASCII string
   representing the hex value of the Sequence number. This field
   MUST be sent as lower case because it is not urgent.

TCP_Ackl - The 32-bit Acknowledgement Number, encoded as ASCII string
   representing the value of the Acknowledgement number.

TCP_DODO - The 4-bit Data Offset value, encoded as an ASCII string
   representing the base 32 value of the actual length of TCP header
   in bits. (Normally this is the Data value times 32.)

TCP_6Os - The 6 reserved bits, encoded as a string of 6 ASCII
   characters. A "O" ("Oh") represents an "Off" bit and "O" ("Oh")
   represents an "On" bit. (Note these characters MUST all be sent
   as "off" and MUST be ignored on receipt.)

TCP_FlgBts - The TCP Flags, encoded as the set of 5 comma-separated
   ASCII strings: [{URG|urg}, {ACK|ack}, {PSH|psh}, {RST|rst},
   {SYN|syn}, {FIN|fin}]. Capital letters imply the flag is set,
   lowercase means the flag is not set.

TCP_Windex - The 16-bit TCP Window Size, encoded as an ASCII string
   representing the value of the number of bytes in the window.

TCP_Checkit - The 16-bit TCP Checksum field, encoded as an ASCII
   string representing the decimal value of the ones-complement of
   the checksum field.

TCP_UP - The 16-bit TCP Urgent Pointer, encoded as the hex
   representation of the value of the field. The hex string MUST be
   capitalized since it is urgent.

TCP_Opp_Lst - A comma-separated list of any TCP options that may be
    present. Each option is encoded as an ASCII string representing
    the name of the option followed by option-specific information
    enclosed in square brackets. Representative options and their
    encoding follow, other IP options follow the same form:

    End of Options option: ["End of Options"]

    Window scale option: ["Window scale", shift_count], where
        shift_count is the window scaling factor represented as the
        ASCII string in decimal.

3.2 IPv4 Header Encapsulation:

    This proposal defines the following new HTTP headers for representing
    IPv4 header information:

    These optional headers are used to encode the IPv4 [5] header for
    better readability. These fields are encoded in a manner similar to
    the above TCP header fields.

    Since the base IP packet is already present in an HTTP header, the
    following headers are optional. None, some or all of them may be
    used depending on the whim of the programmer.

    IP_value_opt - This ASCII string represents the encoding type for the
        following fields where a mandatory encoding type is not
        specified. The legitimate values are the same as for
        TCP_value_opt.

    IP_Ver - The IP Version number, encoded as an UTF-8 string. The
        legitimate values for the string are "four", "five", and "six."
        The encapsulation of the fields in the IP header are defined in
        this section if the value is "four", and in section 3.3 if the
        value is "six". Encapsulations for headers with IP_Ver value of
        "five" will be developed if the right orders are received.
        Encapsulations for headers with the IP_Ver value of "eight" are
        empty. Implementations MUST be able to support arbitrary native
        languages for these strings.

    IP4_Hlen - The IP Internet Header Length field, it is encoded in the
        same way as TCP_DODO.

    IP4_Type_of_Service (this name is case sensitive) - This is an
        obsolete name for a field in the IPv4 header, which has been
        replaced with IP_$$ and IP_CU.

IP_$$ - The 6-bit Differentiated Services field, encapsulated as an
    UTF-8 string representing the name of the DS codepoint in the
    field.

IP_CU - The 2-bit field that was the two low-order bits of the TOS
    field. Since this field is currently being used for experiments
    it has to be coded in the most general way possible, thus it is
    encoded as two ASCII strings of the form "bit0=X" and "bit1=X,"
    where "X" is "on" or "off." Note that bit 0 is the MSB.

IP4_Total - The 16-bit Total Length field, encoded as an ASCII string
    representing the value of the field.

IP4_SSN - The IP Identification field, encoded as an ASCII string
    representing the value of the field.

IP4_Flags - The IP Flags, encoded as the set of 3 comma separated
    ASCII strings: [{"Must Be Zero"}, {"May Fragment"|"Don't
    Fragment"}, {"Last Fragment"|"More Fragments"}]

IP4_Frager - The 13-bit Fragment Offset field, encoded as an ASCII
    string representing the value of the field.

IP4_TTL - The 8-bit Time-to-Live field, encoded as an UTF-8 string of
    the form "X hops to destruction." Where "X" is the decimal value
    -1 of the field. Implementations MUST be able to support
    arbitrary languages for this string.

IP4_Proto - The 8-bit Protocol field, encoded as an UTF-8 string
    representing the common name for the protocol whose header
    follows the IP header.

IP4_Checkit - The 16-bit Checksum field, encoded in the same way as
    TCP_Checkit.

IP4_Apparent_Source - The 32-bit Source Address field. For user
    friendliness this is encoded as an UTF-8 string representing the
    domain name of the apparent sender of the packet. An alternate
    form, to be used when the domain name itself might be blocked by a
    firewall programmed to protect the innocence of the corporate
    users, is an ASCII string representing the dotted quad form of the
    IPv4 address.

IP4_Dest_Addr - The 32-bit Destination Address field, encoded in the
    same way as is IP4_Apparent_Source.

   IP4_Opp_Lst - A comma-separated list of all IPv4 options that are
      present. Each option is encoded as an ASCII string representing
      the name of the option followed by option-specific information
      enclosed in square brackets. Representative options and their
      encoding follow, other IP options follow the same form:

      End of Options option: ["End of Options"]

      Loose Source Routing option: ["Loose Source Routing", length,
         pointer, IP4_addr1, IP4_addr2, ...], where length and pointer
         are ASCII strings representing the value of those fields.

3.3 IPv6 Header Encapsulation:

   This proposal defines the following new HTTP headers for representing
   IPv6 header information:

   These optional headers encode the IPv6 [5] header for better
   readability. These fields are encoded in a manner similar to the
   above TCP header fields.

   Since the base IP packet is already present in an HTTP header the
   following headers are optional. None, some or all of them may be
   used depending on the whim of the programmer. At this time only the
   base IPv6 header is supported. If there is sufficient interest,
   support will be developed for IPv6 extension headers.

   IP_$$ - the 6-bit Differentiated Services field - see above

   IP_CU - the 2-bit unused field - see above

   IP6_Go_with_the_Flow - The 20-bit Flow Label field. Since this field
      is not currently in use it should be encoded as the UTF-8 string
      "do not care".

   IP6_PayLd - The 16-bit Payload Length field, encoded as an ASCII
      string representing the value of the field. The use of FEP with
      IPv6 jumbograms is not recommended.

   IP6_NxtHdr - The 8-bit Next Header field, encoded in the same way as
      IP4_Proto.

   IP6_Hopping - The 8-bit Hop Limit field, encoded in the same way as
      IP4_TTL.

   IP6_Apparent_Source - The 128-bit Source Address field. For user
      friendliness, this is encoded as an UTF-8 string representing the
      domain name of the apparent sender of the packet. An alternate
      form, to be used when the domain name itself might be blocked by a
      Firewall programmed to protect the innocence of the corporate
      users, is an ASCII string representing any one of the legitimate
      forms of representing an IPv6 address.

   IP6_Dest_Addr - The 128-bit Destination Address field, encoded the
      same way as IP6_Apparent_Source.

3.4 TCP Header Compression

   Compressing TCP headers in the face of a protocol such as this one
   that explodes the size of packets is silly, so we ignore it.

4.0 Security Considerations

   Since this protocol deals with Firewalls there are no real security
   considerations.

5.0 Acknowledgements

   We wish to thank the many Firewall vendors who have supported our
   work to re-enable the innovation that made the Internet great,
   without giving up the cellophane fig leaf of security that a Firewall
   provides.

6.0 Authors' Addresses

   Mark Gaynor
   Harvard University
   Cambridge MA 02138

   EMail gaynor@eecs.harvard.edu

   Scott Bradner
   Harvard University
   Cambridge MA 02138

   Phone +1 617 495 3864
   EMail sob@harvard.edu

References

[1] Carpenter, B., "Internet Transparency", RFC 2775, February 2000.

[2] Saltzer, J., Reed, D., and D. Clark, "End-to-End Arguments in
     System Design". 2nd International Conference on Distributed
     Systems, Paris, France, April 1981.

[3] Eastlake, D., "IP over MIME", Work in Progress.

[4] Postel, J., "Transmission Control Protocol", STD 7, RFC 793,
     September 1981.

[5] Postel, J., "Internet Protocol", STD 5, RFC 791, September 1981.

[6] Clark, D. and M. Blumenthal, "Rethinking the Design of the
     Internet: The end-to-end argument vs. the brave new world". 2000.

Full Copyright Statement

Acknowledgement

Funding for the RFC Editor function is currently provided by the
Internet Society.

Network Working Group   B. Rajagopalan
Request for Comments: 3251   Tellium, Inc.
Category: Informational   1 April 2002

Electricity over IP

Status of this Memo

Copyright Notice

Abstract

   Mostly Pointless Lamp Switching (MPLampS) is an architecture for
   carrying electricity over IP (with an MPLS control plane). According
   to our marketing department, MPLampS has the potential to
   dramatically lower the price, ease the distribution and usage, and
   improve the manageability of delivering electricity. This document
   is motivated by such work as SONET/SDH over IP/MPLS (with apologies
   to the authors). Readers of the previous work have been observed
   scratching their heads and muttering, "What next?". This document
   answers that question.

   This document has also been written as a public service. The "Sub-
   IP" area has been formed to give equal opportunity to those working
   on technologies outside of traditional IP networking to write
   complicated IETF documents. There are possibly many who are
   wondering how to exploit this opportunity and attain high visibility.
   Towards this goal, we see the topics of "foo-over-MPLS" (or MPLS
   control for random technologies) as highly amenable for producing a
   countless number of unimplementable documents. This document
   illustrates the key ingredients that go into producing any "foo-
   over-MPLS" document and may be used as a template for all such work.

1. Conventions used in this document

   The key words "MUST", "MUST NOT", "DO", "DON'T", "REQUIRED", "SHALL",
   "SHALL NOT", "SHOULD", "SHOULD NOT", "RECOMMENDED", "MAY", "MAY BE"
   and "OPTIONAL" in this document do not mean anything.

2. Pre-requisite for reading this document

   While reading this document, at various points the readers may have
   the urge to ask questions like, "does this make sense?", "is this
   feasible?," and "is the author sane?". The readers must have the
   ability to suppress such questions and read on. Other than this, no
   specific technical background is required to read this document. In
   certain cases (present document included), it may be REQUIRED that
   readers have no specific technical background.

3. Introduction

   It was recently brought to our attention that the distribution
   network for electricity is not an IP network! After absorbing the
   shock that was delivered by this news, the following thoughts
   occurred to us:

   1. Electricity distribution must be based on some outdated technology
      (called "Legacy Distribution System" or LDS in the rest of the
      document).
   2. An LDS not based on the Internet technology means that two
      different networks (electricity and IP) must be administered and
      managed. This leads to inefficiencies, higher cost and
      bureaucratic foul-ups (which possibly lead to blackouts in
      California. We are in the process of verifying this using
      simulations as part of a student's MS thesis).
   3. The above means that a single network technology (i.e., IP) must
      be used to carry both electricity and Internet traffic.
   4. An internet draft must be written to start work in this area,
      before someone else does.
   5. Such a draft can be used to generate further drafts, ensuring that
      we (and CCAMP, MPLS or another responsible working group) will be
      busy for another year.
   6. The draft can also be posted in the "white papers" section of our
      company web page, proclaiming us as revolutionary pioneers.

   Hence the present document.

4. Terminology

   MPLampS: Mostly Pointless Lamp Switching - the architecture
   introduced in this document.

   Lamp: An end-system in the MPLampS architecture (clashes with the
   IETF notion of end-system but of course, we DON'T care).

   LER: Low-voltage Electricity Receptor - fancy name for "Lamp".

ES: Electricity source - a generator.

LSR: Load-Switching Router - an MPLampS device used in the core electricity distribution network.

LDS: Legacy Distribution System - an inferior electricity distribution technology that MPLampS intends to replace.

RSVP: Rather Screwed-up, but router Vendors Push it - an IP signaling protocol.

RSVP-TE: RSVP with Tariff Extensions - RSVP adaptation for MPLampS, to be used in the new deregulated utilities environment.

CRLDP: for CRying out Loud, Don't do rsvP - another IP signaling protocol.

OSPF: Often Seizes-up in multiPle area conFigurations - a hierarchical IP routing protocol.

ISIS: It's not oSpf, yet It somehow Survives - another routing protocol.

OSPF-TE, ISIS-TE: OSPF and ISIS with Tariff Extensions.

COPS: Policemen. Folks who scour all places for possibilities to slip in the Common Open Policy Service protocol.

VPN: Voltage Protected Network - allows a customer with multiple sites to receive electricity with negligible voltage fluctuation due to interference from other customers.

SUB-IP: SUBstitute IP everywhere - an effort in the IETF to get involved in technical areas outside of traditional IP networking (such as MPLampS).

ITU: International Tariffed Utilities association - a utilities trade group whose work is often ignored by the IETF.

5. Background

We dug into the electricity distribution technology area to get some background. What we found stunned us, say, with the potency of a bare 230V A/C lead dropped into our bathtub while we were still in it. To put it simply, electricity is generated and distributed along a vast LDS which does not have a single router in it (LSR or otherwise)! Furthermore, the control of devices in this network is mostly manual, done by folks driving around in trucks. After

wondering momentarily about how such a network can exist in the 21st
century, we took a pencil and paper and sketched out a scenario for
integrating the LDS network with the proven Internet technology. The
fundamental points we came up with are:

1. IP packets carry electricity in discrete, digitized form.
2. Each packet would deliver electricity to its destination (e.g., a
   device with an IP address) on-demand.
3. MPLS control will be used to switch packets within the core LDS,
   and in the edge premises. The architecture for this is referred
   to as Mostly-Pointless Lamp Switching (MPLampS).
4. The MPLampS architectural model will accommodate both the overlay
   model, where the electricity consuming devices (referred to as
   "lamps") are operated over a distinct control plane, and the peer
   model, in which the lamps and the distribution network use a
   single control plane.
5. RSVP-TE (RSVP with Tariff Extensions) will be used for
   establishing paths for electricity flow in a de-regulated
   environment.
6. COPS will be used to support accounting and policy.

After jotting these points down, we felt better. We then noted the
following immediate advantages of the proposed scheme:

1. Switches and transformers in the LDS can be replaced by LSRs,
   thereby opening up a new market for routers.
2. Electricity can be routed over the Internet to reach remote places
   which presently do not have electricity connections but have only
   Internet kiosks (e.g., rural India).
3. Electrical technicians can be replaced by highly paid IP network
   administrators, and
4. The IETF can get involved in another unrelated technology area.

In the following, we describe the technical issues in a vague manner.

6. Electricity Encoding

The Discrete Voltage Encoding (DVE) scheme has been specified in ITU
standard G.110/230V [2] to digitize electrical voltages. In essence,
an Electricity Source (ES) such as a generator is connected to a DV
encoder that encodes the voltage and current, and produces a bit
stream. This bit stream can be carried in IP packets to various
destinations (referred to as LERs - Low-voltage Electricity
Receptors) on-demand. At the destination, a DV decoder produces the
right voltage and current based on the received bit stream. It is to
be determined whether the Real-time Transport Protocol (RTP) can be

used for achieving synchronization and end-to-end control. We leave
draft writing opportunities in the RTP area to our friends and
colleagues.

7. MPLampS Architecture

7.1 Overview

   In an LDS, the long-haul transmission of electricity is at high
   voltages. The voltage is stepped down progressively as electricity
   flows into local distribution networks and is finally delivered to
   LERs at a standard voltage (e.g., 110V). Thus, the LDS is a
   hierarchical network. This immediately opens up the possibility of
   OSPF and ISIS extensions for routing electricity in a transmission
   network, but we'll contain the urge to delve into these productive
   internet draft areas until later. For the present, we limit our
   discussion merely to controlling the flow of electricity in an IP-
   based distribution network using MPLampS.

   Under MPLampS, a voltage is equated to a label. In the distribution
   network, each switching element and transformer is viewed as a load-
   switching router (LSR). Each IP packet carrying an electricity flow
   is assigned a label corresponding to the voltage. Electricity
   distribution can then be trivially reduced to the task of label
   (voltage) switching as electricity flows through the distribution
   network. The configuration of switching elements in the distribution
   network is done through RSVP-TE to provide electricity on demand.

   We admit that the above description is vague and sounds crazy. The
   example below tries to add more (useless) details, without removing
   any doubts the reader might have about the feasibility of this
   proposal:

   Example: Turning on a Lamp

   It is assumed that the lamp is controlled by an intelligent device
   (e.g, a (light) switch with an MPLampS control plane). Turning the
   lamp on causes the switch to issue an RSVP-TE request (a PATH message
   with new objects) for the electricity flow. This PATH message
   traverses across the network to the ES. The RESV message issued in
   return sets up the label mappings in LSRs. Finally, electricity
   starts flowing along the path established. It is expected that the
   entire process will be completed within a few seconds, thereby giving
   the MPLampS architecture a distinct advantage over lighting a candle
   with a damp match stick.

7.2 Overlay vs Peer Models

   As noted before, there are two control plane models to be considered.
   Under the overlay model, the lamps and the distribution network
   utilize distinct control planes. Under the peer model, a single
   control plane is used. A number of arguments can be made for one
   model versus the other, and these will be covered in the upcoming
   framework document. We merely observe here that it is the lamp
   vendors who prefer the peer model against the better judgement of the
   LSR vendors. We, however, want to please both camps regardless of
   the usefulness of either model. We therefore note here that MPLampS
   supports both models and also migration scenarios from overlay to
   peer.

7.3 Routing in the Core Network

   The above description of the hierarchical distribution system
   immediately opens up the possibility of applying OSPF and ISIS with
   suitable extensions. The readers may rest assured that we are
   already working on such concepts as voltage bundling, multi-area
   tariff extensions, insulated LSAs, etc. Future documents will
   describe the details.

7.4 Voltage Protected Networks (VPNs)

   VPNs allow a customer with multiple sites to get guaranteed
   electricity supply with negligible voltage fluctuations due to
   interference from other customers. Indeed, some may argue that the
   entire MPLampS architecture may be trashed if not for the possibility
   of doing VPNs. Whatever be the case, VPNs are a hot topic today and
   the readers are forewarned that we have every intention of writing
   several documents on this. Specifically, BGP-support for VPNs is an
   area we're presently eyeing with interest.

8. Multicast

   It has been observed that there is a strong spatial and temporal
   locality in electricity demand. ITU Study Group 55 has studied this
   phenomenon for over a decade and has issued a preliminary report.
   This report states that when a lamp is turned on in one house, it is
   usually the case that lamps are turned on in neighboring houses at
   around the same time (usually at dusk) [3]. This observation has a
   serious implication on the scalability of the signaling mechanism.
   Specifically, the distribution network must be able to handle tens of
   thousands of requests all at once. The signaling load can be reduced
   if multicast delivery is used. Briefly, a request for electricity is
   not sent from the lamp all the way to an ES, but is handled by the
   first LSR that is already in the path to another lamp.

Support for this requires the application of multicast routing
protocols together with RSVP-TE shared reservation styles and the
development of MPLampS multicast forwarding mode. We are currently
studying the following multicast routing protocol:

o DVMRP: Discrete Voltage Multicast Routing Protocol - this protocol
works over existing voltage routing protocols but the danger here is
that electricity is delivered to all lamps when any one lamp is
turned on. Indeed, the switching semantics gets annoying - all lamps
get turned on periodically and those not needed must be switched off
each time manually.

Other protocols we will eventually consider are Current-Based Tree
(CBT) and Practically Irrelevant Multicast (PIM). An issue we are
greatly interested in is multicast scope: we would like support for
distributing electricity with varying scope, from lamps within a
single Christmas tree to those in entire cities. Needless to say, we
will write many detailed documents on these topics as time
progresses.

9. Security Considerations

This document MUST be secured in a locked cabinet to prevent it from
being disposed off with the trash.

10. Summary

This document described the motivation and high level concepts behind
Mostly Pointless Lamp Switching (MPLampS), an architecture for
electricity distribution over IP. MPLampS utilizes DVE (discrete
voltage encoding), and an MPLS control plane in the distribution
network. Since the aim of this document is to be a high-visibility
place-holder, we did not get into many details of MPLampS. Numerous
future documents, unfortunately, will attempt to provide these
details.

11. References

1. A. Malis, et al., "SONET/SDH Circuit Emulation Service Over MPLS
   (CEM) Encapsulation", Internet Draft, Work in Progress.

2. International Tarriffed Utilities association draft standard, ITU
   G.110/230V, "Discrete Voltage Encoding", March, 1999.

3. International Tarriffed Utilities association technical report,
   ITU (SG-55) TR-432-2000, "Empirical Models for Energy
   Utilization", September, 2000.

12. Disclaimer

    The opinions expressed in this document are solely the author's.
    Company's opinions, as always, are proprietary and confidential and
    may be obtained under appropriate NDAs.

13. Author's Address

    Bala Rajagopalan
    Tellium, Inc.
    2 Crescent Place
    Ocean Port, NJ 07757
    Phone: 732-923-4237
    EMail: braja@tellium.com

14. Full Copyright Statement

Acknowledgement

    Funding for the RFC Editor function is currently provided by the
    Internet Society.

133

Network Working Group   H. Kennedy
Request for Comments: 3252   Mimezine
Category: Informational   1 April 2002

Binary Lexical Octet Ad-hoc Transport

Status of this Memo

Copyright Notice

Abstract

   This document defines a reformulation of IP and two transport layer
   protocols (TCP and UDP) as XML applications.

1.   Introduction

1.1. Overview

   This document describes the Binary Lexical Octet Ad-hoc Transport
   (BLOAT): a reformulation of a widely-deployed network-layer protocol
   (IP [RFC791]), and two associated transport layer protocols (TCP
   [RFC793] and UDP [RFC768]) as XML [XML] applications. It also
   describes methods for transporting BLOAT over Ethernet and IEEE 802
   networks as well as encapsulating BLOAT in IP for gatewaying BLOAT
   across the public Internet.

1.2. Motivation

   The wild popularity of XML as a basis for application-level protocols
   such as the Blocks Extensible Exchange Protocol [RFC3080], the Simple
   Object Access Protocol [SOAP], and Jabber [JABBER] prompted
   investigation into the possibility of extending the use of XML in the
   protocol stack. Using XML at both the transport and network layer in
   addition to the application layer would provide for an amazing amount
   of power and flexibility while removing dependencies on proprietary
   and hard-to-understand binary protocols. This protocol unification
   would also allow applications to use a single XML parser for all
   aspects of their operation, eliminating developer time spent figuring
   out the intricacies of each new protocol, and moving the hard work of

parsing to the XML toolset. The use of XML also mitigates concerns
over "network vs. host" byte ordering which is at the root of many
network application bugs.

1.3. Relation to Existing Protocols

The reformulations specified in this RFC follow as closely as
possible the spirit of the RFCs on which they are based, and so MAY
contain elements or attributes that would not be needed in a pure
reworking (e.g. length attributes, which are implicit in XML.)

The layering of network and transport protocols are maintained in
this RFC despite the optimizations that could be made if the line
were somewhat blurred (i.e. merging TCP and IP into a single, larger
element in the DTD) in order to foster future use of this protocol as
a basis for reformulating other protocols (such as ICMP.)

Other than the encoding, the behavioral aspects of each of the
existing protocols remain unchanged. Routing, address spaces, TCP
congestion control, etc. behave as specified in the extant standards.
Adapting to new standards and experimental algorithm heuristics for
improving performance will become much easier once the move to BLOAT
has been completed.

1.4. Requirement Levels

The key words "MUST", "MUST NOT", "REQUIRED", "SHALL", "SHALL NOT",
"SHOULD", "SHOULD NOT", "RECOMMENDED", "MAY", and "OPTIONAL" in this
document are to be interpreted as described in BCP 14, RFC 2119
[RFC2119].

2.   IPoXML

This protocol MUST be implemented to be compliant with this RFC.
IPoXML is the root protocol REQUIRED for effective use of TCPoXML
(section 3.) and higher-level application protocols.

The DTD for this document type can be found in section 7.1.

The routing of IPoXML can be easily implemented on hosts with an XML
parser, as the regular structure lends itself handily to parsing and
validation of the document/datagram and then processing the
destination address, TTL, and checksum before sending it on to its
next-hop.

The reformulation of IPv4 was chosen over IPv6 [RFC2460] due to the
wider deployment of IPv4 and the fact that implementing IPv6 as XML
would have exceeded the 1500 byte Ethernet MTU.

All BLOAT implementations MUST use - and specify - the UTF-8 encoding of RFC 2279 [RFC2279]. All BLOAT document/datagrams MUST be well-formed and include the XMLDecl.

2.1. IP Description

A number of items have changed (for the better) from the original IP specification. Bit-masks, where present have been converted into human-readable values. IP addresses are listed in their dotted-decimal notation [RFC1123]. Length and checksum values are present as decimal integers.

To calculate the length and checksum fields of the IP element, a canonicalized form of the element MUST be used. The canonical form SHALL have no whitespace (including newline characters) between elements and only one space character between attributes. There SHALL NOT be a space following the last attribute in an element.

An iterative method SHOULD be used to calculate checksums, as the length field will vary based on the size of the checksum.

The payload element bears special attention. Due to the character set restrictions of XML, the payload of IP datagrams (which MAY contain arbitrary data) MUST be encoded for transport. This RFC REQUIRES the contents of the payload to be encoded in the base-64 encoding of RFC 2045 [RFC2045], but removes the requirement that the encoded output MUST be wrapped on 76-character lines.

2.2. Example Datagram

    The following is an example IPoXML datagram with an empty payload:

```
<?xml version="1.0" encoding="UTF-8"?>
<!DOCTYPE ip PUBLIC "-//IETF//DTD BLOAT 1.0 IP//EN" "bloat.dtd">
<ip>
<header length="474">
<version value="4"/>
<tos precedence="Routine" delay="Normal" throughput="Normal"
     relibility="Normal" reserved="0"/>
<total.length value="461"/>
<id value="1"/>
<flags reserved="0" df="dont" mf="last"/>
<offset value="0"/>
<ttl value="255"/>
<protocol value="6"/>
<checksum value="8707"/>
<source address="10.0.0.22"/>
<destination address="10.0.0.1"/>
<options>
<end copied="0" class="0" number="0"/>
</options>
<padding pad="0"/>
</header>
<payload>
</payload>
</ip>
```

3.   TCPoXML

    This protocol MUST be implemented to be compliant with this RFC. The
    DTD for this document type can be found in section 7.2.

3.1. TCP Description

    A number of items have changed from the original TCP specification.
    Bit-masks, where present have been converted into human-readable
    values. Length and checksum and port values are present as decimal
    integers.

    To calculate the length and checksum fields of the TCP element, a
    canonicalized form of the element MUST be used as in section 2.1.

    An iterative method SHOULD be used to calculate checksums as in
    section 2.1.

    The payload element MUST be encoded as in section 2.1.

The TCP offset element was expanded to a maximum of 255 from 16 to allow for the increased size of the header in XML.

TCPoXML datagrams encapsulated by IPoXML MAY omit the <?xml?> header as well as the <!DOCTYPE> declaration.

3.2. Example Datagram

The following is an example TCPoXML datagram with an empty payload:

```
<?xml version="1.0" encoding="UTF-8"?>
<!DOCTYPE tcp PUBLIC "-//IETF//DTD BLOAT 1.0 TCP//EN" "bloat.dtd">
<tcp>
<tcp.header>
<src port="31415"/>
<dest port="42424"/>
<sequence number="322622954"/>
<acknowledgement number="689715995"/>
<offset number=""/>
<reserved value="0"/>
<control syn="1" ack="1"/>
<window size="1"/>
<urgent pointer="0"/>
<checksum value="2988"/>
<tcp.options>
<tcp.end kind="0"/>
</tcp.options>
<padding pad="0"/>
</tcp.header>
<payload>
</payload>
</tcp>
```

4.   UDPoXML

This protocol MUST be implemented to be compliant with this RFC. The DTD for this document type can be found in section 7.3.

4.1. UDP Description

A number of items have changed from the original UDP specification. Bit-masks, where present have been converted into human-readable values. Length and checksum and port values are present as decimal integers.

To calculate the length and checksum fields of the UDP element, a
canonicalized form of the element MUST be used as in section 2.1. An
iterative method SHOULD be used to calculate checksums as in section
2.1.

The payload element MUST be encoded as in section 2.1.

UDPoXML datagrams encapsulated by IPoXML MAY omit the <?xml?> header
as well as the <!DOCTYPE> declaration.

4.2. Example Datagram

The following is an example UDPoXML datagram with an empty payload:

```
<?xml version="1.0" encoding="UTF-8"?>
<!DOCTYPE udp PUBLIC "-//IETF//DTD BLOAT 1.0 UDP//EN" "bloat.dtd">
<udp>
<udp.header>
<src port="31415"/>
<dest port="42424"/>
<udp.length value="143"/>
<checksum value="2988"/>
</udp.header>
<payload>
</payload>
</udp>
```

5.   Network Transport

This document provides for the transmission of BLOAT datagrams over
two common families of physical layer transport. Future RFCs will
address additional transports as routing vendors catch up to the
specification, and we begin to see BLOAT routed across the Internet
backbone.

5.1. Ethernet

BLOAT is encapsulated in Ethernet datagrams as in [RFC894] with the
exception that the type field of the Ethernet frame MUST contain the
value 0xBEEF. The first 5 octets of the Ethernet frame payload will
be 0x3c 3f 78 6d 6c ("<?xml".)

5.2. IEEE 802

BLOAT is encapsulated in IEEE 802 Networks as in [RFC1042] except
that the protocol type code for IPoXML is 0xBEEF.

6. Gatewaying over IP

   In order to facilitate the gradual introduction of BLOAT into the
   public Internet, BLOAT MAY be encapsulated in IP as in [RFC2003] to
   gateway between networks that run BLOAT natively on their LANs.

7. DTDs

   The Transport DTDs (7.2. and 7.3.) build on the definitions in the
   Network DTD (7.1.)

   The DTDs are referenced by their PubidLiteral and SystemLiteral (from
   [XML]) although it is understood that most IPoXML implementations
   will not need to pull down the DTD, as it will normally be embedded
   in the implementation, and presents something of a catch-22 if you
   need to load part of your network protocol over the network.

7.1. IPoXML DTD

   <!--
   DTD for IP over XML.
   Refer to this DTD as:

   <!DOCTYPE ip PUBLIC "-//IETF//DTD BLOAT 1.0 IP//EN" "bloat.dtd">
   -->
   <!--
   DTD data types:

      Digits   [0..9]+

      Precedence "NetworkControl | InternetworkControl |
                  CRITIC | FlashOverride | Flash | Immediate |
                  Priority | Routine"

      IP4Addr   "dotted-decimal" notation of [RFC1123]

      Class   [0..3]

      Sec   "Unclassified | Confidential | EFTO | MMMM | PROG |
                  Restricted | Secret | Top Secret | Reserved"

      Compartments [0..65535]

      Handling   [0..65535]

      TCC   [0..16777216]

   -->

```
    <!ENTITY % Digits "CDATA">
    <!ENTITY % Precedence "CDATA">
    <!ENTITY % IP4Addr "CDATA">
    <!ENTITY % Class "CDATA">
    <!ENTITY % Sec "CDATA">
    <!ENTITY % Compartments "CDATA">
    <!ENTITY % Handling "CDATA">
    <!ENTITY % TCC "CDATA">

    <!ELEMENT ip (header, payload)>

    <!ELEMENT header (version, tos, total.length, id, flags, offset, ttl,
                      protocol, checksum, source, destination, options,
                      padding)>
    <!-- length of header in 32-bit words -->
    <!ATTLIST header
            length %Digits; #REQUIRED>

    <!ELEMENT version EMPTY>
    <!-- ip version. SHOULD be "4" -->
    <!ATTLIST version
            value    %Digits;  #REQUIRED>

    <!ELEMENT tos EMPTY>
    <!ATTLIST tos
            precedence    %Precedence;     #REQUIRED
            delay     (normal | low)  #REQUIRED
            throughput    (normal | high) #REQUIRED
            relibility    (normal | high) #REQUIRED
            reserved      CDATA #FIXED "0">

    <!ELEMENT total.length EMPTY>
    <!--
     total length of datagram (header and payload) in octets, MUST be
     less than 65,535 (and SHOULD be less than 1024 for IPoXML on local
     ethernets).
    -->
    <!ATTLIST total.length
            value %Digits; #REQUIRED>

    <!ELEMENT id EMPTY>
    <!-- 0 <= id <= 65,535  -->
    <!ATTLIST id
            value %Digits; #REQUIRED>

    <!ELEMENT flags EMPTY>
    <!-- df = don't fragment, mf = more fragments  -->
    <!ATTLIST flags
```

142

```
            reserved CDATA  #FIXED "0"
            df (may|dont)    #REQUIRED
            mf (last|more)   #REQUIRED>

   <!ELEMENT offset EMPTY>
   <!-- 0 <= offset <= 8192 measured in 8 octet (64-bit) chunks -->
   <!ATTLIST offset
            value %Digits; #REQUIRED>

   <!ELEMENT ttl EMPTY>
   <!-- 0 <= ttl <= 255 -->
   <!ATTLIST ttl
            value %Digits; #REQUIRED>

   <!ELEMENT protocol EMPTY>
   <!-- 0 <= protocol <= 255 (per IANA) -->
   <!ATTLIST protocol
            value %Digits; #REQUIRED>

   <!ELEMENT checksum EMPTY>
   <!-- 0 <= checksum <= 65535 (over header only) -->
   <!ATTLIST checksum
            value %Digits; #REQUIRED>

   <!ELEMENT source EMPTY>
   <!ATTLIST source
            address %IP4Addr; #REQUIRED>

   <!ELEMENT destination EMPTY>
   <!ATTLIST destination
            address %IP4Addr; #REQUIRED>

   <!ELEMENT options ( end | noop | security | loose | strict | record
                     | stream | timestamp )*>

   <!ELEMENT end EMPTY>
   <!ATTLIST end
            copied (0|1) #REQUIRED
            class  CDATA #FIXED "0"
            number CDATA #FIXED "0">

   <!ELEMENT noop EMPTY>
   <!ATTLIST noop
            copied (0|1) #REQUIRED
            class  CDATA #FIXED "0"
            number CDATA #FIXED "1">

   <!ELEMENT security EMPTY>
```

```
    <!ATTLIST security
              copied CDATA #FIXED "1"
              class  CDATA #FIXED "0"
              number CDATA #FIXED "2"
              length CDATA #FIXED "11"
              security %Sec; #REQUIRED
              compartments %Compartments; #REQUIRED
              handling %Handling; #REQUIRED
              tcc %TCC; #REQUIRED>
    <!ELEMENT loose (hop)+>
    <!ATTLIST loose
              copied CDATA #FIXED "1"
              class  CDATA #FIXED "0"
              number CDATA #FIXED "3"
              length %Digits; #REQUIRED
              pointer %Digits; #REQUIRED>

    <!ELEMENT hop EMPTY>
    <!ATTLIST hop
              address %IP4Addr; #REQUIRED>

    <!ELEMENT strict (hop)+>
    <!ATTLIST strict
              copied CDATA #FIXED "1"
              class  CDATA #FIXED "0"
              number CDATA #FIXED "9"
              length %Digits; #REQUIRED
              pointer %Digits; #REQUIRED>

    <!ELEMENT record (hop)+>
    <!ATTLIST record
              copied CDATA #FIXED "0"
              class  CDATA #FIXED "0"
              number CDATA #FIXED "7"
              length %Digits; #REQUIRED
              pointer %Digits; #REQUIRED>

    <!ELEMENT stream EMPTY>
    <!-- 0 <= id <= 65,535 -->
    <!ATTLIST stream
              copied CDATA #FIXED "1"
              class  CDATA #FIXED "0"
              number CDATA #FIXED "8"
              length CDATA #FIXED "4"
              id %Digits; #REQUIRED>

    <!ELEMENT timestamp (tstamp)+>
    <!-- 0 <= oflw <=15 -->
```

144

```
<!ATTLIST timestamp
          copied CDATA #FIXED "0"
          class  CDATA #FIXED "2"
          number CDATA #FIXED "4"
          length %Digits;  #REQUIRED
          pointer %Digits; #REQUIRED
          oflw %Digits;    #REQUIRED
          flag (0 | 1 | 3)  #REQUIRED>

<!ELEMENT tstamp EMPTY>
<!ATTLIST tstamp
          time %Digits;   #REQUIRED
          address %IP4Addr; #IMPLIED>
<!--
    padding to bring header to 32-bit boundary.
    pad MUST be "0"*
 -->
<!ELEMENT padding EMPTY>
<!ATTLIST padding
          pad CDATA #REQUIRED>

<!-- payload MUST be encoded as base-64 [RFC2045], as modified
     by section 2.1 of this RFC -->
<!ELEMENT payload (CDATA)>
```

7.2. TCPoXML DTD

```
<!--
    DTD for TCP over XML.
    Refer to this DTD as:

    <!DOCTYPE tcp PUBLIC "-//IETF//DTD BLOAT 1.0 TCP//EN" "bloat.dtd">
 -->

<!-- the pseudoheader is only included for checksum calculations -->
<!ELEMENT tcp (tcp.pseudoheader?, tcp.header, payload)>

<!ELEMENT tcp.header (src, dest, sequence, acknowledgement, offset,
                      reserved, control, window, checksum, urgent,
                      tcp.options, padding)>

<!ELEMENT src EMPTY>
<!-- 0 <= port <= 65,535 -->
<!ATTLIST src
          port %Digits; #REQUIRED>

<!ELEMENT dest EMPTY>
<!-- 0 <= port <= 65,535 -->
```

145

```
    <!ATTLIST dest
            port %Digits; #REQUIRED>

    <!ELEMENT sequence EMPTY>
    <!-- 0 <= number <= 4294967295 -->
    <!ATTLIST sequence
            number %Digits; #REQUIRED>

    <!ELEMENT acknowledgement EMPTY>
    <!-- 0 <= number <= 4294967295 -->
    <!ATTLIST acknowledgement
            number %Digits; #REQUIRED>

    <!ELEMENT offset EMPTY>
    <!-- 0 <= number <= 255 -->
    <!ATTLIST offset
            number %Digits; #REQUIRED>

    <!ELEMENT reserved EMPTY>
    <!ATTLIST reserved
            value CDATA #FIXED "0">

    <!ELEMENT control EMPTY>
    <!ATTLIST control
            urg (0|1) #IMPLIED
            ack (0|1) #IMPLIED
            psh (0|1) #IMPLIED
            rst (0|1) #IMPLIED
            syn (0|1) #IMPLIED
            fin (0|1) #IMPLIED>

    <!ELEMENT window EMPTY>
    <!-- 0 <= size <= 65,535 -->
    <!ATTLIST window
            size %Digits; #REQUIRED>

    <!--
       checksum as in ip, but with
       the following pseudo-header added into the tcp element:
       -->
    <!ELEMENT tcp.pseudoheader (source, destination, protocol,
                               tcp.length)>

    <!--
       tcp header + data length in octets. does not include the size of

       the pseudoheader.
      -->
```

146

```
    <!ELEMENT tcp.length EMPTY>
    <!ATTLIST tcp.length
            value %Digits; #REQUIRED>

    <!ELEMENT urgent EMPTY>
    <!-- 0 <= pointer <= 65,535 -->
    <!ATTLIST urgent
            pointer %Digits; #REQUIRED>

    <!ELEMENT tcp.options (tcp.end | tcp.noop | tcp.mss)+>

    <!ELEMENT tcp.end EMPTY>
    <!ATTLIST tcp.end
            kind CDATA #FIXED "0">

    <!ELEMENT tcp.noop EMPTY>
    <!ATTLIST tcp.noop
            kind CDATA #FIXED "1">

    <!ELEMENT tcp.mss EMPTY>
    <!ATTLIST tcp.mss
            kind CDATA #FIXED "2"
            length CDATA #FIXED "4"
            size %Digits; #REQUIRED>
```

7.3. UDPoXML DTD

```
    <!--
       DTD for UDP over XML.
       Refer to this DTD as:

       <!DOCTYPE udp PUBLIC "-//IETF//DTD BLOAT 1.0 UDP//EN" "bloat.dtd">
    -->

    <!ELEMENT udp (udp.pseudoheader?, udp.header, payload)>

    <!ELEMENT udp.header (src, dest, udp.length, checksum)>

    <!ELEMENT udp.pseudoheader (source, destination, protocol,
                               udp.length)>

    <!--
       udp header + data length in octets. does not include the size of
       the pseudoheader.
    -->
    <!ELEMENT udp.length EMPTY>
    <!ATTLIST udp.length
            value %Digits; #REQUIRED>
```

8. Security Considerations

    XML, as a subset of SGML, has the same security considerations as
    specified in SGML Media Types [RFC1874]. Security considerations
    that apply to IP, TCP and UDP also likely apply to BLOAT as it does
    not attempt to correct for issues not related to message format.

9. References

    [JABBER]   Miller, J., "Jabber", draft-miller-jabber-00.txt,
                 February 2002. (Work in Progress)

    [RFC768]   Postel, J., "User Datagram Protocol", STD 6, RFC 768,
                 August 1980.

    [RFC791]   Postel, J., "Internet Protocol", STD 5, RFC 791,
                 September 1981.

    [RFC793]   Postel, J., "Transmission Control Protocol", STD 7, RFC
                 793, September 1981.

    [RFC894]   Hornig, C., "Standard for the Transmission of IP
                 Datagrams over Ethernet Networks.", RFC 894, April 1984.

    [RFC1042]   Postel, J. and J. Reynolds, "Standard for the
                 Transmission of IP Datagrams Over IEEE 802 Networks", STD
                 43, RFC 1042, February 1988.

    [RFC1123]   Braden, R., "Requirements for Internet Hosts -
                 Application and Support", RFC 1123, October 1989.

    [RFC1874]   Levinson, E., "SGML Media Types", RFC 1874, December
                 1995.

    [RFC2003]   Perkins, C., "IP Encapsulation within IP", RFC 2003,
                 October 1996.

    [RFC2045]   Freed, N. and N. Borenstein, "Multipurpose Internet Mail
                 Extensions (MIME) Part One: Format of Internet Message
                 Bodies", RFC 2045, November 1996.

    [RFC2119]   Bradner, S., "Key words for use in RFCs to Indicate
                 Requirement Levels", BCP 14, RFC 2119, March 1997.

    [RFC2279]   Yergeau, F., "UTF-8, a transformation format of ISO
                 10646", RFC 2279, January 1998.

   [RFC2460]   Deering, S. and R. Hinden, "Internet Protocol, Version 6
                (IPv6) Specification", RFC 2460, December 1998.

   [RFC3080]   Rose, M., "The Blocks Extensible Exchange Protocol Core",
                RFC 3080, March 2001.

   [SOAP]   Box, D., Ehnebuske, D., Kakivaya, G., Layman, A.,
                Mendelsohn, N., Nielsen, H. F., Thatte, S. Winer, D.,
                "Simple Object Access Protocol (SOAP) 1.1" World Wide Web
                Consortium Note, May 2000 http://www.w3.org/TR/SOAP/

   [XML]   Bray, T., Paoli, J., Sperberg-McQueen, C. M., "Extensible
                Markup Language (XML)" World Wide Web Consortium
                Recommendation REC- xml-19980210.
                http://www.w3.org/TR/1998/REC-xml-19980210

10. Author's Address

   Hugh Kennedy
   Mimezine
   1060 West Addison
   Chicago, IL 60613
   USA

   EMail: kennedyh@engin.umich.edu

149

11. Full Copyright Statement

Acknowledgement

Funding for the RFC Editor function is currently provided by the
Internet Society.

Network Working Group   A. Farrel
Request for Comments: 4041   Old Dog Consulting
Category: Informational   1 April 2005

       Requirements for Morality Sections in Routing Area Drafts

Status of This Memo

Copyright Notice

Abstract

   It has often been the case that morality has not been given proper
   consideration in the design and specification of protocols produced
   within the Routing Area. This has led to a decline in the moral
   values within the Internet and attempts to retrofit a suitable moral
   code to implemented and deployed protocols has been shown to be
   sub-optimal.

   This document specifies a requirement for all new Routing Area
   Internet-Drafts to include a "Morality Considerations" section, and
   gives guidance on what that section should contain.

1. Introduction

   It is well accepted by popular opinion and other reliable metrics
   that moral values are declining and that degeneracy is increasing.
   Young people are particularly at risk from the rising depravity in
   society and much of the blame can be squarely placed at the door of
   the Internet. If you do not feel safe on the streets at night, what
   do you think it is like on the Information Superhighway?

   When new protocols or protocol extensions are developed within the
   Routing Area, it is often the case that not enough consideration is
   given to the impact of the protocol on the moral fiber of the
   Internet. The result is that moral consequences are only understood
   once the protocols have been implemented, and sometimes not until
   after they have been deployed.

The resultant attempts to restore appropriate behavior and purge the community of improper activities are not always easy or architecturally pleasant. Further, it is possible that certain protocol designs make morality particularly hard to achieve.

Recognising that moral issues are fundamental to the utility and success of protocols designed within the IETF, and that simply making a wishy-washy liberal-minded statement does not necessarily provide adequate guarantees of a correct and proper outcome for society, this document defines requirements for the inclusion of Morality Considerations sections in all Internet-Drafts produced within the Routing Area. Meeting these requirements will ensure that proper consideration is given to moral issues at all stages of the protocol development process, from Requirements and Architecture, through Specification and Applicability.

The remainder of this document describes the necessary subsections of the Morality Considerations sections, and gives guidance about what information should be contained in those subsections.

1.1. Conventions Used in This Document

The key words "MUST", "MUST NOT", "REQUIRED", "SHALL", "SHALL NOT", "SHOULD", "SHOULD NOT", "RECOMMENDED", "MAY", and "OPTIONAL" in this document are to be interpreted as described in RFC 2119 [RFC2119].

The key words "SHALT", "SHALT NOT", "SMITE", and "PILLAR OF SALT" in this document are to be interpreted as expected.

2. Presence and Placement of Morality Considerations Sections

2.1. Null Morality Considerations Sections

It may be the case that the authors of Internet-Drafts have no or few morals. This does not relieve them of their duty to understand the consequences of their actions.

The more likely an author is to say that a null Morality Considerations section is acceptable, the more pressure must be exerted on him by the Area and the appropriate Working Group to ensure that he gives full consideration to his actions, and reflects long and hard on the consequences of his writing and the value of his life.

On the other hand, some authors are well known to have the highest moral pedigree: a fact that is plainly obvious from the company they keep, the Working Groups they attend, and their eligibility for NomCom. It is clearly unnecessary for such esteemed persons to waste effort on Morality Considerations sections. It is inconceivable that anything that they write would have anything other than a beneficial effect on the Routing Area and the Internet in general.

2.2. Mandatory Subsections

   If the Morality Considerations section is present, it MUST contain at least the following subsections. The content of these subsections is surely self-evident to any right-thinking person. Further guidance can be obtained from your moral guardian, your household gods, or from any member of the IMM (Internet Moral Majority).

   - Likelihood of misuse by depraved or sick individuals. This subsection must fully address the possibility that the proposed protocols or protocol extensions might be used for the distribution of blue, smutty, or plain disgusting images.

   - Likelihood of misuse by misguided individuals. There is an obvious need to protect minors and people with misguided thought processes from utilising the protocols or protocol extensions for purposes that would inevitably do them harm.

   - Likelihood of misuse by large, multi-national corporations. Such a thought is, of course, unthinkable.

   - Availability of oversight facilities. There are those who would corrupt our morals motivated as they are by a hatred of the freedom of Internet access with which we are graced. We place a significant burden of responsibility on those who guard our community from these evil-doers and it is only fitting that we give them as much support as is possible. Therefore, all encryption and obfuscation techniques MUST be excluded - individuals who have nothing to hide need to fear the oversight of those whose morals are beyond doubt.

   - Inter-SDO impact. We must allow for other moral frameworks and fully respect other people's right to subscribe to other belief systems. Such people are, however, wrong and doomed to spend eternity in a dark corner with only dial-up access. So it has been written.

   - Care and concern for avian carriers. A duck may be somebody's mother.

   Even if one or more of these subsections are considered irrelevant, they MUST all still be present, and MUST contain a full rebuttal of this deviant thought.

153

2.3. Optional Subsections

Additional subsections may be added to accommodate zealots.

2.4. Placement of Morality Considerations Sections

The Morality Considerations section MUST be given full prominence in each Internet Draft.

3. Applicability Scenarios

This section outlines, by way of example, some particular areas that are in dire need of reform and where a short, sharp shock could make a really big difference.

3.1. Provision of Services

We must do our utmost to ensure that services are delivered in a timely and reliable way. Emphasis should be placed on Quality of Service (QoS) and meeting the needs of the consumer of the service.

Arrangements should be made for regular provision of services, and sermons should be to the point and contain a strong moral message.

3.2. Political Correctness (PC)

Political correctness has gone too far. This problem can be traced way back to the 1970s when the desktop PC was invented. It is necessary for Internet-Drafts to observe a form of political correctness, but note that you do not always have to mean what you say.

3.2.1. Differentiated Services

Segregation of packets on the grounds of color is now banned and Internet-Drafts must not make use of this technique.

If you follow all of the recommendations in this document, you will find that "packets of color" (as we must now refer to them) tend to avoid your points of presence, and you will no longer be troubled by them.

3.2.2. Jumbo Packets

It is no longer appropriate to refer to "jumbo packets". Please use the term "capacitorially challenged".

3.2.3. Byte Ordering

Note that within Internet-Drafts, bytes (and bits) progress from the
left to the right. This is how things should be.

3.3. Protection or Abstinence

Much has been made recently of the need to provide protection within
the Internet. It is the role of the IMM to determine when protection
is required, and the role of the IESG bulldogs to ensure that we are
all protected.

However, protection is only one way to prevent unplanned outages and,
as we all know, the ready availability of protection schemes such as
1:1 (one-on-one) or 1:n (orgy-mode) have lead to a belief that it is
acceptable to switch (or swing) at will. It should be noted that
protection can fail, and under no circumstances should extra traffic
be countenanced.

In reality, the only safe way to avoid passing data to your friends
is to agree to pledge to have no control plane before marriage. Join
our campaign and sign up for the SONET Ring Thing.

3.4. Promiscuity

Various disgusting protocols indulge in promiscuity. This appears to
happen most often when an operator is unwilling to select a single
partner and wants to play the field.

Promiscuous modes of operation are an abomination, exceeded only by
multicast.

4. Terminology

Admission Control
    The caring investigative arm of the IMM.

Doom
    Port 666. Need we say more?

ECMP
    What is this? Some kind of Communism?

Money
    The root of all evil.

MPLS
>   What is with this "layer two-and-a-half" nonsense? The world is
>   flat, just accept the fact.

Packet Switching
>   Sounds like fraud to me.

Path
>   The route of all LSPs.

Policy Control
>   The administrative arm of the IMM.

Random Walk
>   Substance abuse is to be avoided.

Rendezvous Point
>   Poorly lit street corner. Not to be confused with the root of all
>   multicast.

Standard Body
>   What we should all strive for.

Strawberry Ice Cream
>   Something that wills the void between rational discussion and
>   all-out thermo nuclear war [SCREAM].

5. Morality Considerations

    The moral pedigree of the author of this document places him and his
    writings beyond question.

6. IANA Considerations

    IANA should think carefully about the protection of their immortal
    souls.

7. Security Considerations

    Security is of the utmost importance.

    A secure Internet community will ensure the security of all of its
    members.

8. Acknowledgements

   I would like to thank my guru Alex Dipandra-Zinin.

   Jozef Wroblewski, who clearly knows promiscuous behavior when he sees
   it, pointed out some of the dangers in promiscuous operation.

   No avian carriers were harmed in the production of this document.

9. Intellectual Property Considerations

   Property is theft. What is yours is mine. What is mine, you keep
   your hands off.

10. Normative References

   I don't need to be told how to formulate my morals.

   [RFC2119] Bradner, S., "Key words for use in RFCs to Indicate
             Requirement Levels", BCP 14, RFC 2119, March 1997.

11. Informative References

   To be frank, I don't find many other documents informative.

   [SCREAM] Farrel, A., "Observations on Proposing Protocol
             Enhancements that Address Stated Requirements but also go
             Further by Meeting more General Needs", Work in Progress,
             June 2003.

Author's Address

   Adrian Farrel
   Old Dog Consulting

   Phone: I'm not telling you that. Why do you ask, anyway?
   EMail: adrian@olddog.co.uk

Full Copyright Statement

Intellectual Property

Acknowledgement

    Funding for the RFC Editor function is currently provided by the
    Internet Society.

Network Working Group   M. Crispin
Request for Comments: 4042   Panda Programming
Category: Informational   1 April 2005

UTF-9 and UTF-18
Efficient Transformation Formats of Unicode

Status of This Memo

Copyright Notice

Abstract

   ISO-10646 defines a large character set called the Universal
   Character Set (UCS), which encompasses most of the world's writing
   systems. The same set of codepoints is defined by Unicode, which
   further defines additional character properties and other
   implementation details. By policy of the relevant standardization
   committees, changes to Unicode and amendments and additions to
   ISO/IEC 646 track each other, so that the character repertoires and
   code point assignments remain in synchronization.

   The current representation formats for Unicode (UTF-7, UTF-8, UTF-16)
   are not storage and computation efficient on platforms that utilize
   the 9 bit nonet as a natural storage unit instead of the 8 bit octet.

   This document describes a transformation format of Unicode that takes
   advantage of the nonet so that the format will be storage and
   computation efficient.

1. Introduction

   A number of Internet sites utilize platforms that are not based upon
   the traditional 8-bit byte or octet. One such platform is the PDP-
   10, which is based upon a 36-bit word. On these platforms, it is
   wasteful to represent data in octets, since 4 bits are left unused in
   each word. The 9-bit nonet is a much more sensible representation.

   Although these platforms support IETF standards, many of these
   platforms still utilize a text representation based upon the septet,

which is only suitable for [US-ASCII] (although it has been used for
various ISO 10646 national variants).

To maximize international and multi-lingual interoperability, the IAB
has recommended ([IAB-CHARACTER]) that [ISO-10646] be the default
coded character set.

Although other transformation formats of [UNICODE] exist, and
conceivably can be used on nonet-oriented machines (most notably
[UTF-8]), they suffer significant disadvantages:

   [UTF-8]
      requires one to three octets to represent codepoints in the
      Basic Multilingual Plane (BMP), four octets to represent
      [UNICODE] codepoints outside the BMP, and six octets to
      represent non-[UNICODE] codepoints. When stored in nonets,
      this results in as many as four wasted bits per [UNICODE]
      character.

   [UTF-16]
      requires a hexadecet to represent codepoints in the BMP, and
      two hexadecets to represent [UNICODE] codepoints outside the
      BMP. When stored in nonet pairs, this results in as many as
      four wasted bits per [UNICODE] character. This transformation
      format requires complex surrogates to represent codepoints
      outside the BMP, and can not represent non-[UNICODE] codepoints
      at all.

   [UTF-7]
      requires one to five septets to represent codepoints in the
      BMP, and as many as eight septets to represent codepoints
      outside the BMP. When stored in nonets, this results in as
      many as sixteen wasted bits per character. This transformation
      format requires very complex and computationally expensive
      shifting and "modified BASE64" processing, and can not
      represent non-[UNICODE] codepoints at all.

By comparison, UTF-9 uses one to two nonets to represent codepoints
in the BMP, three nonets to represent [UNICODE] codepoints outside
the BMP, and three or four nonets to represent non-[UNICODE]
codepoints. There are no wasted bits, and as the examples in this
document demonstrate, the computational processing is minimal.

Transformation between [UTF-8] and UTF-9 is straightforward, with
most of the complexity in the handling of [UTF-8]. It is hoped that
future extensions to protocols such as SMTP will permit the use of
UTF-9 in these protocols between nonet platforms without the use of
[UTF-8] as an "on the wire" format.

Similarly, transformation between [UNICODE] codepoints and UTF-18 is
also quite simple. Although (like UCS-2) UTF-18 only represents a
subset of the available [UNICODE] codepoints, it encompasses the
non-private codepoints that are currently assigned in [UNICODE].

1.1. Conventions Used in This Document

The key words "MUST", "MUST NOT", "REQUIRED", "SHALL", "SHALL NOT",
"SHOULD", "SHOULD NOT", "RECOMMENDED", "MAY", and "OPTIONAL" in this
document are to be interpreted as described in BCP 14, RFC 2119
[KEYWORDS].

2. Overview

UTF-9 encodes [UNICODE] codepoints in the low order 8 bits of a
nonet, using the high order bit to indicate continuation. Surrogates
are not used.

[UNICODE] codepoints in the range U+0000 - U+00FF ([US-ASCII] and
Latin 1) are represented by a single nonet; codepoints in the range
U+0100 - U+FFFF (the remainder of the BMP) are represented by two
nonets; and codepoints in the range U+1000 - U+10FFFF (remainder of
[UNICODE]) are represented by three nonets.

Non-[UNICODE] codepoints in [ISO-10646] (that is, codepoints in the
range 0x110000 - 0x7fffffff) can also be represented in UTF-9 by
obvious extension, but this is not discussed further as these
codepoints have been removed from [ISO-10646] by ISO.

UTF-18 encodes [UNICODE] codepoints in the Basic Multilingual Plane
(BMP, plane 0), Supplementary Multilingual Plane (SMP, plane 1),
Supplementary Ideographic Plane (SIP, plane 2), and Supplementary
Special-purpose Plane (SSP, plane 14) in a single 18-bit value. It
does not encode planes 3 though 13, which are currently unused; nor
planes 15 or 16, which are private spaces.

Normally, UTF-9 and UTF-18 should only be used in the context of 9
bit storage and transport. Although some protocols, e.g., [FTP],
support transport of nonets, the current IETF protocol suite is quite
deficient in this area. The IETF is urged to take action to improve
IETF protocol support for nonets.

3. UTF-9 Definition

A UTF-9 stream represents [ISO-10646] codepoints using 9 bit nonets.
The low order 8-bits of a nonet is an octet, and the high order bit
indicates continuation.

161

UTF-9 does not use surrogates; consequently a UTF-16 value must be
transformed into the UCS-4 equivalent, and U+D800 - U+DBFF are never
transmitted in UTF-9.

Octets of the [UNICODE] codepoint value are then copied into
successive UTF-9 nonets, starting with the most-significant non-zero
octet. All but the least significant octet have the continuation bit
set in the associated nonet.

Examples:

Character	Name	UTF-9 (in octal)
U+0041	LATIN CAPITAL LETTER A	101
U+00C0	LATIN CAPITAL LETTER A WITH GRAVE	300
U+0391	GREEK CAPITAL LETTER ALPHA	403 221
U+611B	<CJK ideograph meaning "love">	541 33
U+10330	GOTHIC LETTER AHSA	401 403 60
U+E0041	TAG LATIN CAPITAL LETTER A	416 400 101
U+10FFFD	<Plane 16 Private Use, Last>	420 777 375
0x345ecf1b	(UCS-4 value not in [UNICODE])	464 536 717 33

4. UTF-18 Definition

A UTF-18 stream represents [ISO-10646] codepoints using a pair of 9
bit nonets to form an 18-bit value.

UTF-18 does not use surrogates; consequently a UTF-16 value must be
transformed into the UCS-4 equivalent, and U+D800 - U+DBFF are never
transmitted in UTF-18.

[UNICODE] codepoint values in the range U+0000 - U+2FFFF are copied
as the same value into a UTF-18 value. [UNICODE] codepoint values in
the range U+E0000 - U+EFFFF are copied as values 0x30000 - 0x3ffff;
that is, these values are shifted by 0x70000. Other codepoint values
can not be represented in UTF-18.

Examples:

Character	Name	UTF-18 (in octal)
U+0041	LATIN CAPITAL LETTER A	000101
U+00C0	LATIN CAPITAL LETTER A WITH GRAVE	000300
U+0391	GREEK CAPITAL LETTER ALPHA	001621
U+611B	<CJK ideograph meaning "love">	060433
U+10330	GOTHIC LETTER AHSA	201460
U+E0041	TAG LATIN CAPITAL LETTER A	600101

162

5. Sample Routines

5.1. [UNICODE] Codepoint to UTF-9 Conversion

   The following routines demonstrate conversion from UCS-4 to UTF-9.
   For simplicity, these routines do not do any validity checking.
   Routines used in applications SHOULD reject invalid UTF-9 sequences;
   that is, the first nonet with a value of 400 octal (0x100), or
   sequences that result in an overflow (exceeding 0x10ffff for
   [UNICODE]), or codepoints used for UTF-16 surrogates.

   ; Return UCS-4 value from UTF-9 string (PDP-10 assembly version)
   ; Accepts: P1/ 9-bit byte pointer to UTF-9 string
   ; Returns +1: Always, T1/ UCS-4 value, P1/ updated byte pointer
   ; Clobbers T2

```
   UT92U4: TDZA T1,T1              ; start with zero
   U92U41:  XOR T1,T2             ; insert octet into UCS-4 value
           LSH T1,^D8             ; shift UCS-4 value
           ILDB T2,P1             ; get next nonet
           TRZE T2,400            ; extract octet, any continuation?
            JRST U92U41           ; yes, continue
           XOR T1,T2              ; insert final octet
           POPJ P,
```

```
   /* Return UCS-4 value from UTF-9 string (C version)
    * Accepts: pointer to pointer to UTF-9 string
    * Returns: UCS-4 character, nonet pointer updated
    */

   UINT31 UTF9_to_UCS4 (UINT9 **utf9PP)
   {
     UINT9 nonet;
     UINT31 ucs4;
     for (ucs4 = (nonet = *(*utf9PP)++) & 0xff;
         nonet & 0x100;
         ucs4 |= (nonet = *(*utf9PP)++) & 0xff)
       ucs4 <<= 8;
     return ucs4;
   }
```

5.2. UTF-9 to UCS-4 Conversion

   The following routines demonstrate conversion from UTF-9 to UCS-4.
   For simplicity, these routines do not do any validity checking.
   Routines used in applications SHOULD reject invalid UCS-4 codepoints;
   that is, codepoints used for UTF-16 surrogates or codepoints with
   values exceeding 0x10ffff for [UNICODE].

163

```
; Write UCS-4 character to UTF-9 string (PDP-10 assembly version)
; Accepts: P1/ 9-bit byte pointer to UTF-9 string
;          T1/ UCS-4 character to write
; Returns +1: Always, P1/ updated byte pointer
; Clobbers T1, T2; (T1, T2) must be an accumulator pair

U42UT9: SETO T2,              ; we'll need some of these 1-bits later
        ASHC T1,-^D8          ; low octet becomes nonet with high 0-bit
U32U91: JUMPE T1,U42U9X       ; done if no more octets
        LSHC T1,-^D8          ; shift next octet into T2
        ROT T2,-1            ; turn it into nonet with high 1 bit
        PUSHJ P,U42U91        ; recurse for remainder
U42U9X: LSHC T1,^D9           ; get next nonet back from T2
        IDPB T1,P1            ; write nonet
        POPJ P,

/* Write UCS-4 character to UTF-9 string (C version)
 * Accepts: pointer to nonet string
 *          UCS-4 character to write
 * Returns: updated pointer
 */

UINT9 *UCS4_to_UTF9 (UINT9 *utf9P,UINT31 ucs4)
{
  if (ucs4 > 0x100) {
    if (ucs4 > 0x10000) {
      if (ucs4 > 0x1000000)
        *utf9P++ = 0x100 | ((ucs4 >> 24) & 0xff);
      *utf9P++ = 0x100 | ((ucs4 >> 16) & 0xff);
    }
    *utf9P++ = 0x100 | ((ucs4 >> 8) & 0xff);
  }
  *utf9P++ = ucs4 & 0xff;
  return utf9P;
}
```

6. Implementation Experience

    As the sample routines demonstrate, it is quite simple to implement
    UTF-9 and UTF-18 on a nonet-based architecture. More sophisticated
    routines can be found in ftp://panda.com/tops-20/utools.mac.txt or
    from lingling.panda.com via the file <UTF9>UTOOLS.MAC via ANONYMOUS
    [FTP].

We are now in the process of implementing support for nonet-based
text files and automated transformation between septet, octet, and
nonet textual data.

7. References

7.1. Normative References

   [FTP]   Postel, J. and J. Reynolds, "File Transfer Protocol",
                      STD 9, RFC 959, October 1985.

   [IAB-CHARACTER] Weider, C., Preston, C., Simonsen, K., Alvestrand,
                      H., Atkinson, R., Crispin, M., and P. Svanberg, "The
                      Report of the IAB Character Set Workshop held 29
                      February - 1 March, 1996", RFC 2130, April 1997.

   [ISO-10646]   International Organization for Standardization,
                      "Information Technology - Universal Multiple-octet
                      coded Character Set (UCS)", ISO/IEC Standard 10646,
                      comprised of ISO/IEC 10646-1:2000, "Information
                      technology - Universal Multiple-Octet Coded Character
                      Set (UCS) - Part 1: Architecture and Basic
                      Multilingual Plane", ISO/IEC 10646-2:2001,
                      "Information technology - Universal Multiple-Octet
                      Coded Character Set (UCS) - Part 2: Supplementary
                      Planes" and ISO/IEC 10646-1:2000/Amd 1:2002,
                      "Mathematical symbols and other characters".

   [KEYWORDS]   Bradner, S., "Key words for use in RFCs to Indicate
                      Requirement Levels", BCP 14, RFC 2119, March 1997.

   [UNICODE]   The Unicode Consortium, "The Unicode Standard -
                      Version 3.2", defined by The Unicode Standard,
                      Version 3.0 (Reading, MA, Addison-Wesley, 2000. ISBN
                      0-201-61633-5), as amended by the Unicode Standard
                      Annex #27: Unicode 3.1 and by the Unicode Standard
                      Annex #28: Unicode 3.2, March 2002.

7.2. Informative References

   [US-ASCII]   American National Standards Institute, "Coded
                      Character Set - 7-bit American Standard Code for
                      Information Interchange", ANSI X3.4, 1986.

   [UTF-16]   Hoffman, P. and F. Yergeau, "UTF-16, an encoding of
                      ISO 10646", RFC 2781, February 2000.

    [UTF-7]   Goldsmith, D. and M. Davis, "UTF-7 A Mail-Safe
                       Transformation Format of Unicode", RFC 2152, May
                       1997.

    [UTF-8]   Sollins, K., "Architectural Principles of Uniform
                       Resource Name Resolution", RFC 2276, January 1998.

8. Security Considerations

    As with UTF-8, UTF-9 can represent codepoints that are not in
    [UNICODE]. Applications should validate UTF-9 strings to ensure that
    all codepoints do not exceed the [UNICODE] maximum of U+10FFFF.

    The sample routines in this document are for example purposes, and
    make no attempt to validate their arguments, e.g., test for overflow
    ([UNICODE] values great than 0x10ffff) or codepoints used for
    surrogates. Besides resulting in invalid data, this can also create
    covert channels.

9. IANA Considerations

    The IANA shall reserve the charset names "UTF-9" and "UTF-18" for
    future assignment.

Author's Address

    Mark R. Crispin
    Panda Programming
    6158 NE Lariat Loop
    Bainbridge Island, WA 98110-2098

    Phone: (206) 842-2385
    EMail: UTF9@Lingling.Panda.COM

Full Copyright Statement

Intellectual Property

Acknowledgement

    Funding for the RFC Editor function is currently provided by the
    Internet Society.

Network Working Group   R. Glenn
Request for Comments: 2410   NIST
Category: Standards Track   S. Kent
                                                              BBN Corp
                                                         November 1998

             The NULL Encryption Algorithm and Its Use With IPsec

Status of this Memo

Copyright Notice

Abstract

   This memo defines the NULL encryption algorithm and its use with the
   IPsec Encapsulating Security Payload (ESP). NULL does nothing to
   alter plaintext data. In fact, NULL, by itself, does nothing. NULL
   provides the means for ESP to provide authentication and integrity
   without confidentiality.

   Further information on the other components necessary for ESP
   implementations is provided by [ESP] and [ROAD].

1. Introduction

   This memo defines the NULL encryption algorithm and its use with the
   IPsec Encapsulating Security Payload [ESP] to provide authentication
   and integrity without confidentiality.

   NULL is a block cipher the origins of which appear to be lost in
   antiquity. Despite rumors that the National Security Agency
   suppressed publication of this algorithm, there is no evidence of
   such action on their part. Rather, recent archaeological evidence
   suggests that the NULL algorithm was developed in Roman times, as an
   exportable alternative to Ceaser ciphers. However, because Roman
   numerals lack a symbol for zero, written records of the algorithm's
   development were lost to historians for over two millennia.

[ESP] specifies the use of an optional encryption algorithm to
provide confidentiality and the use of an optional authentication
algorithm to provide authentication and integrity. The NULL
encryption algorithm is a convenient way to represent the option of
not applying encryption. This is referred to as ESP_NULL in [DOI].

The IPsec Authentication Header [AH] specification provides a similar
service, by computing authentication data which covers the data
portion of a packet as well as the immutable in transit portions of
the IP header. ESP_NULL does not include the IP header in
calculating the authentication data. This can be useful in providing
IPsec services through non-IP network devices. The discussion on how
ESP_NULL might be used with non-IP network devices is outside the
scope of this document.

In this memo, NULL is used within the context of ESP. For further
information on how the various pieces of ESP fit together to provide
security services, refer to [ESP] and [ROAD].

The key words "MUST", "MUST NOT", "REQUIRED", "SHALL", "SHALL NOT",
"SHOULD", "SHOULD NOT", "RECOMMENDED", "MAY", and "OPTIONAL" in this
document are to be interpreted as described in [RFC 2119].

2. Algorithm Definition

NULL is defined mathematically by the use of the Identity function I
applied to a block of data b such that:

    NULL(b) = I(b) = b

2.1 Keying Material

Like other modern ciphers, e.g., RC5 [RFC-2040], the NULL encryption
algorithm can make use of keys of varying lengths. However, no
measurable increase in security is afforded by the use of longer key
lengths.

2.2 Cryptographic Synchronization

Because of the stateless nature of the NULL encryption algorithm, it
is not necessary to transmit an IV or similar cryptographic
synchronization data on a per packet (or even a per SA) basis. The
NULL encryption algorithm combines many of the best features of both
block and stream ciphers, while still not requiring the transmission
of an IV or analogous cryptographic synchronization data.

2.3 Padding

   NULL has a block size of 1 byte, thus padding is not necessary.

2.4. Performance

   The NULL encryption algorithm is significantly faster than other
   commonly used symmetric encryption algorithms and implementations of
   the base algorithm are available for all commonly used hardware and
   OS platforms.

2.5 Test Vectors

   The following is a set of test vectors to facilitate in the
   development of interoperable NULL implementations.

```
test_case =         1
data =              0x123456789abcdef
data_len =          8
NULL_data =         0x123456789abcdef

test_case =         2
data =              "Network Security People Have A Strange Sense Of Humor"
data_len =          53
NULL_data =         "Network Security People Have A Strange Sense Of Humor"
```

3. ESP_NULL Operational Requirements

   ESP_NULL is defined by using NULL within the context of ESP. This
   section further defines ESP_NULL by pointing out particular
   operational parameter requirements.

   For purposes of IKE [IKE] key extraction, the key size for this
   algorithm MUST be zero (0) bits, to facilitate interoperability and
   to avoid any potential export control problems.

   To facilitate interoperability, the IV size for this algorithm MUST
   be zero (0) bits.

   Padding MAY be included on outgoing packets as specified in [ESP].

4. Security Considerations

   The NULL encryption algorithm offers no confidentiality nor does it
   offer any other security service. It is simply a convenient way to
   represent the optional use of applying encryption within ESP. ESP
   can then be used to provide authentication and integrity without
   confidentiality. Unlike AH these services are not applied to any

part of the IP header. At the time of this writing there is no
evidence to support that ESP_NULL is any less secure than AH when
using the same authentication algorithm (i.e. a packet secured using
ESP_NULL with some authentication algorithm is as cryptographically
secure as a packet secured using AH with the same authentication
algorithm).

As stated in [ESP], while the use of encryption algorithms and
authentication algorithms are optional in ESP, it is imperative that
an ESP SA specifies the use of at least one cryptographically strong
encryption algorithm or one cryptographically strong authentication
algorithm or one of each.

At the time of this writing there are no known laws preventing the
exportation of NULL with a zero (0) bit key length.

5. Intellectual Property Rights

Pursuant to the provisions of [RFC-2026], the authors represent that
they have disclosed the existence of any proprietary or intellectual
property rights in the contribution that are reasonably and
personally known to the authors. The authors do not represent that
they personally know of all potentially pertinent proprietary and
intellectual property rights owned or claimed by the organizations
they represent or third parties.

6. Acknowledgments

Steve Bellovin suggested and provided the text for the Intellectual
Property Rights section.

Credit also needs to be given to the participants of the Cisco/ICSA
IPsec & IKE March 1998 Interoperability Workshop since it was there
that the need for this document became apparent.

7. References

    [ESP]   Kent, S., and R. Atkinson, "IP Encapsulating Security
                 Payload", RFC 2406, November 1998.

    [AH]   Kent, S., and R. Atkinson, "IP Authentication Header",
                 RFC 2402, November 1998.

    [ROAD]   Thayer, R., Doraswamy, N., and R. Glenn, "IP Security
                 Document Roadmap", RFC 2411, November 1998.

    [DOI]   Piper, D., "The Internet IP Security Domain of
                 Interpretation for ISAKMP", RFC 2408, November 1998.

    [IKE]   Harkins, D., and D. Carrel, "The Internet Key Exchange
                    (IKE)", RFC 2409, November 1998.

    [RFC-2026]   Bradner, S., "The Internet Standards Process -- Revision
                    3", BCP 9, RFC 2026, October 1996.

    [RFC-2040]   Baldwin, R., and R. Rivest, "The RC5, RC5-CBC, RC5-CBC-
                    Pad, and RC5-CTS Algorithms", RFC 2040, October 1996

    [RFC-2119]   Bradner, S., "Key words for use in RFCs to Indicate
                    Requirement Levels", BCP 14, RFC 2119, March 1997.

6. Editors' Addresses

    Rob Glenn
    NIST

    EMail: rob.glenn@nist.gov

    Stephen Kent
    BBN Corporation

    EMail: kent@bbn.com

    The IPsec working group can be contacted through the chairs:

    Robert Moskowitz
    ICSA

    EMail: rgm@icsa.net

    Ted T'so
    Massachusetts Institute of Technology

    EMail: tytso@mit.edu

7. Full Copyright Statement

   Copyright (C) The Internet Society (1998). All Rights Reserved.

   This document and translations of it may be copied and furnished to
   others, and derivative works that comment on or otherwise explain it
   or assist in its implementation may be prepared, copied, published
   and distributed, in whole or in part, without restriction of any
   kind, provided that the above copyright notice and this paragraph are
   included on all such copies and derivative works. However, this
   document itself may not be modified in any way, such as by removing
   the copyright notice or references to the Internet Society or other
   Internet organizations, except as needed for the purpose of
   developing Internet standards in which case the procedures for
   copyrights defined in the Internet Standards process must be
   followed, or as required to translate it into languages other than
   English.

   The limited permissions granted above are perpetual and will not be
   revoked by the Internet Society or its successors or assigns.

   This document and the information contained herein is provided on an
   "AS IS" basis and THE INTERNET SOCIETY AND THE INTERNET ENGINEERING
   TASK FORCE DISCLAIMS ALL WARRANTIES, EXPRESS OR IMPLIED, INCLUDING
   BUT NOT LIMITED TO ANY WARRANTY THAT THE USE OF THE INFORMATION
   HEREIN WILL NOT INFRINGE ANY RIGHTS OR ANY IMPLIED WARRANTIES OF
   MERCHANTABILITY OR FITNESS FOR A PARTICULAR PURPOSE.

Part III

Poetry in Motion

In June 1973 there were 45 hosts on the ARPAnet. So we know what the critical mass is, before verse breaks out. The authorship of RFC 527 is unclear: Keith Lim has said that it was originally written by D.L. Coville in May 1973, and edited by R. Merryman the next month. The original poem, *Jabberwocky,* by Lewis Carroll is part of *Through the Looking-Glass and What Alice Found There*, 1872.

Vint Cerf has been called "The Father of the Internet." Certainly, he has been at the forefront—he was in Kleinrock's lab in 1969; together with Bob Kahn, he invented TCP/IP; and so on. His imaginative work, RFCs 968, 1607, and his part of 1121, however, is of remarkable significance.

It is possible that Craig Partridge and Paul Mockapetris had something to do with RFC 1605, but who can be certain? Jay Ashcroft, however, gets full blame for RFC 2100, despite his cowardly attempt to fob off blame on Thomas Stearns Eliot.

ARPAWOCKY

Twas brillig, and the Protocols
    Did USER-SERVER in the wabe.
All mimsey was the FTP,
    And the RJE outgrabe,

Beware the ARPANET, my son;
    The bits that byte, the heads that scratch;
Beware the NCP, and shun
    the frumious system patch,

He took his coding pad in hand;
    Long time the Echo-plex he sought.
When his HOST-to-IMP began to limp
    he stood a while in thought,

And while he stood, in uffish thought,
    The ARPANET, with IMPish bent,
Sent packets through conditioned lines,
    And checked them as they went,

One-two, one-two, and through and through
    The IMP-to-IMP went ACK and NACK,
When the RFNM came, he said "I'm game",
    And sent the answer back,

Then hast thou joined the ARPANET?
    Oh come to me, my bankrupt boy!
Quick, call the NIC! Send RFCs!
    He chortled in his joy.

Twas brillig, and the Protocols
    Did USER-SERVER in the wabe.
All mimsey was the FTP,
    And the RJE outgrabe.

                                           D.L. COVILL
                                           May 1973

Network Working Group   V. Cerf
Request for Comments: 968   MCI
                                                   December 1985

'Twas the Night Before Start-up'

STATUS OF THIS MEMO

    This memo discusses problems that arise and debugging techniques used
    in bringing a new network into operation. Distribution of this memo
    is unlimited.

DISCUSSION

    Twas the night before start-up and all through the net,
        not a packet was moving; no bit nor octet.
    The engineers rattled their cards in despair,
        hoping a bad chip would blow with a flare.
    The salesmen were nestled all snug in their beds,
        while visions of data nets danced in their heads.
    And I with my datascope tracings and dumps
        prepared for some pretty bad bruises and lumps.
    When out in the hall there arose such a clatter,
        I sprang from my desk to see what was the matter.

    There stood at the threshold with PC in tow,
        An ARPANET hacker, all ready to go.
    I could see from the creases that covered his brow,
        he'd conquer the crisis confronting him now.
    More rapid than eagles, he checked each alarm
        and scrutinized each for its potential harm.

    On LAPB, on OSI, X.25!
        TCP, SNA, V.35!

    His eyes were afire with the strength of his gaze;
        no bug could hide long; not for hours or days.
    A wink of his eye and a twitch of his head,
        soon gave me to know I had little to dread.
    He spoke not a word, but went straight to his work,
        fixing a net that had gone plumb berserk;
    And laying a finger on one suspect line,
        he entered a patch and the net came up fine!

    The packets flowed neatly and protocols matched;
        the hosts interfaced and shift-registers latched.
    He tested the system from Gateway to PAD;
        not one bit was dropped; no checksum was bad.
    At last he was finished and wearily sighed

Cerf   [Page 1]

181

        and turned to explain why the system had died.
    I twisted my fingers and counted to ten;
        an off-by-one index had done it again...

    Vint Cerf
    December 1985

Network Working Group   J. Postel (ISI)
Request for Comments: 1121   L. Kleinrock (UCLA)
                                                        V. Cerf (NRI)
                                                     B. Boehm (UCLA)
                                                      September 1989

                        Act One - The Poems

Status of this Memo

    This RFC presents a collection of poems that were presented at "Act
    One", a symposium held partially in celebration of the 20th
    anniversary of the ARPANET. Distribution of this memo is unlimited.

Introduction

    The Computer Science Department of the University of California, Los
    Angeles (UCLA) organized a Symposium on Very High Speed Information
    Networks as the first in a projected series of meetings on Advanced
    Computer Technologies, thus ACT ONE. The time was chosen to also
    commemorate the 20th anniversary of the installation of the first
    Interface Message Processor (IMP) on the ARPANET which took place at
    UCLA.

    The Symposium took on a theatrical theme and a few of the speakers
    could not resist the temptation to commit poetry. This memo is an
    attempt to capture the result.

The Poems

                               WELCOME
                                  by
                          Leonard Kleinrock

    We've gathered here for two days to examine and debate
    And reflect on data networks and as well to celebrate.
    To recognize the leaders and recount the path we took.
    We'll begin with how it happened; for it's time to take a look.

    Yes, the history is legend and the pioneers are here.
    Listen to the story - it's our job to make it clear.
    We'll tell you where we are now and where we'll likely go.
    So welcome to ACT ONE, folks. Sit back - enjoy the show!!

                                183

                         ODE TO A QUEUE
                              by
                       Leonard Kleinrock

         In the 20 years of funding
         Many fields has DARPA led.
         But the finest thing that they did bring
         Was the analytic thread.

         By that I mean they nurtured
         Quantitative research tools.
         And they always felt for all their gelt
         They got principles and rules.

         Indeed a wealth of knowledge
         Was uncovered and was new.
         And the common thread with which we led
         Was the analytic queue!

         Now a queue may have one server.
         If there's more, they form a team.
         Its dearest wish is just to fish
         In a quiet Poisson stream.

         If you want to model networks
         Or a complex data flow
         A queue's the key to help you see
         All the things you need to know.

         So the next time you feel lonely
         And wonder what to do,
         You'll soon feel fine if you join the line
         Of an analytic queue!

                       THE PAST IS PROLOGUE
                              by
                       Leonard Kleinrock

         The past is prologue so they say.
         So Scene 1 was played today.
         It set the stage to point the way
         To high speed nets on Friday.

         And old slow IMP, a costly link,
         Codes to fix the lines that stink,
         Ideas born in tanks that think,
         Tomorrow's distance sure to shrink.

                              184

But first tonight we'll drink and eat.
We'll take some time good friends to greet.
Hear Bible class from Danny's seat.
Those good old days were bittersweet!

THE BIG BANG!
(or the birth of the ARPANET)
by
Leonard Kleinrock

It was back in '67 that the clan agreed to meet.
The gangsters and the planners were a breed damned hard to beat.
The goal we set was honest and the need was clear to all:
Connect those big old mainframes and the minis, lest they fall.

The spec was set quite rigid: it must work without a hitch.
It should stand a single failure with an unattended switch.
Files at hefty throughput 'cross the ARPANET must zip.
Send the interactive traffic on a quarter second trip.

The spec went out to bidders and t'was BBN that won.
They worked on soft and hardware and they all got paid for fun.
We decided that the first node would be we who are your hosts
And so today you're gathered here while UCLA boasts.

I suspect you might be asking "What means FIRST node on the net?"
Well frankly, it meant trouble, 'specially since no specs were set.
For you see the interface between the nascent IMP and HOST
Was a confidential secret from us folks on the West coast.

BBN had promised that the IMP was running late.
We welcomed any slippage in the deadly scheduled date.
But one day after Labor Day, it was plopped down at our gate!
Those dirty rotten scoundrels sent the damned thing out air freight!

As I recall that Tuesday, it makes me want to cry.
Everybody's brother came to blame the other guy!
Folks were there from ARPA, GTE and Honeywell.
UCLA and ATT and all were scared as hell.

We cautiously connected and the bits began to flow.
The pieces really functioned - just why I still don't know.
Messages were moving pretty well by Wednesday morn.
All the rest is history - packet switching had been born!

ROSENCRANTZ AND ETHERNET
by
Vint Cerf

All the world's a net! And all the data in it merely packets
come to store-and-forward in the queues a while and then are
heard no more. 'Tis a network waiting to be switched!

To switch or not to switch? That is the question. Whether
'tis wiser in the net to suffer the store and forward of
stochastic networks or to raise up circuits against a sea
of packets and, by dedication, serve them.

To net, to switch. To switch, perchance to slip!
Aye, there's the rub. For in that choice of switch,
what loops may lurk, when we have shuffled through
this Banyan net? Puzzles the will, initiates symposia,
stirs endless debate and gives rise to uncontrolled
flights of poetry beyond recompense!

UNTITLED
by
Barry Boehm

Paul Baran came out of the wood
With a message first misunderstood
    But despite dangers lurking
    The IMP's were soon working
And ARPA did see it was good.

So in place of our early myopia
We now have a net cornucopia
    With IMP's, TIP's, and LAN's
    Wideband VAN's, MAN's, and WAN's
And prospects of World Net Utopia.

But though we must wind up the clock
With thoughts of downstream feature shock
    We all be can mollified
    For there's no one more qualified
To discuss this than Leonard Kleinrock.

Notes

   The Symposium was held August 17 & 18, 1989, a Thursday and Friday.

   "Welcome" was presented on Thursday morning during the Overture.

   "Ode to a Queue" was presented in the Thursday morning session on
   "Giant Steps Forward: Technology Payoffs".

   "The Past is Prologue" was presented at the end of the Thursday
   afternoon sessions.

   "The Big Bang!" was presented during the after dinner events on
   Thursday night.

   "Rosencrantz and Ethernet" was presented at the morning session on
   Friday on "Communication Technologies in the next Millenium" (note
   that this version may differ slightly from the actual presentation
   since it was reconstructed from human memory several weeks later).

   The untitled poem by Barry Boehm was presented in the Friday
   afternoon session on "Impact on Government, Commerce and Citizenry".
   Barry gave his talk on "The Software Challenge to Our Technical
   Aspirations" then introduced the next speaker with this poem.

Security Considerations

   None.

Authors' Addresses

   Jon Postel
   USC/Information Sciences Institute
   4676 Admiralty Way
   Marina del Rey, CA 90292-6695

   Phone: 213-822-1511

   EMail: Postel@ISI.EDU

Leonard Kleinrock
University of California
Computer Science Department
3732G Boelter Hall
Los Angeles, CA 90024-1600

Phone: 213-825-2543

EMail: lk@CS.UCLA.EDU

Vinton G. Cerf
Corporation for National Research Initiatives
1895 Preston White Drive, Suite 100
Reston, VA 22091

Phone: 703-620-8990

EMail: VCerf@NRI.RESTON.VA.US

Barry Boehm
University of California
Computer Science Department
3732 Boelter Hall
Los Angeles, CA 90024-1600

Phone: 213-825-8137

EMail: boehm@CS.UCLA.EDU

Network Working Group   W. Shakespeare
Request for Comments: 1605   Globe Communications
Category: Informational   1 April 1994

                        SONET to Sonnet Translation

Status of this Memo

   This memo provides information for the Internet community. This memo
   does not specify an Internet standard of any kind. Distribution of
   this memo is unlimited.

Abstract

   Because Synchronous Optical Network (SONET) transmits data in frames
   of bytes, it is fairly easy to envision ways to compress SONET frames
   to yield higher bandwidth over a given fiber optic link. This memo
   describes a particular method, SONET Over Novel English Translation
   (SONNET).

Protocol Overview

   In brief, SONNET is a method for compressing 810-byte (9 lines by 90
   bytes) SONET OC-1 frames into approximately 400-byte (fourteen line
   decasyllabic) English sonnets. This compression scheme yields a
   roughly 50% average compression, and thus SONNET compression speeds
   are designated OCh-#, where 'h' indicates 50% (one half) compression
   and the # is the speed of the uncompressed link. The acronym is
   pronounced "owch."

   Mapping of the $2**704$ possible SONET payloads is achieved by matching
   each possible payload pattern with its equivalent Cerf catalog number
   (see [1], which lists a vast number of sonnets in English, many of
   which are truly terrible but suffice for the purposes of this memo).

Basic Transmission Rules

   The basic transmission rules are quite simple. The basic SONET OC-1
   frame is replaced with the corresponding sonnet at the transmission
   end converted back from the sonnet to SONET at the receiving end.
   Thus, for example, SONET frame 12 is transmitted as:

        When do I count the clock that tells the time
        And see the brave day sunk in hideous night;
        When I behold the violet past prime,
        And sable curls,...

For rates higher than OC-1, the OC-1 frames may either come
interleaved or concatenated into larger frames. Under SONNET
conversion rules, interleaved frames have their corresponding sonnet
representations interleaved. Thus SONET frames 33, 29 and 138 in an
OC-3 frame would be converted to the sequence:

        Full many a glorious morning have I seen
        When, in disgrace with fortune and men's eyes,
        When my loves swears that she is made of truth
        Flatter the mountain-tops with sovereign eye
        I all alone beweep my outcast state,
        I do believe her, though I know she lies
        Kissing with golden face...

while in an OC-3c frame, the individual OC-1 frames concatenated, one
after another, viz.:

        Full many a glorious morning have I seen Flatter the mountain-
        tops with sovereign eye Kissing with golden face...

        When, in disgrace with fortune and men's eyes, I all alone
        beweep my outcast state,...

        When my loves swears that she is made of truth I do believe her,
        though I know she lies...

(This example, perhaps, makes clear why data communications experts
consider concatenated SONET more efficient and esthetically
pleasing).

Timing Issues

    It is critical in this translation scheme to maintain consistent
    timing within a frame. If SONET frames or converted sonnets shift in
    time, the SONET pointers, or worse, poetic meter, may suffer.

References

    [1] Cerf, B., "A Catalog of All Published English Sonnets to 1950",
        Random House, 1953. (Now out of print.)

Security Considerations

    Security issues are not discussed in this memo.

Author's Address

    William Shakespeare
    Globe Communications
    London, United Kingdom

    Any suggestions that this, or any other work by this author, might
    be the work of a third party such as C. Marlow, R. Bacon, or
    C. Partridge or based on a previously developed theme by
    P.V. Mockapetris are completely spurious.

Network Working Group   B. Hancock
Request for Comments: 1882   Network-1 Software and Technology, Inc.
Category: Informational   December 1995

                The 12-Days of Technology Before Christmas

Status of this Memo

    This memo provides information for the Internet community. This memo
    does not specify an Internet standard of any kind. Distribution of
    this memo is unlimited.

Discussion

    On the first day of Christmas, technology gave to me:
          A database with a broken b-tree (what the hell is a b-tree
          anyway?)

    On the second day of Christmas, technology gave to me:
          Two transceiver failures (CRC errors? Collisions? What is
          going on?)
          And a database with a broken b-tree (Rebuild WHAT? It's a
          10GB database!)

    On the third day of Christmas, technology gave to me:
          Three French users (who, of course, think they know
          everything)
          Two transceiver failures (which are now spewing packets all
          over the net)
          And a database with a broken b-tree (Backup? What backup?)

    On the fourth day of Christmas, technology gave to me:
          Four calls for support (playing the same Christmas song over
          and over)
          Three French users (Why do they like to argue so much over
          trivial things?)
          Two transceiver failures (How the hell do I know which ones
          they are?)
          And a database with a broken b-tree (Pointer error? What's a
          pointer error?)

On the fifth day of Christmas, technology gave to me:
        Five golden SCSI contacts (Of course they're better than
        silver!)
        Four support calls (Ever notice how time stands still when on
        hold?
        Three French users (No, we don't have footpedals on PC's. Why
        do you ask?)
        Two transceiver failures (If I knew which ones were bad, I
        would know which ones to fix!)
        And a database with a broken b-tree (Not till next week? Are
        you nuts?!?!)

On the sixth day of Christmas, technology gave to me:
        Six games a-playing (On the production network, of course!)
        Five golden SCSI contacts (What do you mean "not terminated!")
        Four support calls (No, don't transfer me again - do you HEAR?
        Damn!)
        Three French users (No, you cannot scan in by putting the page
        to the screen...)
        Two transceiver failures (I can't look at the LEDs - they're
        in the ceiling!)
        And a database with a broken b-tree (Norway? That's where this
        was written?)

On the seventh day of Christmas, technology gave to me:
        Seven license failures (Expired? When?)
        Six games a-playing (Please stop tying up the PBX to talk to
        each other!)
        Five golden SCSI contacts (What do you mean I need "wide"
        SCSI?)
        Four support calls (At least the Muzak is different this
        time...)
        Three French Users (Well, monsieur, there really isn't an
        "any" key, but...)
        Two transceiver failures (SQE? What is that? If I knew I would
        set it myself!)
        And a database with a broken b-tree (No, I really need to talk
        to Lars - NOW!)

194

On the eighth day of Christmas, technology gave to me:
        Eight MODEMs dialing (Who bought these? They're a security
        violation!)
        Seven license failures (How many WEEKS to get a license?)
        Six games a-playing (What do you mean one pixel per packet on
        updates?!?)
        Five golden SCSI contacts (Fast SCSI? It's supposed to be
        fast, isn't it?)
        Four support calls (I already told them that! Don't transfer
        me back - DAMN!)
        Three French users (No, CTL-ALT-DEL is not the proper way to
        end a program)
        Two transceiver failures (What do you mean "babbling
        transceiver"?)
        And a database with a broken b-tree (Does anyone speak English
        in Oslo?)

On the ninth day of Christmas, technology gave to me:
        Nine lady executives with attitude (She said do WHAT with the
        servers?)
        Eight MODEMs dialing (You've been downloading WHAT?)
        Seven license failures (We sent the P.O. two months ago!)
        Six games a-playing (HOW many people are doing this to the
        network?)
        Five golden SCSI contacts (What do you mean two have the same
        ID?)
        Four support calls (No, I am not at the console - I tried that
        already.)
        Three French users (No, only one floppy fits at a time? Why do
        you ask?)
        Two transceiver failures (Spare? What spare?)
        And a database with a broken b-tree (No, I am trying to find
        Lars! L-A-R-S!)

On the tenth day of Christmas, technology gave to me:
        Ten SNMP alerts flashing (What is that Godawful beeping?)
        Nine lady executives with attitude (No, it used to be a mens
        room? Why?)
        Eight MODEMs dialing (What Internet provider? We don't allow
        Internet here!)
        Seven license failures (SPA? Why are they calling us?)
        Six games a-playing (No, you don't need a graphics accelerator
        for Lotus!)
        Five golden SCSI contacts (You mean I need ANOTHER cable?)
        Four support calls (No, I never needed an account number
        before...)
        Three French users (When the PC sounds like a cat, it's a head
        crash!)
        Two transceiver failures (Power connection? What power
        connection?)
        And a database with a broken b-tree (Restore what index
        pointers?)

On the eleventh day of Christmas, technology gave to me:
        Eleven boards a-frying (What is that terrible smell?)
        Ten SNMP alerts flashing (What's a MIB, anyway? What's an
        extension?)
        Nine lady executives with attitude (Mauve? Our computer room
        tiles in mauve?)
        Eight MODEMs dialing (What do you mean you let your roommate
        dial-in?)
        Seven license failures (How many other illegal copies do we
        have?!?!)
        Six games a-playing (I told you - AFTER HOURS!)
        Five golden SCSI contacts (If I knew what was wrong, I
        wouldn't be calling!)
        Four support calls (Put me on hold again and I will slash your
        credit rating!)
        Three French users (Don't hang your floppies with a magnet
        again!)
        Two transceiver failures (How should I know if the connector
        is bad?)
        And a database with a broken b-tree (I already did all of
        that!)

On the twelfth day of Christmas, technology gave to me:
        Twelve virtual pipe connections (There's only supposed to be
        two!)
        Eleven boards a-frying (What a surge suppressor supposed to
        do, anyway?)
        Ten SNMP alerts flashing (From a distance, it does kinda look
        like XMas lights.)
        Nine lady executives with attitude (What do you mean aerobics
        before backups?)
        Eight MODEMs dialing (No, we never use them to connect during
        business hours.)
        Seven license failures (We're all going to jail, I just know
        it.)
        Six games a-playing (No, no - my turn, my turn!)
        Five golden SCSI contacts (Great, just great! Now it won't
        even boot!)
        Four support calls (I don't have that package! How did I end
        up with you!)
        Three French users (I don't care if it is sexy, no more nude
        screen backgrounds!)
        Two transceiver failures (Maybe we should switch to token
        ring...)
        And a database with a broken b-tree (No, operator - Oslo,
        Norway. We were just talking and were cut off...)

Security Considerations

    Security issues are not discussed in this memo.

Author's Address

    Bill Hancock, Ph.D.
    Network-1 Software & Technology, Inc.
    DFW Research Center
    878 Greenview Dr.
    Grand Prairie, TX 75050

    EMail: hancock@network-1.com
    Phone: (214) 606-8200
    Fax: (214) 606-8220

Network Working Group   J. Ashworth
Request for Comments: 2100   Ashworth & Associates
Category: Informational   1 April 1997

                        The Naming of Hosts

Status of this Memo

Introduction

    This RFC is a commentary on the difficulty of deciding upon an
    acceptably distinctive hostname for one's computer, a problem which
    grows in direct proportion to the logarithmically increasing size of
    the Internet.

    Distribution of this memo is unlimited.

    Except to TS Eliot.

    And, for that matter, to David Addison, who hates iambic pentameter.

Poetry

        The Naming of Hosts is a difficult matter,
            It isn't just one of your holiday games;
        You may think at first I'm as mad as a hatter
            When I tell you, a host must have THREE DIFFERENT NAMES.

        First of all, there's the name that the users use daily,
            Such as venus, athena, and cisco, and ames,
        Such as titan or sirius, hobbes or europa--
            All of them sensible everyday names.

        There are fancier names if you think they sound sweeter,
            Some for the web pages, some for the flames:
        Such as mercury, phoenix, orion, and charon--
            But all of them sensible everyday names.

        But I tell you, a host needs a name that's particular,
            A name that's peculiar, and more dignified,
        Else how can it keep its home page perpendicular,
            And spread out its data, send pages world wide?

    Of names of this kind, I can give you a quorum,
        Like lothlorien, pothole, or kobyashi-maru,
    Such as pearly-gates.vatican, or else diplomatic-
        Names that never belong to more than one host.

    But above and beyond there's still one name left over,
        And that is the name that you never will guess;
    The name that no human research can discover--
        But THE NAMESERVER KNOWS, and will us'ually confess.

    When you notice a client in rapt meditation,
        The reason, I tell you, is always the same:
    The code is engaged in a deep consultation
        On the address, the address, the address of its name:

                    It's ineffable,
                    effable,
                    Effanineffable,
                    Deep and inscrutable,
                    singular
                    Name.

Credits

    Thanks to Don Libes, Mark Lottor, and a host of twisted
    individuals^W^Wcreative sysadmins for providing source material for
    this memo, to Andrew Lloyd-Webber, Cameron Mackintosh, and a cast of
    thousands (particularly including Terrance Mann) who drew my
    attention to the necessity, and of course, to Thomas Stearns Eliot,
    for making this all necessary.

References

    [1] Libes, D., "Choosing a Name for Your Computer", Communications
         of the ACM, Vol. 32, No. 11, Pg. 1289, November 1989.

    [2] Lottor, M. et al., "Domain Name Survey, Jan 1997",
         namedroppers@internic.net

    [3] Wong, M. et. al., "Cool Hostnames",
         http://www.seas.upenn.edu/~mengwong/coolhosts.html

    [4] Stearns, TS, _Old Possum's Book of Practical Cats_.

Security Considerations

    Security issues are not discussed in this memo.

    Particularly the cardiac security of certain famous poets.

Author's Address

    Jay R. Ashworth
    Ashworth & Associates
    Advanced Technology Consulting
    St. Petersburg FL 33709-4819

    Phone: +1 813 790 7592

    EMail: jra@scfn.thpl.lib.fl.us

Part IV

The IPng Process and IPv6

As the ARPAnet became the Internet and as clear and easily-recalled bang-addressing gave way to the obscurities of the Domain Name System, the Internet Protocol itself started to evolve. What most of us currently use is IPv4. But for well over a decade, something has been in the works: IP next generation, IPng, and IPv6. Look on the IESG's work, and despair!

RFC 1606 illustrates just how far network-assignment still has to go. RFC 1607 lets us see just where it will go (or has gone; or went).

As belied by its number, RFC 1776 is truly revolutionary. Written by Steve Crocker, the author of RFC 1, which allocated 5 bits for address space, RFC 1776 includes 1696 bytes of address space. This should suffice for now.

Robert Elz, a stalwart of the Australian Unix User Group and the author of Berkeley's disk quotas, went in the opposite direction (which we attribute to his being in the Southern Hemisphere). RFC 1924 condenses IPv6 addresses to a mere 20 bytes.

Network Working Group   J. Onions
Request for Comments: 1606   Nexor Ltd.
Category: Informational   1 April 1994

       A Historical Perspective On The Usage Of IP Version 9

Status of this Memo

    This memo provides information for the Internet community. This memo
    does not specify an Internet standard of any kind. Distribution of
    this memo is unlimited.

Abstract

    This paper reviews the usages of the old IP version protocol. It
    considers some of its successes and its failures.

Introduction

    The take-up of the network protocol TCP/IPv9 has been phenomenal over
    the last few years. Gone are the days when there were just a few
    million hosts, and the network was understood. As the IP version 9
    protocol comes to the end of its useful life, once again due to
    address space exhaustion, we look back at some of the success of the
    protocol.

Routing

    The up to 42 deep hierarchy of routing levels built into IPv9 must
    have been one of the key features for its wide deployment. The
    ability to assign a whole network, or group of networks to an
    electronic component must be seen as one of the reasons for its
    takeup. The use of the Compact Disk Hologram units is typical of the
    usage. They typically have a level 37 network number assigned to each
    logical part, and a level 36 network number assigned to the whole
    device. This allows the CDH management protocol to control the unit
    as a whole, and the high-street vendor to do remote diagnostics on
    discreet elements of the device. This still allows sub-chip routing
    to be done using the 38th level addressing to download new nanocode.
    As yet, no requirement has been found for levels 40-42, with level 39
    still being used for experimental interrogation of atomic structure
    of components where required.

Allocation

   The vast number space of the IPv9 protocol has also allowed
   allocation to be done in a straight forward manner. Typically, most
   high street commercial internet providers issue a range of 1 billion
   addresses to each house. The addresses are then dynamically
   partitioned into subnet hierarchies allowing groups of a million
   addresses to be allocated for each discreet unit (e.g., room/floor
   etc.) The allocation of sub groups then to controllers such as light
   switches, mains sockets and similar is then done from each pool.

   The allocation process is again done in a hierarchical zoned way,
   with each major application requesting a block of addresses from its
   controller. In this way the light bulb requests an address block from
   the light switch, the light switch in turn from the electrical system
   which in turn requests one from the room/floor controller. This has
   been found to be successful due to the enormous range of addresses
   available, and contention for the address space being without
   problems typically.

   Whilst there are still many addresses unallocated the available space
   has been sharply decreased. The discovery of intelligent life on
   other solar systems with the parallel discovery of a faster-than-
   light transport stack is the main cause. This enables real time
   communication with them, and has made the allocation of world-size
   address spaces necessary, at the level 3 routing hierarchy. There is
   still only 1 global (spatial) level 2 galaxy wide network required
   for this galaxy, although the establishment of permanent space
   stations in deep space may start to exhaust this. This allows level 1
   to be used for inter-galaxy routing. The most pressing problem now is
   the case of parallel universes. Of course there is the danger of
   assuming that there is no higher extrapolation than parallel
   universes...

   Up to now, the hacking into, and setting of holo-recorder devices to
   the wrong channel from remote galaxies, has not been confirmed, and
   appears to be attributable to finger problem with the remote control
   whilst travelling home from the office.

Applications

   The introduction of body monitors as IPv9 addresseable units injected
   into the blood stream has been rated as inconclusive. Whilst being
   able to have devices lodged in the heart, kidneys, brain, etc.,
   sending out SNMPv9 trap messages at critical events has been a useful
   monitoring tool for doctors, the use of the blood stream as both a
   delivery and a communication highway, has been problematic. The
   crosstalk between the signals moving through the blood stream and the

close proximity of nerves has meant that patients suffering multiple
events at once, can go into violent spasm. This, coupled with early
problems with broadcasts storms tending to make patients blood boil,
have led to a rethink on this whole procedure. Also, the requirement
to wear the silly satellite dish hat has led to feelings of
embarrassment except in California, where it is now the latest trend.

The usage of IPv9 addresseable consumer packaging has been a topic of
hot debate. The marketing people see it as a godsend, being able to
get feedback on how products are actually used. Similarly, the
recycling is much improved by use of directed broadcast, "All those
packages composed of cardboard respond please." Consumers are not so
keen on this seeing it as an invasion of privacy. The introduction of
the handy-dandy directed stack zapper (which is also rumoured to be
IPv9 aware) sending directed broadcasts on the local food package net
effectively resetting the network mask to all 1's has made this an
area of choice.

The advent of the IPv9 magazine was universally approved of. Being
able to ask a magazine where its contents page was the most useful of
the features. However combined with the networked newspaper/magazine
rack, the ability to find out where you left the magazine with the
article that was concerned with something about useage of lawn mowers
in outer space is obvious. The ability to download reading habits
automatically into the house controller and therefore alert the
reader of articles of similar ilk is seen as marginal. Alleged
querying of this information to discover "deviant" behaviour in
persons within political office by members of contending parties is
suspected

Sneakernet, as pioneered by shoe specialists skholl is seen to be a
failure. The market was just not ready for shoes that could forward
detailed analysis of foot odour to manufacturers...

Manufacture

Of course, cost is one of the issues that was not considered when
IPv9 was designed. It took a leap of imagination to believe that one
day anything that wished to be could be IPv9 addresseable. It was
assumed that IPv9 protocol machines would drop in price as with
general chip technology. Few people would have forseen the advance in
genetic manipulation that allowed viruses to be instructed to build
nano-technology IPv9 protocol machines by the billion for the price
or a grain of sugar. Or similarly, the nano-robots that could insert
and wire these in place.

The recent research in quark-quark transistors, shows some promise and may allow specially built atoms to be used as switches. The manufacture of these will be so expensive (maybe up to 10cent an IPv9 stack) as to be prohibitive except for the most highly demanding niches.

Conclusions

Those who do not study history, are doomed to repeat it.

Security Considerations

Security issues are not discussed in this memo.

Author's Address

Julian Onions
Nexor Ltd.
PO Box 132
Nottingham NG7 2UU, ENGLAND

Phone: +44 602 520580
EMail: j.onions@nexor.co.uk

```
Network Working Group                                      V. Cerf
Request for Comments: 1607                         Internet Society
Category: Informational                               1 April 1994
```

A VIEW FROM THE 21ST CENTURY

Status of this Memo

   This memo provides information for the Internet community. This memo
   does not specify an Internet standard of any kind. Distribution of
   this memo is unlimited.

A NOTE TO THE READER

   The letters below were discovered in September 1993 in a reverse
   time-capsule apparently sent from 2023. The author of this paper
   cannot vouch for the accuracy of the letter contents, but spectral
   and radiation analysis are consistent with origin later than 2020. It
   is not known what, if any, effect will arise if readers take actions
   based on the future history contained in these documents. I trust
   you will be particularly careful with our collective futures!

THE LETTERS

   To: "Jonathan Bradel" <jbradel@astro.luna.edu>
   CC: "Therese Troisema" <ttroisema@inria.fr>
   From: "David Kenter" <dkenter@xob.isea.mr>
   Date: September 8, 2023 08:47.01 MT
   Subject: Hello from the Exobiology Lab!

   Hi Jonathan!

   I just wanted to let you know that I have settled in my new
   offices at the Exobiology Lab at the Interplanetary Space
   Exploration Agency's base here on Mars. The trip out was
   uneventful and did let me get through an awful lot of
   reading in preparation for my three year term here. There
   is an excellent library of material here at the lab and
   reasonable communications back home, thanks to the CommRing
   satellites that were put up last year here. The transfer
   rates are only a few terabits per second, but this is
   usually adequate for the most part.

   We've been doing some simulation work to test various
   theories of bio-history on Mars and I have attached the
   output of one of the more interesting runs. The results are

best viewed with a model VR-95HR/OS headset with the
peripheral glove adapter. I would recommend finding an
outdoor location if you activate the olfactory simulator
since some of the outputs are pretty rank! You'll notice
that atmospheric outgassing seriously interfered with any
potential complex life form development.

We tried a few runs to see what would happen if an
atmospheric confinement/replenishment system had been in
place, but the results are too speculative to be more than
entertaining at this point. There has been some serious
discussion of terra-forming options, but the economics are
still very unclear, as are the time-frames for realizing
any useful results.

I have also been trying out some new exercises to recover
from the effects of the long trip out. I've attached a
sample neuroscan clip which will give you some feeling for
the kinds of gymnastics that are possible in this gravity
field. My timing is still pretty lousy, but I hope it will
improve with practice.

I'd appreciate it very much if you could track down the
latest NanoConstructor ToolKit from MIT. I have need of
some lab gear which isn't available here and which would be
a lot easier to fabricate with the tool kit. The version I
have is NTK-R5 (2020) and I know there has been a lot added
since then.

Therese,

I wanted you to see the simulation runs, too. You may be
able to coax better results from the EXAFLOP array at CERN,
if you still have an account there. We're still limping
along with the 50 PFLOP system that Danny Hillis donated to
the agency a few years back.

The attached HD video clip shows the greenhouse efforts
here to grow grapes from the cuttings that were brought out
five years ago. We're still a long ways from '82
Beaucastel!

Gotta get ready for a sampling trip to Olympus Mons, so
will send this off for now.

Warmest regards,

David

Cerf   [Page 2]

212

-=-

To: "David Kenter" <dkenter@xob.isea.mr>
CC: "Therese Troisema" <ttroisema@inria.fr>
From: "Jonathan Bradel" <jbradel@astro.luna.edu>
Date: September 10, 2023 12:30:14 LT
Subject: Re: Hello from the Exobiology Lab!

David,

Many thanks for your note and all its news and interesting
data! Melanie and I are glad to know you are settled now
and back at work. We've been making heavy use of the new
darkside reflector telescope and, thanks to the new petabit
fiber links that were introduced last year, we have very
effective controls from Luna City. We've been able to run
some really interesting synthetic aperture observations by
linking the results from the darkside array and the Earth-
orbiting telescopes, giving us an effective diameter of
about 200,000 miles. I can hardly wait to see what we can
make of some of the most distant Quasars with this set-up.

We had quite a scare last month when Melanie complained of
a recurring vertigo. None of the usual treatments seemed to
help so a molecular-level brain bioscan was done. An
unexpectedly high level of localized neuro-transmitter
synthesis was discovered but has now been corrected by
auto-gene therapy.

As you requested, I have attached the latest
NanoConstructor ToolKit from MIT. This version integrates
the Knowbot control subsystem which allows the NanoSystem
to be fully linked to the Internet for control, data
sharing and inter-system communication. By the way, the
Internet Society has negotiated a nice discount for nano-
fab services if you need something more elaborate than the
ISEA folks have available at XOB. I could put the
NanoSystem on the Solex Mars/Luna run and have it to you
pretty quickly.

Keep in touch!

Jon and Melanie

-=-

To: "David Kenter" <dkenter@xob.isea.mr>
CC: "Jonathan Bradel" <jbradel@astro.luna.edu>
CC: "Troisema" <rm1023@geosync.hyatt.com>
From: "Therese Troisema" <ttroisema@inria.fr>
Date: September 10, 2023 12:30:14 UT
Subject: Re: Hello from the Exobiology Lab!

Bon Jour, David!

I am writing to you from the Hyatt Geosync where your email
was forwarded to me from INRIA. Louis and I are here
vacationing for two weeks. I have some time available and
will set up a simulation run on my EXAFLOP account. They
have the VR-95HR/OS headsets here for entertainment
purposes, but they will work fine for examining the results
of the simulation.

I have been taking time to do some research on the
development of the Interplanetary Internet and have found
some rather interesting results. I guess this counts as a
kind of paleo-networking effort, since some of the early
days reach back to the 1960s. It's hard to believe that
anyone even knew what a computer network was back then!

Did you know that the original work on Internet was
intended for military network use? One would never guess it
from the current state of affairs, but a lot of the
original packet switching work on ARPANET was done under
the sponsorship of something called the Advanced Research
Projects Agency of the US Department of Defense back in
1968. During the 1970s, a number of packet networks were
built by ARPA and others (including work by the predecessor
to INRIA, IRIA, which developed a packet network called
CIGALE on which the CYCLADES network operating system was
built). There was also work done by the French PTT on an
experimental system called RCP that later became a
commercial system called TRANSPAC. Some seminal work was
done in the mid-late 1960s in England at the National
Physical Laboratory on a single node switch that apparently
served as the first local area network! It's very hard to
believe that this all happened over 50 years ago.

A radio-based network was developed in the same 1960s/early
1970s time period called ALOHANET which featured use of a
randomly-shared radio channel. This idea was later realized
on a coaxial cable at XEROX PARC and called Ethernet. By
1978, the Internet research effort had produced 4 versions
of a set of protocols called "TCP/IP" (Transmission Control

Protocol/Internet Protocol"). These were used in
conjunction with devices called gateways, back then, but
which became known as "routers". The gateways connected
packet networks to each other. The combination of gateways
and TCP/IP software was implemented on a lot of different
operating systems, especially something called UNIX. There
was enough confidence in the resulting implementations that
all the computers on the ARPANET and any networks linked to
the ARPANET by gateways were required to switch over to use
TCP/IP at the beginning of 1983. For many historians, 1983
marks the start of global Internet growth although it had
its origins in the research effort started at Stanford
University in 1973, ten years earlier.

I am going to read more about this and, if you are
interested, I can report on what happened after 1983.

I will leave any simulation results from the EXAFLOP runs
in the private access directory in the CERN TERAFLEX
archive. It will be accessible using the JIT-ticket I have
attached, protected with your public key.

Au revoir, mon ami, Therese

```
-=-=-=-=-=-=-=-=-=-=-=-=-=-=-=-=-=-=-=-=-=-=-=-
```

To: "Troisema" <rm1023@geosync.hyatt.com>
CC: "Jonathan Bradel" <jbradel@astro.luna.edu>
CC: "Therese Troisema" <ttroisema@inria.fr>
From: "David Kenter" <dkenter@xob.isea.mr>
Date: September 10, 2023 17:26:35 MT
Subject: Internet History

Dear Therese,

I am so glad you have had a chance to take a short
vacation; you and Louis work too hard! I changed the
subject line to reflect the new thread this discussion
seems to be leading in. It sounds as if the whole system
started pretty small. How did it ever get to the size it is
now?

David


```
-=-=-=-=-=-=-=-=-=-=-=-=-=-=-=-=-=-=-=-=-=-=-=-
```

To: "David Kenter" <dkenter@xob.isea.mr>
CC: "Therese Troisema" <ttroisema@inria.fr>
CC: "Troisema" <rm1023@geosync.hyatt.com>
From: "Jonathan Bradel" <jbradel@astro.luna.edu>
Date: September 11, 2023 09:45:26 LT
Subject: Re: Internet History

Hello everyone! I have been following the discussion with
great interest. I seem to remember that there was an effort
to connect what people thought were "super computers" back
in the mid-1980's and that had something to do with the way
in which the system evolved. Therese, did your research
tell you anything about that?

Jon

-=-

To: "Jonathan Bradel" <jbradel@astro.luna.edu>
CC: "David Kenter" <dkenter@xob.isea.mr>
CC: "Troisema" <rm1023@geosync.hyatt.com>
From: "Therese Troisema" <ttroisema@inria.fr>
Date: September 12, 2023 16:05:02 UT
Subject: Re: Internet History

Jon,

Yes, the US National Science Foundation (NSF) set up 5
super computer centers around the US and also provided some
seed funding for what they called "intermediate level"
packet networks which were, in turn, connected to a
national backbone network they called "NSFNET." The
intermediate level nets connected the user community
networks (mostly in research labs and universities at that
time) to the backbone to which the super computer sites
were linked. According to my notes, NSF planned to reduce
funding for the various networking activities over time on
the presumption that they could become self-sustaining.
Many of the intermediate level networks sought to create a
larger market by turning to industry, which NSF permitted.
There was a rapid growth in the equipment market during the
last half of the 1980s, for routers (the new name for
gateways), work stations, network servers, and local area
networks. The penetration of the equipment market led to a
new market in commercial Internet services. Some of the
intermediate networks became commercial services, joining
others that were created to meet a growing demand for
Internet access.

By mid-1993, the system had grown to include over 15,000
networks, world-wide, and over 2 million computers. They
must have thought this was a pretty big system, back then.
Actually, it was, at the time, the largest collection of
networks and computers ever interconnected. Looking back
from our perspective, though, this sounds like a very
modest beginning, doesn't it? Nobody knew, at the time,
just how many users there were, but the system was doubling
annually and that attracted a lot of attention in many
different quarters.

There was an interesting report produced by the US National
Academy of Science about something they called

Cerf   [Page 7]

"Collaboratories" which was intended to convey the idea
that people and computers could carry out various kinds of
collaborative work if they had the right kinds of networks
to link their computer systems and the right kinds of
applications to deal with distributed applications. Of
course, we take that sort of thing for granted now, but it
was new and often complicated 30 years ago.

I am going to try to find out how they dealt with the
problem of explosive growth.

Louis and I will be leaving shortly for a three-day
excursion to the new vari-grav habitat but I will let you
know what I find out about the 1990s period in Internet
history when we get back.

Therese

-=-

To: "Troisema" <rm1023@geosync.hyatt.com>
CC: "David Kenter" <dkenter@xob.isea.mr>
CC: "Therese Troisema" <ttroisema@inria.fr>
From: "Jonathan Bradel" <jbradel@astro.luna.edu>
Date: September 13, 2023 10:34:05 LT
Subject: Re: Internet History

Therese,

I sent a few Knowbot programs out looking for Internet
background and found an interesting archive at the Postel
Historical Institute in Pacific Palisades, California.
These folks have an incredible collection of old documents,
some of them actually still on paper, dating as far back as
1962! This stuff gets addicting after a while.

Postel apparently edited a series of reports called
"Request for Comments" or "RFC" for short. These seem to be
one of the principal means by which the technology of the
Internet has been documented, and also, as nearly as I can
tell, a lot of its culture. The Institute also has a
phenomenal archive of electronic mail going back to about
1970 (do you believe it? Email from over 50 years ago!). I
don't have time to set up a really good automatic analysis
of the contents, but I did leave a couple of Knowbots
running to find things related to growth, scaling, and

increased capacity of the Internet.

It turns out that the technical committee called the
Internet Engineering Task Force was very pre-occupied in
the 1991-1994 period with the whole problem of
accommodating exponential growth in the size of the
Internet. They had a bunch of different options for replacing the then-existing IP layer with something that
could support a larger address space. There were a lot of
arguments about how soon they would run out of addresses
and a lot of uncertainty about how much functionality to
add on while solving the primary growth problem. Some folks
thought the scaling problem was so critical that it should
take priority while others thought there was still some
time and that new functionality would help motivate the
massive effort needed to replace the then-current version 4
IP.

As it happens, they were able to achieve multiple
objectives, as we now know. They found a way to increase
the space for identifying logical end-points in the system
as well increasing the address space needed to identify
physical end-points. That gave them a hook on which to base
the mobile, dynamic addressing capability that we now rely
on so heavily in the Internet. According to the notes I
have seen, they were also experimenting with new kinds of
applications that required different kinds of service than
the usual "best efforts" they were able to obtain from the
conventional router systems.

I found an absolutely hilarious "packet video clip" in one
of the archives. It's a black-and-white, 6 frame per second
shot of some guy taking off his coat, shirt and tie at one
of the engineering committee meetings. His T-shirt says "IP
on everything" which must have been some kind of slogan for
Internet expansion back then. Right at the end, some big
bearded guy comes up and stuffs some paper money in the
other guy's waistband. Apparently, there are quite a few
other archives of the early packet video squirreled away at
the PHI. I can't believe how primitive all this stuff
looks. I have attached a sample for you to enjoy. They
didn't have TDV back then, so you can't move the point of
view around the room or anything. You just have to watch
the figures move jerkily across the screen.

You can dig into this stuff if you send a Knowbot program
to concierge@phi.pacpal.ca.us. This Postel character must
have never thrown anything away!!

Jon

-=-

To: "Jonathan Bradel" <jbradel@astro.luna.edu>
CC: "David Kenter" <dkenter@xob.isea.mr>
CC: "Troisema" <rm1023@geosync.hyatt.com>
From: "Therese Troisema" <ttroisema@inria.fr>
Date: September 15, 2023 07:55:45 UT
Subject: Re: Internet History

Jon,

thanks for the pointer. I pulled up a lot of very useful
material from PHI. You're right, they did manage to solve a
lot of problems at once with the new IP. Once they got the
bugs out of the prototype implementations, it spread very
quickly from the transit service companies outward towards
all the host computers in the system. I also discovered
that they were doing research on primitive gigabit-per-
second networks at that same general time. They had been
relying on unbelievably slow transmission systems around
100 megabits-per-second and below. Can you imagine how long
it would take to send a typical 3DV image at those glacial
speeds?

According to the notes I found, a lot of the wide-area
system was moved over to operate on top of something they
called Asynchronous Transfer Mode Cell Switching or ATM for
short. Towards the end of the decade, they managed to get
end to end transfer rates on the order of a gigabyte per
second which was fairly respectable, given the technology
they had at the time. Of course, the telecommunications
business had been turned totally upside down in the process
of getting to that point.

It used to be the case that broadcast and cable television,
telephone and publishing were different businesses. In some
countries, television and telephone were monopolies
operated by the government or operated in the private
sector with government regulation. That started changing
drastically as the 1990s unfolded, especially in the United
States where telephone companies bought cable companies,
publishers owned various communication companies and it got
to be very hard to figure out just what kind of company it

was that should or could be regulated. There grew up an
amazing number of competing ways to deliver information in
digital form. The same company might offer a variety of
information and communication services.

With regard to the Internet, it was possible to reach it
through mobile digital radio, satellite, conventional wire
line access (quaintly called "dial-up") using Integrated
Services Digital Networking, specially-designed modems,
special data services on television cable, and new fiber-
based services that eventually made it even into
residential settings. All the bulletin board systems got
connected to the Internet and surprised everyone, including
themselves, when the linkage created a new kind of
publishing environment in which authors took direct responsibility for making their work accessible.

Interestingly, this didn't do away either with the need for
traditional publishers, who filter and evaluate material
prior to publication, nor for a continuing interest in
paper and CD-ROM. As display technology got better and more
portable, though, paper became much more of a specialty
item. Most documents were published on-line or on high-
density digital storage media. The basic publishing
process retained a heavy emphasis on editorial selection,
but the mechanics shifted largely in the direction of the
author - with help from experts in layout and
accessibility. Of course, it helped to have a universal
reference numbering plan which allowed authors to register
documents in permanent archives. References could be made
to these from any other on-line context and the documents
retrieved readily, possiblyat some cost for copying rights.

By the end of the decade, "multimedia" was no longer a
buzz-word but a normal way of preparing and presenting
information. One unexpected angle: multimedia had been
thought to be confined to presentation in visual and
audible forms for human consumption, but it turned out that
including computers as senders and recipients of these
messages allowed them to use the digital email medium as an
enabling technology for deferred, inter-computer
interaction.

Just based on what I have been reading, one of the toughest
technical problems was finding good standards to represent
all these different modalities. Copyright questions, which
had been thought to be what they called "show-stoppers,"
turned out to be susceptible to largely-established case

221

law. Abusing access to digital information was impeded in
large degree by wrapping publications in software shields,
but in the end, abuses were still possible and abusers were
prosecuted.

On the policy side, there was a strong need to apply
cryptography for authentication and for privacy. This was a
big struggle for many governments, including ours here in
France, where there are very strong views and laws on this
subject, but ultimately, the need for commonality on a
global basis outweighed many of the considerations that
inhibited the use of this valuable technology.

Well, that takes us up to about 20 years ago, which still
seems a far cry from our current state of technology. With
over a billion computers in the system and most of the
populations of information-intensive countries fully
linked, some of the more technically-astute back at the
turn of the millennium may have had some inkling of what
was in store for the next two decades.

Therese

-=-

To: "Therese Troisema" <ttroisema@inria.fr>
CC: "Jonathan Bradel" <jbradel@astro.luna.edu>
From: "David Kenter" <dkenter@xob.isea.mr>
Date: September 17, 2023 06:43:13 MT
Subject: Re: Internet History

Therese and Jon,

This is really fascinating! I found some more material,
thanks to the Internet Society, which summarizes the
technical developments over the last 20 years. Apparently
one of the key events was the development of all-optical
transmission, switching and computing in a cost-effective
way. For a long time, this technology involved rather
bulky equipment - some of the early 3DV clips from 2000-
2005 showed rooms full of gear required to steer beams
around. A very interesting combination of fiber optics and
three-dimensional electro-optical integrated circuits
collapsed a lot of this to sizes more like what we are
accustomed to today. Using pico- and femto- molecular
fabrication methods, it has been possible to build very
compact, extremely high speed computing and communication

Cerf

devices.

I guess those guys at Xerox PARC who imagined that there
might be hundreds of millions of computers in the world,
hundreds or even thousands of them for each person, would
be pleased to see how clear their vision was. The only
really bad thing, as I see it, is that those guys who were
trying to figure out how to deal with Internet expansion
really blew it when they picked a measly 64 bit address
space. I hear we are running really tight again. I wonder
why they didn't have enough sense just to allocate at least
1024 bits to make sure we'd have enough room for the
obvious applications we can see we want, now?

David

    -=-

Final Comments

The letters end here, so we are left to speculate about many of the
loose ends not tied up in this informal exchange. Obviously, our
current struggles ultimately will be resolved and a very different,
information-intensive world will evolve from the present. There are a
great many policy, technical and economic questions that remain to be
answered to guide our progress towards the environment described in
part in these messages. It will be an interesting two or three
decades ahead!

Security Considerations

    Security issues are not discussed in this memo.

Author's Address

    Vinton Cerf
    President, Internet Society
    12020 Sunrise Valley Drive, Suite 270
    Reston, VA 22091

    EMail: +1 703 648 9888
    Fax: +1 703 648 9887
    EMail: vcerf@isoc.org

    or

    Vinton Cerf
    Sr. VP Data Architecture
    MCI Data Services Division
    2100 Reston Parkway, Room 6001
    Reston, VA 22091

    Phone: +1 703 715 7432
    Fax: +1 703 715 7436
    EMail: vinton_cerf@mcimail.com

Network Working Group   S. Crocker
Request for Comments: 1776   CyberCash, Inc.
Category: Informational   1 April 1995

The Address is the Message

Status of this Memo

   This memo provides information for the Internet community. This memo
   does not specify an Internet standard of any kind. Distribution of
   this memo is unlimited.

Discussion

   Declaring that the address is the message, the IPng WG has selected a
   packet format which includes 1696 bytes of address space. This
   length is a multiple of 53 and is completely compatible with ATM
   architecture. Observing that it's not what you know but who you
   know, the IPng focused on choosing an addressing scheme that makes it
   possible to talk to everyone while dispensing with the irrelevant
   overhead of actually having to say anything.

   Security experts hailed this as a major breakthrough. With no
   content left in the packets, all questions of confidentiality and
   integrity are moot. Intelligence and law enforcement agencies
   immediately refocused their efforts to detect who's talking to whom,
   and are silently thankful they can avoid divisive public debate about
   key escrow, export control and related matters.

   Although the IPng WG declared there should be more than enough
   address space for everyone, service providers immediately began vying
   for reserved portions of the address space.

Security Considerations

   Security issues are not discussed in this memo.

Author's Address

    Steve Crocker
    CyberCash, Inc.
    2086 Hunters Crest Way
    Vienna, VA 22181

    Phone: +1 703 620 1222
    EMail: crocker@cybercash.com

Network Working Group   R. Elz
Request for Comments: 1924   University of Melbourne
Category: Informational   1 April 1996

A Compact Representation of IPv6 Addresses

Status of this Memo

1. Abstract

   IPv6 addresses, being 128 bits long, need 32 characters to write in
   the general case, if standard hex representation, is used, plus more
   for any punctuation inserted (typically about another 7 characters,
   or 39 characters total). This document specifies a more compact
   representation of IPv6 addresses, which permits encoding in a mere 20
   bytes.

2. Introduction

   It is always necessary to be able to write in characters the form of
   an address, though in actual use it is always carried in binary. For
   IP version 4 (IP Classic) the well known dotted quad format is used.
   That is, 10.1.0.23 is one such address. Each decimal integer
   represents a one octet of the 4 octet address, and consequently has a
   value between 0 and 255 (inclusive). The written length of the
   address varies between 7 and 15 bytes.

   For IPv6 however, addresses are 16 octets long [IPv6], if the old
   standard form were to be used, addresses would be anywhere between 31
   and 63 bytes, which is, of course, untenable.

   Because of that, IPv6 had chosen to represent addresses using hex
   digits, and use only half as many punctuation characters, which will
   mean addresses of between 15 and 39 bytes, which is still quite long.
   Further, in an attempt to save more bytes, a special format was
   invented, in which a single run of zero octets can be dropped, the
   two adjacent punctuation characters indicate this has happened, the
   number of missing zeroes can be deduced from the fixed size of the
   address.

   In most cases, using genuine IPv6 addresses, one may expect the
   address as written to tend toward the upper limit of 39 octets, as
   long strings of zeroes are likely to be rare, and most of the other

groups of 4 hex digits are likely to be longer than a single non-zero
digit (just as MAC addresses typically have digits spread throughout
their length).

This document specifies a new encoding, which can always represent
any IPv6 address in 20 octets. While longer than the shortest
possible representation of an IPv6 address, this is barely longer
than half the longest representation, and will typically be shorter
than the representation of most IPv6 addresses.

3. Current formats

[AddrSpec] specifies that the preferred text representation of IPv6
addresses is in one of three conventional forms.

The preferred form is x:x:x:x:x:x:x:x, where the 'x's are the
hexadecimal values of the eight 16-bit pieces of the address.

Examples:

    FEDC:BA98:7654:3210:FEDC:BA98:7654:3210   (39 characters)

    1080:0:0:0:8:800:200C:417A   (25 characters)

The second, or zero suppressed, form allows "::" to indicate multiple
groups of suppressed zeroes, hence:

    1080:0:0:0:8:800:200C:417A

may be represented as

    1080::8:800:200C:417A

a saving of just 5 characters from this typical address form, and
still leaving 21 characters.

In other cases the saving is more dramatic, in the extreme case, the
address:

    0:0:0:0:0:0:0:0

that is, the unspecified address, can be written as

    ::

This is just 2 characters, which is a considerable saving. However
such cases will rarely be encountered.

The third possible form mixes the new IPv6 form with the old IPv4
form, and is intended mostly for transition, when IPv4 addresses are
embedded into IPv6 addresses. These can be considerably longer than
the longest normal IPv6 representation, and will eventually be phased
out. Consequently they will not be considered further here.

4. The New Encoding Format

The new standard way of writing IPv6 addresses is to treat them as a
128 bit integer, encode that in base 85 notation, then encode that
using 85 ASCII characters.

4.1. Why 85?

2^128 is 340282366920938463463374607431768211456. 85^20 is
3875953108451435587312317848205566406 25, and thus in 20 digits of
base 85 representation all possible 2^128 IPv6 addresses can clearly
be encoded.

84^20 is 30590439823849990868308784932451883417 6, clearly not
sufficient, 21 characters would be needed to encode using base 84,
this wastage of notational space cannot be tolerated.

On the other hand, 94^19 is just
3086236607781508759287901645469541990 4, also insufficient to encode
all 2^128 different IPv6 addresses, so 20 characters would be needed
even with base 94 encoding. As there are just 94 ASCII characters
(excluding control characters, space, and del) base 94 is the largest
reasonable value that can be used. Even if space were allowed, base
95 would still require 20 characters.

Thus, any value between 85 and 94 inclusive could reasonably be
chosen. Selecting 85 allows the use of the smallest possible subset
of the ASCII characters, enabling more characters to be retained for
other uses, eg, to delimit the address.

4.2. The Character Set

The character set to encode the 85 base85 digits, is defined to be,
in ascending order:

            '0'..'9', 'A'..'Z', 'a'..'z', '!', '#', '$', '%', '&', '(',
            ')', '*', '+', '-', ';', '<', '=', '>', '?', '@', '^', '_',
            '`', '{', '|', '}', and '~'.

This set has been chosen with considerable care. From the 94
printable ASCII characters, the following nine were omitted:

'"' and "'", which allow the representation of IPv6 addresses to
be quoted in other environments where some of the characters in
the chosen character set may, unquoted, have other meanings.

',' to allow lists of IPv6 addresses to conveniently be written,
and '.' to allow an IPv6 address to end a sentence without
requiring it to be quoted.

'/' so IPv6 addresses can be written in standard CIDR
address/length notation, and ':' because that causes problems when
used in mail headers and URLs.

'[' and ']', so those can be used to delimit IPv6 addresses when
represented as text strings, as they often are for IPv4,

And last, '\', because it is often difficult to represent in a way
where it does not appear to be a quote character, including in the
source of this document.

5. Converting an IPv6 address to base 85.

The conversion process is a simple one of division, taking the
remainders at each step, and dividing the quotient again, then
reading up the page, as is done for any other base conversion.

For example, consider the address shown above

    1080:0:0:0:8:800:200C:417A

In decimal, considered as a 128 bit number, that is
21932261930451111902915077091070067066.

As we divide that successively by 85 the following remainders emerge:
51, 34, 65, 57, 58, 0, 75, 53, 37, 4, 19, 61, 31, 63, 12, 66, 46, 70,
68, 4.

Thus in base85 the address is:

    4-68-70-46-66-12-63-31-61-19-4-37-53-75-0-58-57-65-34-51.

Then, when encoded as specified above, this becomes:

    4)+k&C#VzJ4br>0wv%Yp

This procedure is trivially reversed to produce the binary form of
the address from textually encoded format.

6. Additional Benefit

   Apart from generally reducing the length of an IPv6 address when
   encode in a textual format, this scheme also has the benefit of
   returning IPv6 addresses to a fixed length representation, leading
   zeroes are never omitted, thus removing the ugly and awkward variable
   length representation that has previously been recommended.

7. Implementation Issues

   Many current processors do not find 128 bit integer arithmetic, as
   required for this technique, a trivial operation. This is not
   considered a serious drawback in the representation, but a flaw of
   the processor designs.

   It may be expected that future processors will address this defect,
   quite possibly before any significant IPv6 deployment has been
   accomplished.

8. Security Considerations

   By encoding addresses in this form, it is less likely that a casual
   observer will be able to immediately detect the binary form of the
   address, and thus will find it harder to make immediate use of the
   address. As IPv6 addresses are not intended to be learned by humans,
   one reason for which being that they are expected to alter in
   comparatively short timespan, by human perception, the somewhat
   challenging nature of the addresses is seen as a feature.

   Further, the appearance of the address, as if it may be random
   gibberish in a compressed file, makes it much harder to detect by a
   packet sniffer programmed to look for bypassing addresses.

9. References

    [IPv6]   Internet Protocol, Version 6 (IPv6) Specification,
                    S. Deering, R. Hinden, RFC 1883, January 4, 1996.

    [AddrSpec]   IP Version 6 Addressing Architecture,
                    R. Hinden, S. Deering, RFC 1884, January 4, 1996.

10. Author's Address

    Robert Elz
    Computer Science
    University of Melbourne
    Parkville, Victoria, 3052
    Australia

    EMail: kre@munnari.OZ.AU

Part V

History and Future Internet

In the first decade or so of the 'Net, packets and (occasionally) whole messages/files might go astray or be lost. M. Crispin wrote RFC 748 to codify such such random events.

B. Miller's RFC 1097 ensures that subliminal messages are (or, are not) appropriately displayed.

RFC 1216 and RFC 1217 are a vital coupling of Ultra-Low-Speed Networking and Slow Commotion Research as announced by "Poorer Richard" and "Professor Kynikos" and responded to by the insufferable (uh...irrepressible) Vint Cerf. Mashed Potato Routing, replacing the common Hot-Potato Routing, and Airline Baggage Routing (taking the most obscure and inconvenient route to reach the intended destination) are important aspects of the CSCR's work.

Craig Partridge's RFC 1313, a day's programming on KRFC, the Bay Area's Internet Talk Radio station, precedes Internet chat and the Web. And RFC 3271 sees Vint Cerf, hard at work, proselytizing for a free and democratic Internet, including Martians!

Network Working Group   M. Crispin
Request for Comments 748   SU-AI
NIC 44125   1 April 1978

                    TELNET RANDOMLY-LOSE Option

1. Command name and code.

    RANDOMLY-LOSE   256

2. Command meanings.

    IAC WILL RANDOMLY-LOSE

        The sender of this command REQUESTS permission to, or confirms
        that it will, randomly lose.

    IAC WON'T RANDOMLY-LOSE

        The sender of this command REFUSES to randomly lose.

    IAC DO RANDOMLY-LOSE

        The sender of this command REQUESTS that the receiver, or grants
        the receiver permission to, randomly lose.

    IAC DON'T RANDOMLY-LOSE

        The command sender DEMANDS that the receiver not randomly lose.

3. Default.

    WON'T RANDOMLY-LOSE

    DON'T RANDOMLY-LOSE

    i.e., random lossage will not happen.

4. Motivation for the option.

    Several hosts appear to provide random lossage, such as system
    crashes, lost data, incorrectly functioning programs, etc., as part
    of their services.   These services are often undocumented and are in
    general quite confusing to the novice user.   A general means is
    needed to allow the user to disable these features.

5. Description of the option.

    The normal mode does not allow random lossage; therefore the system
    is not allowed to crash, mung user files, etc. If the server wants
    to provide random lossage, it must first ask for permission from the
    user by sending IAC WILL RANDOMLY-LOSE.

    If the user wants to permit the server to randomly lose, it replys
    with IAC DO   RANDOMLY-LOSE.   Otherwise   it   sends   IAC   DONT
    RANDOMLY-LOSE, and the server is forbidden from randomly losing.

    Alternatively, the user could request the server to randomly lose, by
    sending IAC DO RANDOMLY-LOSE, and the server will either reply with
    IAC WILL RANDOMLY-LOSE, meaning that it will then proceed to do some
    random lossage (garbaging disk files is recommended for an initial
    implementation).   Or, it could send IAC WONT RANDOMLY-LOSE, meaning
    that it insists upon being reliable.

    Since this is implemented as a TELNET option, it is expected that
    servers which do not implement this option will not randomly lose;
    ie, they will provide 100% reliable uptime.

Network Working Group   B. Miller
Request for Comments: 1097   CMU-NetDev
                                                            1 April 1989

                    TELNET SUBLIMINAL-MESSAGE Option

Status of this Memo

   This RFC specifies a standard for the Internet community. Hosts on
   the Internet that display subliminal messages within the Telnet
   protocol are expected to adopt and implement this standard.
   Distribution of this memo is unlimited.

1. Command name and code.

   SUBLIMINAL-MESSAGE   257

2. Command meanings.

   IAC WILL SUBLIMINAL-MESSAGE

      The sender of this command REQUESTS permission to, or confirms
      that it will, display subliminal messages.

   IAC WONT SUBLIMINAL-MESSAGE

      The sender of this command REFUSES to display subliminal messages.

   IAC DO SUBLIMINAL-MESSAGE

      The sender of this command REQUESTS that the receiver, or grants
      the receiver permission to, display subliminal messages.

   IAC DONT SUBLIMINAL-MESSAGE

      The sender of this command DEMANDS that the receiver not display
      subliminal messages.

   IAC SB SUBLIMINAL-MESSAGE <16-bit value> <16-bit value> <string> IAC
   SE

      The sender specifies a message to be subliminaly displayed by the
      remote host. If the client has agreed (via the standard WILL WONT
      DO DONT mechanism) to display subliminal messages, it must accept
      this subnegotiation and attempt to display the message string on
      the users console for the specified duration and continue to do so
      at fixed intervals until another SUBLIMINAL-MESSAGE subnegotiation
      is received. The position and rendering of the message of

implementation dependent.

The first 16-bit value specifies the duration of the message in milliseconds. It is sent MSB first. The second 16-bit value specifies the frequency with which the message is displayed. It represents the number of seconds between displays and is also sent MSB first. The final parameter is the message itself.

The syntax for this subnegotiation is:

```
        IAC SB SUBLIMINAL-MESSAGE
            DURATION[1] DURATION[0]
            FREQUENCY[1] FREQUENCY[0]
            MESSAGE_STRING
        IAC SE
```

As required by the Telnet protocol, any occurence of 255 in the subnegotiation must be doubled to destinguish it from the IAC character (which has a value of 255).

3. Default.

    WONT SUBLIMINAL-MESSAGE

    DONT SUBLIMINAL-MESSAGE

    i.e., subliminal messages will not be displayed.

4. Motivation for the option

    Frequently the use of "Message of the day" banners and newsletters is insufficient to convince stubborn users to upgrade to the latest version of telnet. Some users will use the same outdated version for years. I ran across this problem trying to convince people to use the REMOTE-FLOW-CONTROL Telnet option. These users need to be gently "persuaded".

5. Description and implementation notes.

    The quality of the client implementation will depend on it's ability to display and erase text strings in a small amount of time. The current implementation at CMU takes into acount terminal line speed, advanced video capabilities, and screen phospher persistance when calculating how long to wait before erasing a message.

    While it is permitted for the client to display the message text "in-line", best results at obtained by printing the message at the top or side of console screen where it will just catch the corner of the user's visual field.

A version is currently under development at CMU to display the
message using morse-code over the keyboard caps-lock LED.

6. Examples

In the following example all numbers are in decimal notation.

1. Server suggests and client agrees to use SUBLIMINAL-MESSAGE.

   (Server sends) IAC DO SUBLIMINAL-MESSAGE
   (Client sends) IAC WILL SUBLIMINAL-MESSAGE
   (Server sends) IAC SB SUBLIMINAL-MESSAGE 0 5 0 20 "Use VMS" IAC SE

      [The server is "suggesting" that the user employ a stable
       operating system, not an unreasonable request...]

   The client should immediately begin displaying the message and
   should continue to do so at regular intervals.

2. Server preempts previous subliminal message.

   (Server sends) IAC SB SUBLIMINAL-MESSAGE 0 5 0 20 "Go home" IAC SE

   The client should now no longer display the previous message and
   should immediately begin displaying the new one.

3. Server has messed with user enough for one day.

   (Server sends) IAC SB SUBLIMINAL-MESSAGE 0 0 0 0 "" IAC SE

   The client must cease display of any subliminal messages.

7. Acknowledgements.

We do things just a little sneakier here at CMU.

Network Working Group   Poorer Richard
Request for Comments: 1216   Almanac Institute
                                                       Prof. Kynikos
                                               Miskatonic University
                                                       1 April 1991

Gigabit Network Economics and Paradigm Shifts

Status of this Memo

   This memo proposes a new standard paradigm for the Internet
   Activities Board (IAB) standardization track. Distribution of this
   memo is unlimited.

1. Introduction

   The history of computer communication contains many examples of
   efforts to align the capabilities of processors to that of
   communication media. Packet switching is the classic case of a
   careful tradeoff between the costs of memory, processing, and
   communications bandwidth.

   With all of the attention and publicity focused on gigabit networks,
   not much notice has been given to small and largely unfunded research
   efforts which are studying innovative approaches for dealing with
   technical issues within the constraints of economic science. This
   memo defines one such paradigm.

2. Contemporary Network Economics

   Recent cost estimates predict a continuing decline in the cost for
   processing, memory, and communication. One recent projection put the
   decline for $/bit and $/MIP at 99% per decade and put the decline for
   $/bps at 90% per decade. Scalable parallel processor designs may
   accelerate the cost declines for CPU and memory, but no similar
   accelerated decline should be expected in the cost of communications.
   Such a decline would imply eventual declines in the cost of 56Kbps
   service used for voice, resulting in a negative rate of return for
   telecommunications carriers, an unlikely eventuality even if free-
   market forces are carried to their logical extreme.

   Increases in processing power create additional demand for
   communications bandwidth, but do nothing to pay for it. While we
   will sell no paradigm before its time, the 9% difference,
   particularly after compounding is taken into account, will bankrupt
   the internet community unless a paradigm shift takes place.

3. The ULS Paradigm Shift

   The ULS paradigm shift breaks the downward spiral by concentrating on
   end-to-end datagrams and virtual circuit services operating in the
   .01 uGbps region, namely Ultra Low Speed networking.

   However,

   "The worlds best technological paradigm shifts are useless unless
   they (a) are economically viable, (b) have clear applicability, (c)
   are technically feasible."

              --Milton John in "Paradigms Lost"

3.1 Economic Viability

   Cost projections indicate that individual ULS circuits can be
   provided at a cost of <$.03/month due to the unusually high
   multiplexing that will be possible on Gbit links. The 10 THz
   bandwidth of existing optical fibers will be able to support on the
   order of 1 TUser, handling population growth, and even internet
   growth, for some time. Moreover, if $.03/month is a significant
   barrier to entry, substantial discounts appear to be economically
   feasible.

3.2 Clear Applicability

   A fundamental principle of networking is that network speed must
   match the application. We have identified a number of critical
   applications that are matched to ULS technology. Below we itemize a
   few of these, but we provide a brief description for only the first;
   the match for the others should be equally obvious.

   - Low priority facsimile: A large percentage of documents and letters
     are sent via facsimile not because they need sub-minute delivery,
     but because they carry signatures or graphics. In these cases, a
     three-hour delivery (comparable to the value reliably achieved on
     many of today's packet-based email systems) is sufficient. With
     proper compression, this delivery time can be achieved over a
     ULSnet.

   - Real time data (e.g., tracking glaciers)

   - US postal service

   - Contracting for research

   To be truly viable, ULS networking must scale, and indeed it does.

Richard & Kynikos   [Page 2]

244

With some effort, we envision extending the technology to the
extremely-low-speed regime. Applications that scale from the ULS
applications above are:

- Real time data (e.g., gravity wave detectors)
- Italian postal service
- Congressional budget process

3.3 Technical Feasibility

The hardware issues are well in hand. The remaining issues are
protocol related. To examine them, we must extrapolate backward from
some well known networking principles.

"Gigabit networks require new protocols."

The clear inference here is that ULS will require old protocols, so
as we recede into the future, we should expect the following:

ULS will require minimal development. Although we may need research
in storage technology to recover the software from old media such as
decayed magnetic dump tapes, paper tape, and partially recycled card
decks, this effort will be more than offset by the savings.

ULS protocols will be well documented, amenable to verification, and
suitable for MSI implementation in Silicon, or even Germanium or
relays. In particular, the alternating bit protocol [1] is a leading
contender.

"Bad news travel fast."

Therefore, ULS gives preferential treatment to good news. While this
will delay the delivery of bills, notices from timeshare
condominiums, and contest announcements, it will also produce
immediate productivity gains on several mailing lists.

3.4 Problems Requiring Work

ULS is not without problems.

Some other well-known protocol suites are well ahead of ULS in
exploring the desired performance operating point. We note our
concern about the dearth of domestic (U.S.-based) research and
development in this important area. This is particularly disturbing
in light of the level of work now underway in other countries.

Efficiency is a problem:

Richard & Kynikos   [Page 3]

245

- All ULS protocols incorporate slow-start.

- Lower data rates mean fewer errors.

- Whereas modern protocols use 32 bit sequence numbers, acknowledgment fields, etc., ULS headers can be quite small (1 bit sequence numbers for the alternating-bit protocol). Thus the header/data ratio shrinks.

The net result is "creeping efficiency" which tends to push us away from the proper ULS operating point. While we have no definitive solution, there are several promising palliatives:

- Forward Error Insertion (FEI)

- Negative window scaling factors

- New protocol layers

- Multiple presentation layers

4. Conclusions

The road to Ultra Low Speed (ULS) technology is long, slow, and easy.

REFERENCES and BIBLIOGRAPHY

[1] Lynch, W. "Reliable full-duplex file transmission over half-duplex telephone lines", CACM, pp. 407-410, June 1968.

Security Considerations

Security issues are not discussed in this memo.

Authors' Addresses

Dr. Poorer Richard
Almanac Institute
Center against Misoneoism
Campo Imperatore, Italy
EMail: none

Prof. Kynikos
Miskatonic University
Arkham, MA.
Email: Kynikos@Cthulu.Miskatonic.EDU

Memo from the Consortium for Slow Commotion Research (CSCR)

Status of this Memo

   This RFC is in response to RFC 1216, "Gigabit Network Economics and
   Paradigm Shifts". Distribution of this memo is unlimited.

To: Poorer Richard and Professor Kynikos

Subject: ULSNET BAA

From: Vint Cerf/CSCR

Date: 4/1/91

   The Consortium for Slow Commotion Research (CSCR) [1] is pleased to
   respond to your research program announcement (RFC 1216) on Ultra
   Low-Speed Networking (ULSNET). CSCR proposes to carry out a major
   research and development program on low-speed, low-efficiency
   networks over a period of several eons. Several designs are
   suggested below for your consideration.

1. Introduction

   Military requirements place a high premium on ultra-robust systems
   capable of supporting communication in extremely hostile
   environments. A major contributing factor in the survivability of
   systems is a high degree of redundancy. CSCR believes that the
   system designs offered below exhibit extraordinary redundancy
   features which should be of great interest to DARPA and the
   Department of Defense.

2. Jam-Resistant Land Mobile Communications

   This system uses a highly redundant optical communication technique
   to achieve ultra-low, ultra-robust transmission. The basic unit is
   the M1A1 tank. Each tank is labelled with the number 0 or 1 painted
   four feet high on the tank turret in yellow, day-glo luminescent
   paint. Several detection methods are under consideration:

      (a) A tree or sand-dune mounted forward observer (FO) radios
           to a reach echelon main frame computer the binary values

247

of tanks moving in a serial column. The mainframe decodes
the binary values and voice-synthesizes the alphameric
ASCII-encoded messages which is then radioed back to the
FO. The FO then dispatches a runner to his unit HQ with
the message. The system design includes two redundant,
emergency back-up forward observers in different trees
with a third in reserve in a foxhole.

   (b)   Wide-area communication by means of overhead
reconnaissance satellites which detect the binary signals
from the M1A1 mobile system and download this
information for processing in special U.S. facilities in the
Washington, D.C. area. A Convection Machine [2] system
will be used to perform a codebook table look-up to decode
the binary message. The decoded message will be relayed
by morse-code over a packet meteor burst communications
channel to the appropriate Division headquarters.

   (c)   An important improvement in the sensitivity of this system
can be obtained by means of a coherent detection strategy.
Using long baseline interferometry, phase differences
among the advancing tank column elements will be used to
signal a secondary message to select among a set of
codebooks in the Convection Machine. The phase analysis
will be carried out using Landsat imagery enhanced by
suitable processing at the Jet Propulsion Laboratory. The
Landsat images (of the moving tanks) will be correlated
with SPOT Image images to obtain the phase-encoded
information. The resulting data will be faxed to
Washington, D.C., for use in the Convection Machine
decoding step. The remainder of this process is as for (b)
above.

   (d)   It is proposed to use SIMNET to simulate this system.

3. Low Speed Undersea Communication

Using the 16" guns of the Battleship Missouri, a pulse-code modulated
message will be transmitted via the Pacific Ocean to the Ames
Research Center in California. Using a combination of fixed and
towed acoustic hydrophone arrays, the PCM signal will be detected,
recorded, enhanced and analyzed both at fixed installations and
aboard undersea vessels which have been suitably equipped. An
alternative acoustic source is to use M1A1 main battle tanks firing
150 mm H.E. ordnance. It is proposed to conduct tests of this method
in the Persian Gulf during the summer of 1991.

4. Jam-Resistant Underwater Communication

   The ULS system proposed in (2) above has the weakness that it is
   readily jammed by simple depth charge explosions or other sources of
   acoustic noise (e.g., Analog Equipment Corporation DUCK-TALK voice
   synthesizers linked with 3,000 AMP amplifiers). An alternative is to
   make use of the ultimate in jam resistance: neutrino transmission.
   For all practical purposes, almost nothing (including several light-
   years of lead) will stop a neutrino. There is, however, a slight
   cross-section which can be exploited provided that a cubic mile of
   sea water is available for observing occasional neutrino-chlorine
   interactions which produce a detectable photon burst. Thus, we have
   the basis for a highly effective, extremely low speed communication
   system for communicating with submarines.

   There are a few details to be worked out:

      (a) the only accelerator available to us to generate neutrino
           bursts is located at Batavia National Laboratory (BNL).

      (b) the BNL facility can only send neutrino bursts in one
           direction (through the center of the Earth) to a site near
           Tierra del Fuego, Chile. Consequently, all submarines must
           be scheduled to pass near Tierra del Fuego on a regular
           basis to coincide with the PCM neutrino signalling from
           the BNL source.

      (c) the maximum rate of neutrino burst transmission is
           approximately once every 20 seconds. This high rate can be
           reduced considerably if the pwer source for the accelerator
           is limited to a rate sustainable by discharging a large
           capacitor which is trickle charged by a 2 square foot solar
           panel mounted to face north.

5. Options for Further Reducing Effective Throughput

      (a) Anti-Huffman Coding. The most frequent symbol is
           assigned the longest code, with code lengths reducing with
           symbol probability.

      (b) Minimum likelihood decoding. The least likely
           interpretation of the detected symbol is selected to
           maximize the probability of decoding error.

      (c) Firefly cryptography. A random signal (mason jar full of
           fireflies) is used to encipher the transmitted signal by
           optical combining. At the receiving site, another jar of
           fireflies is used to decipher the message. Since the

correlation between the transmitting and receiving firefly
jars is essentially nil, the probability of successful
decipherment is quite low, yielding a very low effective
transmission rate.

(d) Recursive Self-encapsulation. Since it is self-evident that
     layered communication is a GOOD THING, more layers
     must be better. It is proposed to recursively encapsulate
     each of the 7 layers of OSI, yielding a 49 layer
     communications model. The redundancy and
     retransmission and flow control achieved by this means
     should produce an extremely low bandwidth system if,
     indeed, any information can be transmitted at all. It is
     proposed that the top level application layer utilize ASN.1
     encoded in a 32 bit per character set.

(e) Scaling. The initial M1A1 tank basis for the land mobile
     communication system can be improved. It is proposed to
     reduce the effective data rate further by replacing the
     tanks with shuttle launch vehicles. The only slower method
     of signalling might be the use of cars on any freeway in the
     Los Angeles area.

(f) Network Management. It is proposed to adopt the Slow
     Network Management Protocol (SNMP) as a standard for
     ULSNET. All standard Management Information Base
     variables will be specified in Serbo-Croatian and all
     computations carried-out in reverse-Polish.

(g) Routing. Two alternatives are proposed:

         (1) Mashed Potato Routing
         (2) Airline Baggage Routing [due to S. Cargo]

     The former is a scheme whereby any incoming packets are
     stored for long periods of time before forwarding. If space
     for storage becomes a problem, packets are compressed by
     removing bits at random. Packets are then returned to the
     sender. In the latter scheme, packets are mislabelled at the
     initial switch and randomly labelled as they are moved
     through the network. A special check is made before
     forwarding to avoid routing to the actual intended
     destination.

CSCR looks forward to a protracted and fruitless discussion with you
on this subject as soon as we can figure out how to transmit the
proposal.

NOTES

    [1] The Consortium was formed 3/27/91 and includes David Clark,
        John Wroclawski, and Karen Sollins/MIT, Debbie Deutsch/BBN,
        Bob Braden/ISI, Vint Cerf/CNRI and several others whose names
        have faded into an Alzheimerian oblivion...

    [2] Convection Machine is a trademark of Thoughtless Machines, Inc.,
        a joint-venture of Hot-Air Associates and Air Heads International
        using vaporware from the Neural Network Corporation.

Security Considerations

    Security issues are not discussed in this memo.

Author's Address

    Vint Cerf
    Corporation for National Research Initiatives
    1895 Preston White Drive, Suite 100
    Reston, VA 22091

    Phone: (703) 620-8990

    EMail: CERF@NRI.RESTON.VA.US

Network Working Group   S. Greenfield
Request for Comments: 1300   Ziff-Davis
                                                        February 1992

                     Remembrances of Things Past

Status of this Memo

Discussion

                    When Shannon was a river
                       and Turing was a car
                    When Banyan was a tree
                       and buses travelled far

                    dBase was where you ran to
                       after you hit the ball
                    Often we were ANSI
                       RISC aversive not at all

                    Windows were for looking out of
                       in a Tandem, two could take a spin
                    Bridges were for crossing
                       a frame was to keep pictures in

                    A semi-conductor was a maestro
                       not in the big time yet
                    A port you sought in a storm
                       fishermen used a net

                    Woody Guthrie sang of "My LAN"
                       WAN was a despairing mood
                    LATAs were for high places
                       menus featured food

                                253

If a cursor used four letter words
    a sensor cut them out
The sight of a mouse in an office
    was sure to raise a shout

Haloid perfected photocopying
    and thereby made a hoard
Then came Japanese competition
    and its "ox" was gored

Frequency was measured in cycles
    Hertz referred to multiple pain
Modem was a harvesting command
    for bringing in the grain

Modelling was at fashion shows
    bauds were ladies of the night
Prompting was helping actors
    contesting for resources, a fight

Walking and chewing gum concurrently
    requires considerable skill
We called it multi-tasking
    and by gosh we always will

We had no electronic calculators
    just slide rules by Keuffel & Esser
I am still a true believer
    Keufel & Esser war besser

Chips were used for gambling
    von Neuman was a pup
Monte Carlo a place to visit
    squaring the circle ... well, we gave up

A Sprint was less than 880
    a relay was a team
Greene was just a color
    breaking up AT&T a dream

```
        Coherent was applied to speech
           not a spectral line excited
        Multi-media meant prose and song
           and Noel Coward was knighted


        Cerf was found at the beach
           a Rose was a Rose was a Rose
        Jobs were to look for
           and Gates were to close


        "2B" was an elementary school class
           and "D" a failing grade
        A router was a tool
           a server was a maid


        Lotus was a flower
           adobe was a brick
        Postscript was an afterthought
           joy a popsicle stick


        We called a plotter a CAD
           a token ring a sham
        A buffer was for buffing
           a male goat was a ram


        The best noise supressor was ... ssh
           we knew little of egos and ids
        For archival storage and encryption
           we looked to the pyramids


        Now in accordance with Greenfield's Law
           in voice both loud and clear
        Here's to exponential growth in memory
           & operating speed next year.

                        --srg
```

Security Considerations

    Security issues are not discussed in this memo.

Author's Address

    Stanley R. Greenfield
    Ziff-Davis
    One Park Avenue
    New York, NY 10016

    EMail: 0004689513@mcimail.com

Network Working Group   C. Partridge
Request for Comments: 1313   BBN
                                                          1 April 1992

Today's Programming for KRFC AM 1313
Internet Talk Radio

Status of this Memo

Welcome!

Hi and welcome to KRFC Internet Talk Radio, your place on the AM dial
for lively talk and just-breaking news on internetworking. Sponsored
by the Internet Society, KRFC serves the San Francisco Bay Area. For
those of you outside the Bay Area, copies of program transcripts can
be anonymously FTPed from archives.krfc.com the day after the
program, or you can listen in via vat.

Here's today's programming for today, Wednesday, 1 April 1992.

Hacker's Hour with Phil Karn (Midnight)

Phil's special guest today is Dr. David Mills, who will explain the
special problems of correcting for the Doppler effect when trying to
properly synchronize the new WWV receiver chip in your PC while
flying on the Concorde.

Nighttime News (1AM)

Award winning Nighttime News gives you a full hour on those key facts
you need to know before going to bed. Be sure to catch our network
outage report with Elise Gerich. (Elise's report is sponsored by
ANS).

Late At Night With Ole (2 AM)

Call in your favorite Internetwork questions to Ole Jacobsen and his
guests. Tonite's featured guests are John Moy, prime author of OSPF,
and Milo Medin who will talk about how OSPF is great, but you really
need to test it on 1822 networks to understand why.

Marty in the Morning (6 AM)

   Join the irrepressable Marty for five hours of eye-opening talk and
   commentary. Hear the latest on the commercial state of data
   networking in the US and who is at fault for limiting its growth.
   Special guest Kent England plans to drop by the studio today --
   listen in for the flames!

Education Report (11 AM)

   Gordon Cook solicits advice from Prof. David Farber on good ways to
   develop a research career. (In the likely event that Prof. Farber is
   unavailable at the last minute, Prof. Farber has arranged for Prof.
   David Sincoskie to take his place).

Lunch with Lynch (11:30 AM)

   Dan Lynch is on vacation this week and Vint Cerf is taking his place.
   Today Vint has lunch with Mitch Kapor of the EFF, MacArthur genius
   Richard Stallman, and Gen. Norman Schwartzkopf. Don't miss Vint's
   suggestions for wines to go with today's business lunch! [Lunch with
   Lynch is sponsored by Interop. Wines are provided by the vineyards in
   return for promotional considerations].

News (1 PM)

   Join Joyce and Jon as they report on the key networking news of the
   day. Don't miss their update on the latest address and port
   assignments and tips on upcoming RFCs!

Two by Four Time (2 PM)

   Today Marshall Rose will take out his two-by-four and apply it to
   Phill Gross for violating the Internet Standard Meeting Rules at the
   last IETF and starting a session before 9 AM. Additional victims to
   be announced. Today's show will be available as a book from Prentice
   Hall by next Tuesday.

Mike at the Mike (4 PM)

   Listen in to the Marina's favorite local DJ. Hear why They never
   listen and Never will! How come The Book's publishers don't seem to
   be able to add and why ATM is Another Technical Mistake. Then join
   MAP at 7:45 for a wee bit of this week's preferred single malt.

The Protocol Police (8 PM)

   Liven up your evening with the protocol police. Join our intrepid
   team of Stev Knowles and Mike St. Johns as they debug various TCP/IP
   implementations from the comfort of Mike's hot tub using Stev's
   water-proof portable PC. Last week they caught Peter Honeyman
   hijacking an NFS implementation. This week they're joined by Yakov
   Rehkter with his new Roto-Router tool, designed to catch routing
   anomalies. Who will our team nab this week?

Family Hour (10 PM)

   As part of this week's special series on children and networking, Bob
   Morris and Jerry Estrin talk about how much you should teach your
   young children about networking.

Securely Speaking (11 PM)

   Come eavesdrop as Steve Kent and Steve Crocker give you this week's
   latest security news (if they're allowed to talk about it). And
   remember, just after 11 o'clock Steve and Steve will be reading this
   week's encrypted message. If you're the first caller to call in with
   the right DES key to decrypt the message, you'll win $1,000 and an
   all expenses paid trip to Ft. Meade! (US nationals only please).

Security Considerations

   Security issues are discussed in the above section.

Author's Address

   Craig Partridge
   BBN
   824 Kipling St
   Palo Alto, CA 94301

   Phone: 415-325-4541
   EMail: craig@aland.bbn.com

Network Working Group   J. Quarterman
Request For Comments: 1935   S. Carl-Mitchell
Category: Informational   TIC
                                                          April 1996

                    What is the Internet, Anyway?

Status of This Memo

Introduction

   We often mention the Internet, and in the press you read about the
   Internet as the prototype of the Information Highway; as a research
   tool; as open for business; as not ready for prime time; as a place
   your children might communicate with (pick one) a. strangers, b.
   teachers, c. pornographers, d. other children, e. their parents; as
   bigger than Poland; as smaller than Chicago; as a place to surf; as
   the biggest hype since Woodstock; as a competitive business tool; as
   the newest thing since sliced bread.

   A recent New York Times article quoting one of us as to the current
   size of the Internet has particularly stirred up quite a ruckus. The
   exact figures attributed to John in the article are not the ones we
   recommended for such use, but the main point of contention is whether
   the Internet is, as the gist of the article said, smaller than many
   other estimates have said. Clearly lots of people really want to
   believe that the Internet is very large. Succeeding discussion has
   shown that some want to believe that so much that they want to count
   computers and people that are probably *going to be* connected some
   time in the future, even if they are not actually connected now. We
   prefer to talk about who is actually on the Internet and on other
   networks now. We'll get back to the sizes of the various networks
   later, but for now let's discuss a more basic issue that is at the

heart of much confusion and contention about sizes: what is the
Internet, anyway?

Starting at the Center

For real confusion, start trying to get agreement on what is part of
the Internet: NSFNET? CIX? Your company's internal network?
Prodigy? FidoNet? The mainframe in accounting? Some people would
include all of the above, and perhaps even consider excluding
anything politically incorrect. Others have cast doubts on each of
the above.

Let's start some place almost everyone would agree is on the
Internet. Take RIPE, for example. The acronym stands for European
IP Networks. RIPE is a coordinating group for IP networking in
Europe. (IP is the Internet protocol, which is the basis of the
Internet. IP has a suite of associated protocols, including the
Transmission Control Protocol, or TCP, and the name IP, or sometimes
TCP/IP, is often used to refer to the whole protocol suite.) RIPE's
computers are physically located in Amsterdam. The important feature
of RIPE for our purposes is that you can reach RIPE (usually by using
its domain, ripe.net) from just about anywhere anyone would agree is
on the Internet.

Reach it with what? Well, just about any service anyone would agree
is related to the Internet. RIPE has a WWW (World Wide Web) server,
a Gopher server, and an anonymous FTP server. So they provide
documents and other resources by hypertext, menu browsing, and file
retrieval. Their personnel use client programs such as Mosaic and
Lynx to access other people's servers, too, so RIPE is a both
distributor and a consumer of resources via WWW, Gopher, and FTP.
They support TELNET interfaces to some of their services, and of
course they can TELNET out and log in remotely anywhere they have
personal login accounts or someone else has an anonymous TELNET
service such a library catalog available. They also have electronic
mail, they run some mailing lists, and some of their people read and
post news articles to USENET newsgroups.

WWW, Gopher, FTP, TELNET, mail, lists, and news: that's a pretty
characteristic set of major Internet services. There are many more
obscure Internet services, but it's pretty safe to say that an
organization like RIPE that is reachable with all these services is
on the Internet.

Reachable from where? Russia first connected to the Internet in
1992. For a while it was reachable from networks in the Commercial
Internet Exchange (CIX) and from various other networks, but not from
NSFNET, the U.S. National Science Foundation network. At the time,

some people considered NSFNET so important that they didn't count
Russia as reachable because it wasn't accessible through NSFNET.
Since there are now several other backbone networks in the U.S. as
fast (T3 or 45Mbps) as NSFNET, and routing through NSFNET isn't very
restricted anymore, few people would make that distinction anymore.
So for the moment let's just say reachable through NSFNET or CIX
networks, and get back to services.

Looking at Firewalls

Many companies and other organizations run networks that are
deliberately firewalled so that their users can get to servers like
those at ripe.net, but nobody outside the company network can get to
company hosts. A user of such a network can thus use WWW, Gopher,
FTP, and TELNET, but cannot supply resources through these protocols
to people outside the company. Since a network that is owned and
operated by a company in support of its own operations is called an
enterprise network, let's call these networks enterprise IP networks,
since they typically use the Internet Protocol (IP) to support these
services. Some companies integrate their enterprise IP networks into
the Internet without firewalls, but most do use firewalls, and those
are the ones that are of interest here, since they're the ones with
one-way access to these Internet services. Another name for an
enterprise IP network, with or without firewall, is an enterprise
Internet.

For purposes of this distinction between suppliers and consumers, it
doesn't matter whether the hosts behind the firewall access servers
beyond the firewall by direct IP and TCP connections from their own
IP addresses, or whether they use proxy application gateways (such as
SOCKS) at the firewall. In either case, they can use outside
services, but cannot supply them.

So for services such as WWW, Gopher, FTP, and TELNET, we can draw a
useful distinction between supplier or distributor computers such as
those at ripe.net and consumer computers such as those inside
firewalled enterprise IP networks. It might seem more obvious to say
producer computers and consumer computers, since those would be more
clearly paired terms. However, the information distributed by a
supplier computer isn't necessarily produced on that computer or
within its parent organization. In fact, most of the information on
the bigger FTP archive servers is produced elsewhere. So we choose
to say distributors and consumers. Stores and shoppers would work
about as well, if you prefer.

Even more useful than discussing computers that actually are
suppliers or consumers right now may be a distinction between
supplier-capable computers (not firewalled) and consumer-capable

computers (firewalled). This is because a computer that is not
supplying information right now may be capable of doing so as soon as
someone puts information on it and tells it to supply it. That is,
setting up a WWW, Gopher, or FTP server isn't very difficult; much
less difficult than getting corporate permission to breach a
firewall. Similarly, a computer may not be able to retrieve
resources by WWW, Gopher, at the moment, since client programs for
those services usually don't come with the computer or its basic
software, but almost any computer can be made capable of doing so by
adding some software. In both cases, once you've got the basic IP
network connection, adding capabilities for specific services is
relatively easy.

Let's call the non-firewalled computers the core Internet, and the
core plus the consumer-capable computers the consumer Internet. Some
people have referred to these two categories as the Backbone Internet
and the Internet Web. We find the already existing connotations of
"Backbone" and "Web" confusing, so we prefer core Internet and
consumer Internet.

It's true that many companies with firewalls have one or two
computers carefully placed at the firewall so that they can serve
resources. Company employees may be able to place resources on these
servers, but they can't serve resources directly from their own
computers. It's rather like having to reserve space on a single
company delivery truck, instead of owning one yourself. If you're
talking about companies, yes, the company is thus fully on the core
Internet, yet its users aren't as fully on the Internet as users not
behind a firewall.

If you're just interested in computers that can distribute
information (maybe you're selling server software), that's a much
smaller Internet than if you're interested in all the computers that
can retrieve such information for their users (maybe you have
information you want to distribute). A few years ago it probably
wouldn't have been hard to get agreement that firewalled company
networks were a different kind of thing than the Internet itself.
Nowadays, firewalls have become so popular that it's hard to find an
enterprise IP network that is not firewalled, and the total number of
hosts on such consumer-capable networks is probably almost as large
as the number on the supplier-capable core of the Internet. So many
people now like to include these consumer-capable networks along with
the supplier-capable core when discussing the Internet.

Some people claim that you can't measure the number of consumer-
capable computers or users through measurements taken on the Internet
itself. Perhaps not, but you can get an idea of how many actual
consumers there are by simply counting accesses to selected servers

and comparing the results to other known facts about the accessing
organizations. And there are other ways to get useful information
about consumers on the Internet, including asking them.

Mail, Lists, and News

   But what about mail, lists, and news? We carefully left those out of
   the discussion of firewalls, because almost all the firewalled
   networks do let these communications services in and out, so there's
   little useful distinction between firewalled and non-firewalled
   networks on the basis of these services. That's because there's a
   big difference between these communications services and the resource
   sharing (TELNET, FTP) and resource discovery (Gopher, WWW) services
   that firewalls usually filter. The communications services are
   normally batch, asynchronous, or store-and-forward. These
   characterizations mean more or less the same thing, so pick the one
   you like best. The point is that when you send mail, you compose a
   message and queue it for delivery. The actual delivery is a separate
   process; it may take seconds or hours, but it is done after you
   finish composing the message, and you normally do not have to wait
   for the message to be delivered before doing something else. It is
   not uncommon for a mail system to batch up several messages to go
   through a single network link or to the same destination and then
   deliver them all at once. And mail doesn't even necessarily go to
   its final destination in one hop; repeated storing at an intermediate
   destination followed by forwarding to another computer is common;
   thus the term store-and-forward. Mailing lists are built on top of
   the same delivery mechanisms as regular electronic mail. USENET news
   uses somewhat different delivery mechanisms, but ones that are also
   typically batch, asynchronous, and store-and-forward. Because it is
   delivered in this manner, a mail message or a news article is much
   less likely to be a security problem than a TELNET, FTP, Gopher, or
   WWW connection. This is why firewalls usually pass mail, lists, and
   news in both directions, but usually stop incoming connections of
   those interactive protocols.

   Because WWW, Gopher, TELNET, and FTP are basically interactive, you
   need IP or something like it to support them. Because mail, lists,
   and news are asynchronous, you can support them with protocols that
   are not interactive, such as UUCP and FidoNet. In fact, there are
   whole networks that do just that, called UUCP and FidoNet, among
   others. These networks carry mail and news, but are not capable of
   supporting TELNET, FTP, Gopher, or WWW. We don't consider them part
   of the Internet, since they lack the most distinctive and
   characteristic services of the Internet.

   Some people argue that networks such as FidoNet and UUCP should also
   be counted as being part of the Internet, since electronic mail is

the most-used service even on the core, supplier-capable Internet.
They further argue that the biggest benefit of the Internet is the
community of discussion it supports, and mail is enough to join that.
Well, if mail is enough to be on the Internet, why is the Internet
drawing such attention from press and new users alike? Mail has been
around for quite a while (1972 or 1973), but that's not what has made
such an impression on the public. What has is the interactive
services, and interfaces to them such as Mosaic. Asynchronous
networks such as FidoNet and UUCP don't support those interactive
services, and are thus not part of the Internet. Besides, if being
part of a community of discussion was enough, we would have to also
include anyone with a fax machine or a telephone. Recent events have
demonstrated that all readers of the New York Times would also have
to be included. With edges so vague, what would be the point in
calling anything the Internet? We choose to stick with a definition
of the Internet as requiring the interactive services.

Some people argue that anything that uses RFC-822 mail is therefore
using Internet mail and must be part of the Internet. We find this
about as plausible as arguing that anybody who flies in a Boeing 737
is using American equipment and is thus within the United States.
Besides, there are plenty of systems out there that use mail but not
RFC-822.

So what to call systems that can exchange mail, but aren't on the
Internet? We say they are part of the Matrix, which is all computer
systems worldwide that can exchange electronic mail. This term is
borrowed (with permission) from Bill Gibson, the science fiction
writer.

Other people refer to the Matrix as global E-mail. That's accurate,
but is a description, rather than a name. Some even call it the e-
mail Internet. We find that term misleading, since if a system can
only exchange mail, we don't consider it part of the Internet. Not
to mention not everything in the world defines itself in terms of the
Internet, or communicates through the Internet. FidoNet and WWIVnet,
for example, have gateways between themselves that have nothing to do
with the Internet. Referring to the Matrix as the Internet is rather
like referring to the United Kingdom as England. You may call it
convenient shorthand; the Scots may disagree.

What about news? Well, the set of all systems that exchange news
already has a name: USENET. USENET is presumably a subset of the
Matrix, since it's hard to imagine a USENET node without mail, even
though USENET itself is news, not mail. USENET is clearly not the
same thing as the Internet, since many (almost certainly most)
Internet nodes do not carry USENET news, and many USENET nodes are on
other networks, especially UUCP, FidoNet, and BITNET.

A few years ago it was popular in some corners of the press to
attempt to equate USENET and the Internet. They're clearly not the
same. News, like mail, is an asynchronous, batch, store-and-forward
service. The distinguishing services of the Internet are
interactive, not news.

Asynchronous Compared to Dialup

Please note that interactive vs. asynchronous isn't the same thing as
direct vs. dialup connections. Dialup IP is still IP and can support
all the usual IP services. It's true that for the more bandwidth-
intensive services such as WWW, you'll be a lot happier with a *fast*
dialup IP connection, but any dialup IP connection can support WWW.
Some people call these on-demand IP connections, or part-time IP
access. They're typically supported over SLIP, PPP, ISDN, or perhaps
even X.25.

It's also true that it's a lot easier to run a useful interactive
Internet supplier node if you're at least dialed up most of the time
so that consumers can reach your node, but you can run servers that
are accessible over any dialup IP connection whenever it's dialed up.
It's true that some access providers handle low-end dialup IP
connections through a rotary of IP addresses, and that's not
conducive to running servers, since it's difficult for users to know
how to reach them. But given a dedicated IP address, how long you
stay dialed up is a matter of degree more than of quality. A IP
connection that's up the great majority of the time is often called a
dedicated connection regardless of whether it's established by
dialing a modem or starting software over a hardwired link.

It's possible to run UUCP over a dedicated IP connection, but it's
still UUCP, and still does not support interactive services.

Some people object to excluding the asynchronous networks from a
definition of the Internet just because they don't support the
interactive services. The argument they make is that FTP, Gopher,
and WWW can be accessed through mail. This is true, but it's hardly
the same, and hardly interactive in the same sense as using FTP,
Gopher, or WWW over an IP connection. It's rather like saying a
mail-order catalog is the same as going to the store and buying an
item on the spot. Besides, we've yet to see anyone log in remotely
by mail.

Is IP Characteristic?

We further choose to define the Internet as being those networks that
use IP to permit users to use both the communication services and at
least TELNET and FTP among the interactive services we have listed.

This requirement for IP has been questioned by some on the basis that
there are now application gateways for other protocol suites such as
Novell Netware that permit use of such services. This kind of
application gateway is actually nothing new, and is not yet
widespread. We choose to think of such networks, at least for the
moment, as yet another layer of the onion, outside the core and
consumer layers of the Internet.

Others have objected to the use of IP as a defining characteristic of
the Internet because they think it's too technical. Actually, we
find far fewer people confused about whether a software package or
network supports IP than about whether it's part of the Internet or
not.

Some people point out that services like WWW, Gopher, FTP, TELNET,
etc. could easily be implemented on top of other protocol suites.
This is true, and has been done. However, people seem to forget to
ask why these services developed on top of IP in the first place.
There seems to be something about IP and the Internet that is
especially conducive to the development of new protocols. We make no
apologies about naming IP, because we think it is important.

There is also the question of IP to where? If you have a UNIX shell
login account on a computer run by an Internet access provider, and
that system has IP access to the rest of the Internet, then you are
an Internet user. However, you will not be able to use the full
graphical capabilities of protocols such as WWW, because the
provider's system cannot display on a bitmapped screen for you. For
that, you need IP to your own computer with a bitmapped screen.
These are two different degrees of Internet connectivity that are
important to both end users and marketers. Some people refer to them
as text-only interactive access and graphical interactive access.
Some people have gone so far as to say you have to have graphical
capabilities to have a full service Internet connection. That may or
may not be so, but in the interests of keeping the major categories
to a minimum, we are simply going to note these degrees and say no
more about them in this article. However, we agree that the
distinction of graphical access is becoming more important with the
spread of WWW and Mosaic.

Conferencing Systems and Commercial Mail Systems

Conferencing systems such as Prodigy and CompuServe that support mail
and often something like news, plus database and services. But most
of them do not support the characteristic interactive services that
we have listed. The few that do (Delphi and AOL), we simply count as
part of the Internet. The others, we count as part of the Matrix,
since they all exchange mail.

We find that users of conferencing systems have no particular
difficulty in distinguishing between the conferencing system they use
and the Internet. CompuServe users, for example, refer to "Internet
mail", which is correct, since the only off-system mail CompuServe
supports is to the Internet, but they do not in general refer to
CompuServe as part of the Internet.

Similarly, users of the various commercial electronic mail networks,
such as MCI Mail and Sprint-Mail, seem to have no difficulty in
distinguishing between the mail network they use and the Internet.
Since they all seem to have their own addressing syntax, this is
hardly surprising. We count these commercial mail networks as part
of the Matrix, but not part of the Internet. Many of them have IP
links to the Internet, but they don't let their users use them,
instead limiting the services they carry to just mail.

Russian Dolls

So let's think of a series of nested Chinese boxes or Russian dolls;
the kind where inside Boris Yeltsin is Mikhail Gorbachov, inside
Gorbachov is Brezhnev, then Kruschev, Stalin, Lenin, and maybe even
Tsar Nicholas II. Let's not talk about that many concentric layers,
though, rather just three: the Matrix on the outside, the consumer
Internet inside, and the core Internet inside that.

	the core Internet	the consumer Internet	the Matrix
interactive services	supplier-capable	consumer-capable	by mail
	stores and shoppers	shoppers	mail order
asynchronous	yes	yes	yes services

Some people have argued that these categories are bad because they
are not mutually exclusive. Well, we observe that in real life
networks have differing degrees of services, and the ones of most
interest share the least common denominator of electronic mail. Thus
concentric categories are needed to describe the real world. You
can, however, extract three mutually-exclusive categories by
referring to the core Internet, the interactive consumer-only part of
the Internet, and to asynchronous systems.

Other people have argued that these categories are not sequential.
They look sequential to us, since if you start with the core Internet
and move out, you subtract services, and if you start at the outside

of the Matrix and move in, you add services.

Outside the Matrix

In addition to computers and networks that fit these classifications, there are also LANs, mainframes, and BBSes that don't exchange any services with other networks or computers; not even mail. These systems are outside the Matrix. For example, many companies have an AppleTalk LAN in marketing, a Novell NetWare LAN in management, and a mainframe in accounting that aren't connected to talk to anything else. In addition, there are a few large networks such as France's Teletel (commonly known as Minitel) that support very large user populations but don't communicate with anything else. These are all currently outside all our Chinese boxes of the core Internet, the consumer Internet, and the Matrix.

DNS and Mail Addresses

There are other interesting network services that make a difference to end users. For example, DNS (Domain Name System) domain names such as tic.com and domain addresses such tic@tic.com can be set up for systems outside the Internet. We used tic.com when we only had a UUCP connection, and few of our correspondents noticed any difference when we added an IP connection (except our mail was faster). This would be more or less a box enclosing the consumer Internet and within the Matrix. But the other three boxes are arguably the most important.

Some people have claimed that anything that uses DNS addresses is part of the Internet. We note that DNS addresses can be used with the UUCP network, which supports no interactive services, and we reject such an equation.

It is interesting to note that over the years various attempts have been made to equate the Internet with something else. Until the mid-1980s lots of people tried to say the Internet was the ARPANET. In the late 1980s many tried to say the Internet was NSFNET. In the early 1990s many tried to say the Internet was USENET. Now many are trying to say the Internet is anything that can exchange mail. We say the Internet is the Internet, not the same as anything else.

Summary

So, here we have a simple set of categories for several of the categories of network access people talk about most these days. Any such categories are at least somewhat a matter of opinion, and other people will propose other categories and other names. We like these categories, because they fit our experience of what real users actually perceive.

You'll notice we've avoided use of the words "connected" and "reachable" because they mean different things to different people at different times. For either of them to be meaningful, you have to say which services you are talking about. To us, reachable usually means pingable with ICMP ECHO, which is another way to define the core Internet. To others, reachable might mean you can send mail there, which is another way to define the Matrix.

Once we have terms for networks of interest, we can talk about how big those networks are. We think the terms we have defined here refer to groups of computers that people want to use, and that some people want to measure. Many marketers want to know about users. Well, users of mail are in the Matrix, and users of interactive services such as WWW and FTP are in the Internet. Other people are more interested in suppliers or distributors of information. Suppliers of information by mail can be anywhere in the Matrix, but suppliers of information by WWW or FTP are in the core Internet. It is easy to define more and finer degrees of distinctions of capabilities and connectivity, but these three major categories handle the most important cases.

We invite our readers to tell us what distinctions they find important about the various networks and their services.

Security Considerations

Security issues are not discussed in this memo.

Authors' Addresses

John S. Quarterman
Smoot Carl-Mitchell

EMail: tic@tic.com

Network Working Group   V. Cerf
Request for Comments: 3271   Internet Society
Category: Informational   April 2002

                     The Internet is for Everyone

Abstract

   This document expresses the Internet Society's ideology that the
   Internet really is for everyone. However, it will only be such if
   we make it so.

1. The Internet is for everyone

   How easy to say - how hard to achieve!

   How have we progressed towards this noble goal?

   The Internet is in its 14th year of annual doubling since 1988.
   There are over 150 million hosts on the Internet and an estimated 513
   million users, world wide.

   By 2006, the global Internet is likely to exceed the size of the
   global telephone network, if it has not already become the telephone
   network by virtue of IP telephony. Moreover, as many as 1.5 billion
   Internet-enabled appliances will have joined traditional servers,
   desk tops and laptops as part of the Internet family. Pagers, cell
   phones and personal digital assistants may well have merged to become
   the new telecommunications tools of the next decade. But even at the
   scale of the telephone system, it is sobering to realize that only
   half of the Earth's population has ever made a telephone call.

   It is estimated that commerce on the network will reach somewhere
   between $1.8T and $3.2T by 2003. That is only two years from now
   (but a long career in Internet years).

The number of Internet users will likely reach over 1000 million by
the end of the year 2005, but that is only about 16% of the world's
population. By 2047 the world's population may reach about 11
billion. If only 25% of the then world's population is on the
Internet, that will be nearly 3 billion users.

As high bandwidth access becomes the norm through digital subscriber
loops, cable modems and digital terrestrial and satellite radio
links, the convergence of media available on the Internet will become
obvious. Television, radio, telephony and the traditional print
media will find counterparts on the Internet - and will be changed in
profound ways by the presence of software that transforms the one-way
media into interactive resources, shareable by many.

The Internet is proving to be one of the most powerful amplifiers of
speech ever invented. It offers a global megaphone for voices that
might otherwise be heard only feebly, if at all. It invites and
facilitates multiple points of view and dialog in ways
unimplementable by the traditional, one-way, mass media.

The Internet can facilitate democratic practices in unexpected ways.
Did you know that proxy voting for stock shareholders is now commonly
supported on the Internet? Perhaps we can find additional ways in
which to simplify and expand the voting franchise in other domains,
including the political, as access to Internet increases.

The Internet is becoming the repository of all we have accomplished
as a society. It has become a kind of disorganized "Boswell" of the
human spirit. Be thoughtful in what you commit to email, news
groups, and other Internet communication channels - it may well turn
up in a web search some day. Thanks to online access to common
repositories, shared databases on the Internet are acting to
accelerate the pace of research progress.

The Internet is moving off the planet! Already, interplanetary
Internet is part of the NASA Mars mission program now underway at the
Jet Propulsion Laboratory. By 2008 we should have a well-functioning
Earth-Mars network that serves as a nascent backbone of an interplanetary system of Internets - InterPlaNet is a network of
Internets! Ultimately, we will have interplanetary Internet relays
in polar solar orbit so that they can see most of the planets and
their associated interplanetary gateways for most, if not all of the
time.

The Internet Society is launching a new campaign to facilitate access
to and use of Internet everywhere. The campaign slogan is "Internet
is for everyone," but there is much work needed to accomplish this
objective.

Internet is for everyone - but it won't be if it isn't affordable by
all that wish to partake of its services, so we must dedicate
ourselves to making the Internet as affordable as other
infrastructures so critical to our well-being. While we follow
Moore's Law to reduce the cost of Internet-enabling equipment, let us
also seek to stimulate regulatory policies that take advantage of the
power of competition to reduce costs.

Internet is for everyone - but it won't be if Governments restrict
access to it, so we must dedicate ourselves to keeping the network
unrestricted, unfettered and unregulated. We must have the freedom
to speak and the freedom to hear.

Internet is for everyone - but it won't be if it cannot keep up with
the explosive demand for its services, so we must dedicate ourselves
to continuing its technological evolution and development of the
technical standards the lie at the heart of the Internet revolution.
Let us dedicate ourselves to the support of the Internet Architecture
Board, the Internet Engineering Steering Group, the Internet Research
Task Force, the Internet Engineering Task Force and other
organizations dedicated to developing Internet technology as they
drive us forward into an unbounded future. Let us also commit
ourselves to support the work of the Internet Corporation for
Assigned Names and Numbers - a key function for the Internet's
operation.

Internet is for everyone - but it won't be until in every home, in
every business, in every school, in every library, in every hospital
in every town and in every country on the Globe, the Internet can be
accessed without limitation, at any time and in every language.

Internet is for everyone - but it won't be if it is too complex to be
used easily by everyone. Let us dedicate ourselves to the task of
simplifying the Internet's interfaces and to educating all that are
interested in its use.

Internet is for everyone - but it won't be if legislation around the
world creates a thicket of incompatible laws that hinder the growth
of electronic commerce, stymie the protection of intellectual
property, and stifle freedom of expression and the development of
market economies. Let us dedicate ourselves to the creation of a
global legal framework in which laws work across national boundaries
to reinforce the upward spiral of value that the Internet is capable
of creating.

Internet is for everyone - but it won't be if its users cannot
protect their privacy and the confidentiality of transactions
conducted on the network. Let us dedicate ourselves to the
proposition that cryptographic technology sufficient to protect
privacy from unauthorized disclosure should be freely available,
applicable and exportable. Moreover, as authenticity lies at the
heart of trust in networked environments, let us dedicate ourselves
to work towards the development of authentication methods and systems
capable of supporting electronic commerce through the Internet.

Internet is for everyone - but it won't be if parents and teachers
cannot voluntarily create protected spaces for our young people for
whom the full range of Internet content still may be inappropriate.
Let us dedicate ourselves to the development of technologies and
practices that offer this protective flexibility to those who accept
responsibility for providing it.

Internet is for everyone - but it won't be if we are not responsible
in its use and mindful of the rights of others who share its wealth.
Let us dedicate ourselves to the responsible use of this new medium
and to the proposition that with the freedoms the Internet enables
comes a commensurate responsibility to use these powerful enablers
with care and consideration. For those who choose to abuse these
privileges, let us dedicate ourselves to developing the necessary
tools to combat the abuse and punish the abuser.

Internet is for everyone - even Martians!

I hope Internauts everywhere will join with the Internet Society and
like-minded organizations to achieve this, easily stated but hard to
attain goal. As we pass the milestone of the beginning of the third
millennium, what better theme could we possibly ask for than making
the Internet the medium of this new millennium?

Internet IS for everyone - but it won't be unless WE make it so.

2. Security Considerations

This document does not treat security matters, except for reference
to the utility of cryptographic techniques to protect confidentiality
and privacy.

3. References

[1] Internet Society - www.isoc.org

[2] Internet Engineering Task Force - www.ietf.org

[3] Internet Corporation for Assigned Names and Numbers -
www.ICANN.org

[4] Cerf's slides: www.wcom.com/cerfsup

[5] Interplanetary Internet - www.ipnsig.org

[6] Internet history - livinginternet.com

4. Author's Addresses

Vint Cerf
former Chairman and President, Internet Society
January 2002

Sr. Vice President, Internet Architecture and Technology
WorldCom
22001 Loudoun County Parkway, F2-4115
Ashburn, VA 20147

EMail: vinton.g.cerf@wcom.com

5. Full Copyright Statement

Acknowledgement

Funding for the RFC Editor function is currently provided by the
Internet Society.

Part VI

Mocking IETF

The IETF—Internet Engineering Task Force—is so important that it deserves a separate class of ridicule.

The IETF process involves standards RFCs and informational and experimental RFCs. As Chapin and Huitema point out, there is no proviso for RFCs that express deep concern, but carry no information whatsoever. RFC 1438 proposes a new series: SOBs—Statements of Boredom.

Alegre Ramos' RFC 2323 guarantees identification and security resulting from such ambiguities as the inability to differentiate Jon from Scott in a group of facially hirsute hackers.

The importance of RFC 2323 is apparent in RFC 2551 in which Scott (but not Jon) specifies Roman Worst Current Practices, obsoleting RFC MMXXVI, in which Scott (but not Jon) discusses the Internet Standards Process. Just how seriously bad these practices are is illustrated by the misnumbering: this should be RFC MMDLI.

RFC 3092 is of such etymological importance that it has now been cited in the supplement to the OED.

Network Working Group   L. Chapin
Request for Comments: 1438   BBN
                                                          C. Huitema
                                                               INRIA
                                                        1 April 1993

Internet Engineering Task Force
Statements Of Boredom (SOBs)

Discussion

   The current IETF process has two types of RFCs: standards track
   documents and other RFCs (e.g., informational, experimental, FYIs).
   The intent of the standards track documents is clear, and culminates
   in an official Internet Standard. Informational RFCs can be
   published on a less formal basis, subject to the reasonable
   constraints of the RFC Editor. Informational RFCs are not subject to
   peer review and carry no significance whatsoever within the IETF
   process.

   The IETF currently has no mechanism or means of publishing documents
   that express its deep concern about something important, but
   otherwise contain absolutely no useful information whatsoever. This
   document creates a new subseries of RFCs, entitled, IETF Statements
   Of Boredom (SOBs). The SOB process is similar to that of the normal
   standards track. The SOB is submitted to the IAB, the IRSG, the
   IESG, the SOB Editor (Morpheus), and the Academie Francais for
   review, analysis, reproduction in triplicate, translation into ASN.1,
   and distribution to Internet insomniacs. However, once everyone has
   approved the document by falling asleep over it, the process ends and
   the document is discarded. The resulting vacuum is viewed as having
   the technical approval of the IETF, but it is not, and cannot become,
   an official Internet Standard.

References

    [1] Internet Activities Board, "The Internet Standards Process", RFC
         1310, IAB, March 1992.

    [2] Postel, J., Editor, "IAB OFFICIAL PROTOCOL STANDARDS", RFC 1410,
         IAB, March 1993.

Security Considerations

    Security issues are not discussed in this memo, but then again, no
    other issues of any importance are discussed in this memo either.

Authors' Addresses

    A. Lyman Chapin
    Bolt, Beranek & Newman
    Mail Stop 20/5b
    150 Cambridge Park Drive
    Cambridge, MA 02140
    USA

    Phone: 1 617 873 3133
    EMail: Lyman@BBN.COM

    Christian Huitema
    INRIA, Sophia-Antipolis
    2004 Route des Lucioles
    BP 109
    F-06561 Valbonne Cedex
    France

    Phone: +33 93 65 77 15
    EMail: Christian.Huitema@MIRSA.INRIA.FR

Network Working Group   A. Ramos
Request for Comments: 2323   ISI
Category: Informational   1 April 1998

            IETF Identification and Security Guidelines

Status of this Memo

Copyright Notice

1. Abstract

   This RFC is meant to represent a guideline by which the IETF
   conferences may run more effeciently with regards to identification
   and security protocols, with specific attention paid to a particular
   sub-group within the IETF: "facial hairius extremis".

   This document will shed further illumination on these problems and
   provide some possible solutions.

   This memo provides entertainment for the Internet community. It does
   not specify an Internet standard of any kind, but is rather
   unstandard, actually. Please laugh loud and hard.

2. Introduction

   It has come to the attention of THEY [1] that a certain "facial
   hairius extremesis" of the male variety of the species "homo sapien"
   of the sub-culture "computeris extrordinarisis" have overrun the IETF
   conferences and thus led to the break-down of many identification and
   safety protocols.

3. Per Capita (Anecdotal) Evidence

   While collecting research about the sub-group "facial hairius
   extremis" (FHE), it was noted that the per capita appearance of FHEs
   at IETFs was largely disproportional with the existence of FHEs in
   the world-at-large. In fact, the existence of facial hair at all
   within the IETF community is extraordinarily common among the males
   of the group. Apart from ZZ-Top and WWF Wrestling, it is not
   possible to find more facial hair within any occupational group. In

this author's own experience the average amount of men with long-term
facial hair is less than 20%. Long-term versus short-term facial
hair is a very important distinction as short-term facial hair, also
known as the temporary illness "goatee universitis" (which symptoms
range from full goatees to the less popular chin-goatee) is a common
affliction for university-based males. Per capita (temporary) facial
hair can go as high as 40%. However, among the males of the IETF the
per capita long-term facial hair is as high as 60% [2].

Ordinarily, this abundance of long-term FHE would not require that an
RFC be written. However, increasingly there have been issues
regarding mistaken identification. For security purposes as well as
ease of identification, this RFC will serve to clarify these issues
and hopefully provide a solution for them.

4. Mistaken Identification Syndrome (or "Are you --jon. or Scott?")

I was speaking to a very well-known network researcher, I'll call him
--jon., who tells me that he is often mistaken for a SOBbing Harvard
person. --jon. says, "People tell someone to look for me or him and
say that I'm about so-tall with a big white beard, and suddenly
people are coming up to me and saying, 'Hi Scott' and he often tells
me that he is mistakenly hailed as, '--jon.'. Often the mistake is
made solely on the appearance of our facial hair."

Another story --jon. told me is that once a woman called looking for
a computer researcher but only having a first name and physical
description. The recieptionist asked for the description and the
woman said she was looking for an older Caucasian man with a beard.
The receptionist reportedly blurted out, "they all have beards!!!!"

On a more personal note, two researchers who were both employed at
USC/ISI shaved their very famous facial hair and were both
unrecognizable to friends and co-workers alike. If it weren't for
B.M.'s Grateful Dead T-shirts and lack of shoes, or R.V.M.'s voice I
would have never recognized them.

5. Security Considerations

It is obvious to this researcher that facial hair of any variety is a
very recognizable characteristic. Indeed, when giving a description
of a male who has facial hair, it is always one of the first
characteristics given. Ordinarily this would not be a problem, since
facial hair in the world at large is below 20%. However, when used
as a description at IETFs, disaster can insue.

6. Solutions

   There are two parts to my proposed solution: the role of the seeker
   and the role of the FHE.

   For those who are seeking a FHE of known identity:

      -It is important to recognize these men as individuals.

         Just because a man has the facial hair you are looking for,
         please stop to inquire if you have the correct person. Think
         of what a blow it is to a person's ego to be constantly
         misidentified, and think of how annoying it is to be hailed by
         someone across a crowded IETF room and they are yelling the
         WRONG NAME. So remember to look, identify, and ask BEFORE you
         begin rambling on about some Internet stuff.

   For the FHE:

      -Give proper signals when being sought.

         If someone mistakenly calls you the wrong name, do not lose
         heart. Count to 10 and commonly reply, "You must have mistaken
         me for so-and-so, I am not that person.", and walk away. Also,
         if someone calls you from across a room, raise your your arm,
         smile and wave vigorously in affirmation or raise your arm,
         shake your head and give them a sign that you are not who they
         are looking for. As an FHE it is part of your responsibility
         to understand that facial hair is an extremely identifiable
         physical characteristic. Understand that non-FHE people do not
         mean any harm.

7. Conclusion

   In closing, I hope you found this RFC worthwhile and that it raised
   some interesting points. I also hope that I was able to further the
   cause of FHE and to make everyone's life a little bit easier. ;^)

8. References

   [1] THEY
       THEY, "We Who Everyone Quotes But Doesn't Know Who We Are", Pop
       Culture, April 1998.

   [2] 60% of IETF men have facial hair
       A. Ramos, "Damn, A Lot Of Men Here Have Facial Hair", ISI Talk,
       September 1997.

9. Acknowledgements

   I would like to thank the men of ISI who inspired me to write this
   RFC. I hope that my work will make life easier for you, and that the
   cases of mistaken identity will not be as common in the future
   because of this RFC. I understand your plight and feel for you.
   Good luck.

   Thanks to my life partner, Martin, who's reoccuring affliction of
   goatee universitis is a constant source of joy for me.

10. Author's Address

   Alegre Ramos
   USC/ISI
   4676 Admiralty Way #1001
   Marina del Rey, CA 90292

   Phone: 310-822-1511 x153
   EMail: ramos@isi.edu

288

11. Full Copyright Statement

289

Network Working Group   S. Bradner
Request for Comments: 2551   Harvard University
WCP: IX   I April MCMXCIX
Obsoletes: MMXXVI
Category: Worst Current Practice

                    The Roman Standards Process -- Revision III

Status of this Memo

    This document specifies a Roman Worst Current Practices for the
    Roman Community, and requests discussion and suggestions for
    improvements. Distribution of this memo is unlimited.

Copyright Statement

Abstract

    This memo documents the process used by the Roman community for
    the standardization of protocols and procedures. It defines the
    stages in the standardization process, the requirements for moving a
    document between stages and the types of documents used during this
    process. It also addresses the intellectual property rights and
    copyright issues associated with the standards process.

Table of Contents

I. INTRODUCTION

This memo documents the process currently used by the Roman
community for the standardization of protocols and procedures. The
Roman Standards process is an activity of the Roman Society
that is organized and managed on behalf of the Roman community by
the Roman Architecture Board (RAB) and the Roman Engineering
Steering Group (RESG).

I.I Roman Standards

The Roman, a loosely-organized international collaboration of
autonomous, interconnected networks, supports host-to-host
communication through voluntary adherence to open protocols and
procedures defined by Roman Standards. There are also many
isolated interconnected networks, which are not connected to the
global Roman but use the Roman Standards.

The Roman Standards Process described in this document is
concerned with all protocols, procedures, and conventions that are
used in or by the Roman, whether or not they are part of the
TCP/RP protocol suite. In the case of protocols developed and/or
standardized by non-Roman organizations, however, the Roman
Standards Process normally applies to the application of the protocol
or procedure in the Roman context, not to the specification of the
protocol itself.

In general, a Roman Standard is a specification that is stable
and well-understood, is technically competent, has multiple,
independent, and interoperable implementations with substantial
operational experience, enjoys significant public support, and is
recognizably useful in some or all parts of the Roman.

I.II The Roman Standards Process

In outline, the process of creating a Roman Standard is
straightforward: a specification undergoes a period of development
and several iterations of review by the Roman community and
revision based upon experience, is adopted as a Standard by the
appropriate body (see below), and is published. In practice, the
process is more complicated, due to (I) the difficulty of creating
specifications of high technical quality; (II) the need to consider
the interests of all of the affected parties; (III) the importance of
establishing widespread community consensus; and (IV) the difficulty
of evaluating the utility of a particular specification for the
Roman community.

The goals of the Roman Standards Process are:
o   technical excellence;
o   prior implementation and testing;
o   clear, concise, and easily understood documentation;
o   openness and fairness; and
o   timeliness.

The procedures described in this document are designed to be fair,
open, and objective; to reflect existing (proven) practice; and to
be flexible.

o   These procedures are intended to provide a fair, open, and
    objective basis for developing, evaluating, and adopting Roman
    Standards. They provide ample opportunity for participation and
    comment by all interested parties. At each stage of the
    standardization process, a specification is repeatedly discussed
    and its merits debated in open meetings and/or public electronic
    mailing lists, and it is made available for review via world-wide
    on-line directories.

o   These procedures are explicitly aimed at recognizing and adopting
    generally-accepted practices. Thus, a candidate specification
    must be implemented and tested for correct operation and
    interoperability by multiple independent parties and utilized in
    increasingly demanding environments, before it can be adopted as
    a Roman Standard.

o   These procedures provide a great deal of flexibility to adapt to
    the wide variety of circumstances that occur in the
    standardization process. Experience has shown this flexibility to
    be vital in achieving the goals listed above.

The goal of technical competence, the requirement for prior
implementation and testing, and the need to allow all interested
parties to comment all require significant time and effort. On the
other hand, today's rapid development of networking technology
demands timely development of standards. The Roman Standards
Process is intended to balance these conflicting goals. The process
is believed to be as short and simple as possible without sacrificing
technical excellence, thorough testing before adoption of a standard,
or openness and fairness.

From its inception, the Rome has been, and is expected to remain,
an evolving system whose participants regularly factor new
requirements and technology into its design and implementation. Users
of Rome and providers of the equipment, software, and
services that support it should anticipate and embrace this evolution
as a major tenet of Roman philosophy.

   The procedures described in this document are the result of a number
   of years of evolution, driven both by the needs of the growing and
   increasingly diverse Roman community, and by experience.

I.III Organization of This Document

   Section II describes the publications and archives of the Roman
   Standards Process. Section III describes the types of Roman
   standard specifications. Section IV describes the Roman standards
   specifications track. Section V describes Worst Current Practice
   RFCs. Section VI describes the process and rules for Roman
   standardization. Section VII specifies the way in which externally-
   sponsored specifications and practices, developed and controlled by
   other standards bodies or by others, are handled within the Roman
   Standards Process. Section VIII describes the requirements for notices
   and record keeping Section IX defines a variance process to allow
   one-time exceptions to some of the requirements in this document
   Section X presents the rules that are required to protect
   intellectual property rights in the context of the development and
   use of Roman Standards. Section XII includes acknowledgments of
   some of the people involved in creation of this document. Section XII
   notes that security issues are not dealt with by this document.
   Section XII contains a list of numeral references. Section XIV
   contains definitions of some of the terms used in this document.
   Section XV lists the author's email and postal addresses. Appendix A
   contains a list of frequently-used acronyms.

II.   Roman STANDARDS-RELATED PUBLICATIONS

II.I Requests for Comments (RFCs)

   Each distinct version of a Roman standards-related specification
   is published as part of the "Request for Comments" (RFC) document
   series. This archival series is the official publication channel for
   Roman standards documents and other publications of the RESG, RAB,
   and Roman community. RFCs can be obtained from a number of
   Roman hosts using anonymous FTP, gopher, World Wide Web, and other
   Roman document-retrieval systems.

   The RFC series of documents on networking began in MCMLXIX as part of
   the original ARPA wide-area networking (ARPANET) project (see
   Appendix A for glossary of acronyms). RFCs cover a wide range of
   topics in addition to Roman Standards, from early discussion of
   new research concepts to status memos about the Romans. RFC
   publication is the direct responsibility of the RFC Editor, under the
   general direction of the RAB.

The rules for formatting and submitting an RFC are defined in [V].
Every RFC is available in ASCII text. Some RFCs are also available
in other formats. The other versions of an RFC may contain material
(such as diagrams and figures) that is not present in the ASCII
version, and it may be formatted differently.

```
*************************************************************
*                                                           *
*  A stricter requirement applies to standards-track        *
*  specifications:  the ASCII text version is the           *
*  definitive reference, and therefore it must be a         *
*  complete and accurate specification of the standard,     *
*  including all necessary diagrams and illustrations.      *
*                                                           *
*************************************************************
```

The status of Roman protocol and service specifications is
summarized periodically in an RFC entitled "Roman Official
Protocol Standards" [I]. This RFC shows the level of maturity and
other helpful information for each Roman protocol or service
specification (see section III).

Some RFCs document Roman Standards. These RFCs form the 'STD'
subseries of the RFC series [IV]. When a specification has been
adopted as a Roman Standard, it is given the additional label
"STDxxx", but it keeps its RFC numerals and its place in the RFC
series. (see section IV.I.III)

Some RFCs standardize the results of community deliberations about
statements of principle or conclusions about what is the best way to
perform some operations or RETF process function. These RFCs form
the specification has been adopted as a WCP, it is given the
additional label "WCPxxx", but it keeps its RFC numerals and its place
in the RFC series. (see section V)

Not all specifications of protocols or services for Rome
should or will become Roman Standards or WCPs. Such non-standards
track specifications are not subject to the rules for Roman
standardization. Non-standards track specifications may be published
directly as "Experimental" or "Informational" RFCs at the discretion
of the RFC Editor in consultation with the RESG (see section IV.II).

```
***********************************************************
*                                                         *
*    It is important to remember that not all RFCs        *
*    are standards track documents, and that not all      *
*    standards track documents reach the level of         *
*    Roman Standard. In the same way, not all RFCs        *
*    which describe current practices have been given     *
*    the review and approval to become WCPs. See          *
*    RFC-MDCCXCVI [VI] for further information.            *
*                                                         *
***********************************************************
```

II.II Roman-Drafts

   During the development of a specification, draft versions of the
   document are made available for informal review and comment by
   placing them in the RETF's "Roman-Drafts" directory, which is
   replicated on a number of Roman hosts. This makes an evolving
   working document readily available to a wide audience, facilitating
   the process of review and revision.

   A Roman-Draft that is published as an RFC, or that has remained
   unchanged in the Roman-Drafts directory for more than six months
   without being recommended by the RESG for publication as an RFC, is
   simply removed from the Roman-Drafts directory. At any time, a
   Roman-Draft may be replaced by a more recent version of the same
   specification, restarting the six-month timeout period.

   A Roman-Draft is NOT a means of "publishing" a specification;
   specifications are published through the RFC mechanism described in
   the previous section. Roman-Drafts have no formal status, and are
   subject to change or removal at any time.

```
***********************************************************
*                                                         *
*    Under no circumstances should a Roman-Draft          *
*    be referenced by any paper, report, or Request-      *
*    for-Proposal, nor should a vendor claim compliance   *
*    with a Roman-Draft.                                  *
*                                                         *
***********************************************************
```

Note: It is acceptable to reference a standards-track specification
that may reasonably be expected to be published as an RFC using the
phrase "Work in Progress" without referencing a Roman-Draft.
This may also be done in a standards track document itself as long
as the specification in which the reference is made would stand as a
complete and understandable document with or without the reference to
the "Work in Progress".

III. Roman STANDARD SPECIFICATIONS

   Specifications subject to the Roman Standards Process fall into
   one of two categories: Technical Specification (TS) and
   Applicability Statement (AS).

III.I Technical Specification (TS)

   A Technical Specification is any description of a protocol, service,
   procedure, convention, or format. It may completely describe all of
   the relevant aspects of its subject, or it may leave one or more
   parameters or options unspecified. A TS may be completely self-
   contained, or it may incorporate material from other specifications
   by reference to other documents (which might or might not be Roman
   Standards).

   A TS shall include a statement of its scope and the general intent
   for its use (domain of applicability). Thus, a TS that is inherently
   specific to a particular context shall contain a statement to that
   effect. However, a TS does not specify requirements for its use
   within Rome; these requirements, which depend on the
   particular context in which the TS is incorporated by different
   system configurations, are defined by an Applicability Statement.

III.II Applicability Statement (AS)

   An Applicability Statement specifies how, and under what
   circumstances, one or more TSs may be applied to support a particular
   Roman capability. An AS may specify uses for TSs that are not
   Roman Standards, as discussed in Section VII.

   An AS identifies the relevant TSs and the specific way in which they
   are to be combined, and may also specify particular values or ranges
   of TS parameters or subfunctions of a TS protocol that must be
   implemented. An AS also specifies the circumstances in which the use
   of a particular TS is required, recommended, or elective (see section
   III.III).

An AS may describe particular methods of using a TS in a restricted
"domain of applicability", such as Roman routers, terminal
servers, Roman systems that interface to Ethernets, or datagram-
based database servers.

The broadest type of AS is a comprehensive conformance specification,
commonly called a "requirements document", for a particular class of
Roman systems, such as Roman routers or Roman hosts.

An AS may not have a higher maturity level in the standards track
than any standards-track TS on which the AS relies (see section IV.I).
For example, a TS at Draft Standard level may be referenced by an AS
at the Proposed Standard or Draft Standard level, but not by an AS at
the Standard level.

III.III Requirement Levels

An AS shall apply one of the following "requirement levels" to each
of the TSs to which it refers:

(a) Required: Implementation of the referenced TS, as specified by
     the AS, is required to achieve minimal conformance. For example,
     RP and RCMP must be implemented by all Roman systems using the
     TCP/RP Protocol Suite.

(b) Recommended: Implementation of the referenced TS is not
     required for minimal conformance, but experience and/or generally
     accepted technical wisdom suggest its desirability in the domain
     of applicability of the AS. Vendors are strongly encouraged to
     include the functions, features, and protocols of Recommended TSs
     in their products, and should omit them only if the omission is
     justified by some special circumstance. For example, the TELNET
     protocol should be implemented by all systems that would benefit
     from remote access.

(c) Elective: Implementation of the referenced TS is optional
     within the domain of applicability of the AS; that is, the AS
     creates no explicit necessity to apply the TS. However, a
     particular vendor may decide to implement it, or a particular user
     may decide that it is a necessity in a specific environment. For
     example, the DECNET MIB could be seen as valuable in an
     environment where the DECNET protocol is used.

As noted in section IV.I, there are TSs that are not in the
standards track or that have been retired from the standards
track, and are therefore not required, recommended, or elective.
Two additional "requirement level" designations are available for
these TSs:

(d) Limited Use: The TS is considered to be appropriate for use
     only in limited or unique circumstances. For example, the usage
     of a protocol with the "Experimental" designation should generally
     be limited to those actively involved with the experiment.

(e) Not Recommended: A TS that is considered to be inappropriate
     for general use is labeled "Not Recommended". This may be because
     of its limited functionality, specialized nature, or historic
     status.

Although TSs and ASs are conceptually separate, in practice a
standards-track document may combine an AS and one or more related
TSs. For example, Technical Specifications that are developed
specifically and exclusively for some particular domain of
applicability, e.g., for mail server hosts, often contain within a
single specification all of the relevant AS and TS information. In
such cases, no useful purpose would be served by deliberately
distributing the information among several documents just to preserve
the formal AS/TS distinction. However, a TS that is likely to apply
to more than one domain of applicability should be developed in a
modular fashion, to facilitate its incorporation by multiple ASs.

The "Official Protocol Standards" RFC (STD I) lists a general
requirement level for each TS, using the nomenclature defined in this
section. This RFC is updated periodically. In many cases, more
detailed descriptions of the requirement levels of particular
protocols and of individual features of the protocols will be found
in appropriate ASs.

IV. THE ROMAN STANDARDS TRACK

Specifications that are intended to become Roman Standards evolve
through a set of maturity levels known as the "standards track".
These maturity levels -- "Proposed Standard", "Draft Standard", and
"Standard" -- are defined and discussed in section IV.I. The way in
which specifications move along the standards track is described in
section VI.

Even after a specification has been adopted as a Roman Standard,
further evolution often occurs based on experience and the
recognition of new requirements. The nomenclature and procedures of
Roman standardization provide for the replacement of old Roman

Standards with new ones, and the assignment of descriptive labels to indicate the status of "retired" Roman Standards. A set of maturity levels is defined in section IV.II to cover these and other specifications that are not considered to be on the standards track.

IV.I Standards Track Maturity Levels

Roman specifications go through stages of development, testing, and acceptance. Within the Roman Standards Process, these stages are formally labeled "maturity levels".

This section describes the maturity levels and the expected characteristics of specifications at each level.

IV.I.I Proposed Standard

The entry-level maturity for the standards track is "Proposed Standard". A specific action by the RESG is required to move a specification onto the standards track at the "Proposed Standard" level.

A Proposed Standard specification is generally stable, has resolved known design choices, is believed to be well-understood, has received significant community review, and appears to enjoy enough community interest to be considered valuable. However, further experience might result in a change or even retraction of the specification before it advances.

Usually, neither implementation nor operational experience is required for the designation of a specification as a Proposed Standard. However, such experience is highly desirable, and will usually represent a strong argument in favor of a Proposed Standard designation.

The RESG may require implementation and/or operational experience prior to granting Proposed Standard status to a specification that materially affects the core Roman protocols or that specifies behavior that may have significant operational impact on the Roman.

A Proposed Standard should have no known technical omissions with respect to the requirements placed upon it. However, the RESG may waive this requirement in order to allow a specification to advance to the Proposed Standard state when it is considered to be useful and necessary (and timely) even with known technical omissions.

Implementors should treat Proposed Standards as immature
specifications. It is desirable to implement them in order to gain
experience and to validate, test, and clarify the specification.
However, since the content of Proposed Standards may be changed if
problems are found or better solutions are identified, deploying
implementations of such standards into a disruption-sensitive
environment is not recommended.

IV.I.II Draft Standard

A specification from which at least two independent and interoperable
implementations from different code bases have been developed, and
for which sufficient successful operational experience has been
obtained, may be elevated to the "Draft Standard" level. For the
purposes of this section, "interoperable" means to be functionally
equivalent or interchangeable components of the system or process in
which they are used. If patented or otherwise controlled technology
is required for implementation, the separate implementations must
also have resulted from separate exercise of the licensing process.
Elevation to Draft Standard is a major advance in status, indicating
a strong belief that the specification is mature and will be useful.

The requirement for at least two independent and interoperable
implementations applies to all of the options and features of the
specification. In cases in which one or more options or features
have not been demonstrated in at least two interoperable
implementations, the specification may advance to the Draft Standard
level only if those options or features are removed.

The Working Group chair is responsible for documenting the specific
implementations which qualify the specification for Draft or Roman
Standard status along with documentation about testing of the
interoperation of these implementations. The documentation must
include information about the support of each of the individual
options and features. This documentation should be submitted to the
Area Director with the protocol action request. (see Section VI)

A Draft Standard must be well-understood and known to be quite
stable, both in its semantics and as a basis for developing an
implementation. A Draft Standard may still require additional or
more widespread field experience, since it is possible for
implementations based on Draft Standard specifications to demonstrate
unforeseen behavior when subjected to large-scale use in production
environments.

A Draft Standard is normally considered to be a final specification, and changes are likely to be made only to solve specific problems encountered. In most circumstances, it is reasonable for vendors to deploy implementations of Draft Standards into a disruption sensitive environment.

IV.I.III Roman Standard

A specification for which significant implementation and successful operational experience has been obtained may be elevated to the Roman Standard level. A Roman Standard (which may simply be referred to as a Standard) is characterized by a high degree of technical maturity and by a generally held belief that the specified protocol or service provides significant benefit to the Roman community.

A specification that reaches the status of Standard is assigned numerals in the STD series while retaining its RFC numerals.

IV.II Non-Standards Track Maturity Levels

Not every specification is on the standards track. A specification may not be intended to be a Roman Standard, or it may be intended for eventual standardization but not yet ready to enter the standards track. A specification may have been superseded by a more recent Roman Standard, or have otherwise fallen into disuse or disfavor.

Specifications that are not on the standards track are labeled with one of three "off-track" maturity levels: "Experimental", "Informational", or "Historic". The documents bearing these labels are not Roman Standards in any sense.

IV.II.I Experimental

The "Experimental" designation typically denotes a specification that is part of some research or development effort. Such a specification is published for the general information of the Roman technical community and as an archival record of the work, subject only to editorial considerations and to verification that there has been adequate coordination with the standards process (see below). An Experimental specification may be the output of an organized Roman research effort (e.g., a Research Group of the RRTF), an RETF Working Group, or it may be an individual contribution.

IV.II.II Informational

An "Informational" specification is published for the general
information of the Roman community, and does not represent a
Roman community consensus or recommendation. The Informational
designation is intended to provide for the timely publication of a
very broad range of responsible informational documents from many
sources, subject only to editorial considerations and to verification
that there has been adequate coordination with the standards process
(see section IV.II.III).

Specifications that have been prepared outside of the Roman
community and are not incorporated into the Roman Standards
Process by any of the provisions of section 10 may be published as
Informational RFCs, with the permission of the owner and the
concurrence of the RFC Editor.

IV.II.III Procedures for Experimental and Informational RFCs

Unless they are the result of RETF Working Group action, documents
intended to be published with Experimental or Informational status
should be submitted directly to the RFC Editor. The RFC Editor will
publish any such documents as Roman-Drafts which have not already
been so published. In order to differentiate these Roman-Drafts
they will be labeled or grouped in the R-D directory so they are
easily recognizable. The RFC Editor will wait two weeks after this
publication for comments before proceeding further. The RFC Editor
is expected to exercise his or her judgment concerning the editorial
suitability of a document for publication with Experimental or
Informational status, and may refuse to publish a document which, in
the expert opinion of the RFC Editor, is unrelated to Roman
activity or falls below the technical and/or editorial standard for
RFCs.

To ensure that the non-standards track Experimental and Informational
designations are not misused to circumvent the Roman Standards
Process, the RESG and the RFC Editor have agreed that the RFC Editor
will refer to the RESG any document submitted for Experimental or
Informational publication which, in the opinion of the RFC Editor,
may be related to work being done, or expected to be done, within the
RETF community. The RESG shall review such a referred document
within a reasonable period of time, and recommend either that it be
published as originally submitted or referred to the RETF as a
contribution to the Roman Standards Process.

If (a) the RESG recommends that the document be brought within the
RETF and progressed within the RETF context, but the author declines
to do so, or (b) the RESG considers that the document proposes

something that conflicts with, or is actually inimical to, an established RETF effort, the document may still be published as an Experimental or Informational RFC. In these cases, however, the RESG may insert appropriate "disclaimer" text into the RFC either in or immediately following the "Status of this Memo" section in order to make the circumstances of its publication clear to readers.

Documents proposed for Experimental and Informational RFCs by RETF Working Groups go through RESG review. The review is initiated using the process described in section VI.I.I.

IV.II.IV Historic

A specification that has been superseded by a more recent specification or is for any other reason considered to be obsolete is assigned to the "Historic" level. (Purists have suggested that the word should be "Historical"; however, at this point the use of "Historic" is historical.)

Note: Standards track specifications normally must not depend on other standards track specifications which are at a lower maturity level or on non standards track specifications other than referenced specifications from other standards bodies. (See Section VII.)

V. WORST CURRENT PRACTICE (WCP) RFCs

The WCP subseries of the RFC series is designed to be a way to standardize practices and the results of community deliberations. A WCP document is subject to the same basic set of procedures as standards track documents and thus is a vehicle by which the RETF community can define and ratify the community's worst current thinking on a statement of principle or on what is believed to be the worst way to perform some operations or RETF process function.

Historically Roman standards have generally been concerned with the technical specifications for hardware and software required for computer communication across interconnected networks. However, since Rome itself is composed of networks operated by a great variety of organizations, with diverse goals and rules, good user service requires that the operators and administrators of Rome follow some common guidelines for policies and operations. While these guidelines are generally different in scope and style from protocol standards, their establishment needs a similar process for consensus building.

While it is recognized that entities such as the RAB and RESG are composed of individuals who may participate, as individuals, in the technical work of the RETF, it is also recognized that the entities

themselves have an existence as leaders in the community. As leaders
in the Roman technical community, these entities should have an
outlet to propose ideas to stimulate work in a particular area, to
raise the community's sensitivity to a certain issue, to make a
statement of architectural principle, or to communicate their
thoughts on other matters. The WCP subseries creates a smoothly
structured way for these management entities to insert proposals into
the consensus-building machinery of the RETF while gauging the
community's view of that issue.

Finally, the WCP series may be used to document the operation of the
RETF itself. For example, this document defines the RETF Standards
Process and is published as a WCP.

V.I WCP Review Process

Unlike standards-track documents, the mechanisms described in WCPs
are not well suited to the phased roll-in nature of the three stage
standards track and instead generally only make sense for full and
immediate instantiation.

The WCP process is similar to that for proposed standards. The WCP
is submitted to the RESG for review, (see section VI.I.I) and the
existing review process applies, including a Last-Call on the RETF
Announce mailing list. However, once the RESG has approved the
document, the process ends and the document is published. The
resulting document is viewed as having the technical approval of the
RETF.

Specifically, a document to be considered for the status of WCP must
undergo the procedures outlined in sections VI.I, and VI.IV of this
document. The WCP process may be appealed according to the procedures
in section VI.V.

Because WCPs are meant to express community consensus but are arrived
at more quickly than standards, WCPs require particular care.
Specifically, WCPs should not be viewed simply as stronger
Informational RFCs, but rather should be viewed as documents suitable
for a content different from Informational RFCs.

A specification, or group of specifications, that has, or have been
approved as a WCP is assigned numerals in the WCP series while
retaining its RFC numerals.

VI. THE ROMAN STANDARDS PROCESS

    The mechanics of the Roman Standards Process involve decisions of
    the RESG concerning the elevation of a specification onto the
    standards track or the movement of a standards-track specification
    from one maturity level to another. Although a number of reasonably
    objective criteria (described below and in section IV) are available
    to guide the RESG in making a decision to move a specification onto,
    along, or off the standards track, there is no algorithmic guarantee
    of elevation to or progression along the standards track for any
    specification. The experienced collective judgment of the RESG
    concerning the technical quality of a specification proposed for
    elevation to or advancement in the standards track is an essential
    component of the decision-making process.

VI.I Standards Actions

    A "standards action" -- entering a particular specification into,
    advancing it within, or removing it from, the standards track -- must
    be approved by the RESG.

VI.I.I Initiation of Action

    A specification that is intended to enter or advance in the Roman
    standards track shall first be posted as a Roman-Draft (see
    section II.II) unless it has not changed since publication as an RFC.
    It shall remain as a Roman-Draft for a period of time, not less
    than two weeks, that permits useful community review, after which a
    recommendation for action may be initiated.

    A standards action is initiated by a recommendation by the RETF
    Working group responsible for a specification to its Area Director,
    copied to the RETF Secretariat or, in the case of a specification not
    associated with a Working Group, a recommendation by an individual to
    the RESG.

VI.I.II RESG Review and Approval

    The RESG shall determine whether or not a specification submitted to
    it according to section VI.I.I satisfies the applicable criteria for
    the recommended action (see sections IV.I and IV.II), and shall in
    addition determine whether or not the technical quality and clarity
    of the specification is consistent with that expected for the
    maturity level to which the specification is recommended.

    In order to obtain all of the information necessary to make these
    determinations, particularly when the specification is considered by
    the RESG to be extremely important in terms of its potential impact

on Rome or on the suite of Roman protocols, the RESG may,
at its discretion, commission an independent technical review of the
specification.

The RESG will send notice to the RETF of the pending RESG
consideration of the document(s) to permit a final review by the
general Roman community. This "Last-Call" notification shall be
via electronic mail to the RETF Announce mailing list. Comments on a
Last-Call shall be accepted from anyone, and should be sent as
directed in the Last-Call announcement.

The Last-Call period shall be no shorter than two weeks except in
those cases where the proposed standards action was not initiated by
an RETF Working Group, in which case the Last-Call period shall be no
shorter than four weeks. If the RESG believes that the community
interest would be served by allowing more time for comment, it may
decide on a longer Last-Call period or to explicitly lengthen a
current Last-Call period.

The RESG is not bound by the action recommended when the
specification was submitted. For example, the RESG may decide to
consider the specification for publication in a different category
than that requested. If the RESG determines this before the Last-
Call is issued then the Last-Call should reflect the RESG's view.
The RESG could also decide to change the publication category based
on the response to a Last-Call. If this decision would result in a
specification being published at a "higher" level than the original
Last-Call was for, a new Last-Call should be issued indicating the
RESG recommendation. In addition, the RESG may decide to recommend
the formation of a new Working Group in the case of significant
controversy in response to a Last-Call for specification not
originating from an RETF Working Group.

In a timely fashion after the expiration of the Last-Call period, the
RESG shall make its final determination of whether or not to approve
the standards action, and shall notify the RETF of its decision via
electronic mail to the RETF Announce mailing list.

VI.I.III Publication

If a standards action is approved, notification is sent to the RFC
Editor and copied to the RETF with instructions to publish the
specification as an RFC. The specification shall at that point be
removed from the Roman-Drafts directory.

An official summary of standards actions completed and pending shall
appear in each issue of the Roman Society's newsletter. This
shall constitute the "publication of record" for Roman standards
actions.

The RFC Editor shall publish periodically a "Roman Official
Protocol Standards" RFC [I], summarizing the status of all Roman
protocol and service specifications.

VI.II Advancing in the Standards Track

The procedure described in section VI.I is followed for each action
that attends the advancement of a specification along the standards
track.

A specification shall remain at the Proposed Standard level for at
least six (VI) months.

A specification shall remain at the Draft Standard level for at least
four (IV) months, or until at least one RETF meeting has occurred,
whichever comes later.

These minimum periods are intended to ensure adequate opportunity for
community review without severely impacting timeliness. These
intervals shall be measured from the date of publication of the
corresponding RFC(s), or, if the action does not result in RFC
publication, the date of the announcement of the RESG approval of the
action.

A specification may be (indeed, is likely to be) revised as it
advances through the standards track. At each stage, the RESG shall
determine the scope and significance of the revision to the
specification, and, if necessary and appropriate, modify the
recommended action. Minor revisions are expected, but a significant
revision may require that the specification accumulate more
experience at its current maturity level before progressing. Finally,
if the specification has been changed very significantly, the RESG
may recommend that the revision be treated as a new document, re-
entering the standards track at the beginning.

Change of status shall result in republication of the specification
as an RFC, except in the rare case that there have been no changes at
all in the specification since the last publication. Generally,
desired changes will be "batched" for incorporation at the next level
in the standards track. However, deferral of changes to the next
standards action on the specification will not always be possible or
desirable; for example, an important typographical error, or a
technical error that does not represent a change in overall function

of the specification, may need to be corrected immediately. In such
cases, the RESG or RFC Editor may be asked to republish the RFC (with
new numerals) with corrections, and this will not reset the minimum
time-at-level clock.

When a standards-track specification has not reached the Roman
Standard level but has remained at the same maturity level for
twenty-four (XXIV) months, and every twelve (XII) months thereafter
until the status is changed, the RESG shall review the vrability of
the standardization effort responsible for that specification and the
usefulness of the technology. Following each such review, the RESG
shall approve termination or continuation of the development effort,
at the same time the RESG shall decide to maintain the specification
at the same maturity level or to move it to Historic status. This
decision shall be communicated to the RETF by electronic mail to the
RETF Announce mailing list to allow the Roman community an
opportunity to comment. This provision is not intended to threaten a
legitimate and active Working Group effort, but rather to provide an
administrative mechanism for terminating a moribund effort.

VI.III Revising a Standard

A new version of an established Roman Standard must progress
through the full Roman standardization process as if it were a
completely new specification. Once the new version has reached the
Standard level, it will usually replace the previous version, which
will be moved to Historic status. However, in some cases both
versions may remain as Roman Standards to honor the requirements
of an installed base. In this situation, the relationship between
the previous and the new versions must be explicitly stated in the
text of the new version or in another appropriate document (e.g., an
Applicability Statement; see section III.II).

VI.IV Retiring a Standard

As the technology changes and matures, it is possible for a new
Standard specification to be so clearly superior technically that one
or more existing standards track specifications for the same function
should be retired. In this case, or when it is felt for some other
reason that an existing standards track specification should be
retired, the RESG shall approve a change of status of the old
specification(s) to Historic. This recommendation shall be issued
with the same Last-Call and notification procedures used for any
other standards action. A request to retire an existing standard can
originate from a Working Group, an Area Director or some other
interested party.

VI.V Conflict Resolution and Appeals

Disputes are possible at various stages during the RETF process. As
much as possible the process is designed so that compromises can be
made, and genuine consensus achieved, however there are times when
even the most reasonable and knowledgeable people are unable to
agree. To achieve the goals of openness and fairness, such conflicts
must be resolved by a process of open review and discussion. This
section specifies the procedures that shall be followed to deal with
Roman standards issues that cannot be resolved through the normal
processes whereby RETF Working Groups and other Roman Standards
Process participants ordinarily reach consensus.

VI.V.I Working Group Disputes

An individual (whether a participant in the relevant Working Group or
not) may disagree with a Working Group recommendation based on his or
her belief that either (a) his or her own views have not been
adequately considered by the Working Group, or (b) the Working Group
has made an incorrect technical choice which places the quality
and/or integrity of the Working Group's product(s) in significant
jeopardy. The first issue is a difficulty with Working Group
process; the latter is an assertion of technical error. These two
types of disagreement are quite different, but both are handled by
the same process of review.

A person who disagrees with a Working Group recommendation shall
always first discuss the matter with the Working Group's chair(s),
who may involve other members of the Working Group (or the Working
Group as a whole) in the discussion.

If the disagreement cannot be resolved in this way, any of the
parties involved may bring it to the attention of the Area
Director(s) for the area in which the Working Group is chartered.
The Area Director(s) shall attempt to resolve the dispute.

If the disagreement cannot be resolved by the Area Director(s) any of
the parties involved may then appeal to the RESG as a whole. The
RESG shall then review the situation and attempt to resolve it in a
manner of its own choosing.

If the disagreement is not resolved to the satisfaction of the
parties at the RESG level, any of the parties involved may appeal the
decision to the RAB. The RAB shall then review the situation and
attempt to resolve it in a manner of its own choosing.

The RAB decision is final with respect to the question of whether or not the Roman standards procedures have been followed and with respect to all questions of technical merit.

VI.V.II Process Failures

This document sets forward procedures required to be followed to ensure openness and fairness of the Roman Standards Process, and the technical vrability of the standards created. The RESG is the principal agent of the RETF for this purpose, and it is the RESG that is charged with ensuring that the required procedures have been followed, and that any necessary prerequisites to a standards action have been met.

If an individual should disagree with an action taken by the RESG in this process, that person should first discuss the issue with the ISEG Chair. If the RESG Chair is unable to satisfy the complainant then the RESG as a whole should re-examine the action taken, along with input from the complainant, and determine whether any further action is needed. The RESG shall issue a report on its review of the complaint to the RETF.

Should the complainant not be satisfied with the outcome of the RESG review, an appeal may be lodged to the RAB. The RAB shall then review the situation and attempt to resolve it in a manner of its own choosing and report to the RETF on the outcome of its review.

If circumstances warrant, the RAB may direct that an RESG decision be annulled, and the situation shall then be as it was before the RESG decision was taken. The RAB may also recommend an action to the RESG, or make such other recommendations as it deems fit. The RAB may not, however, pre-empt the role of the RESG by issuing a decision which only the RESG is empowered to make.

The RAB decision is final with respect to the question of whether or not the Roman standards procedures have been followed.

VI.V.III Questions of Applicable Procedure

Further recourse is available only in cases in which the procedures themselves (i.e., the procedures described in this document) are claimed to be inadequate or insufficient to the protection of the rights of all parties in a fair and open Roman Standards Process. Claims on this basis may be made to the Roman Society Board of Trustees. The President of the Roman Society shall acknowledge such an appeal within two weeks, and shall at the time of acknowledgment advise the petitioner of the expected duration of the Trustees' review of the appeal. The Trustees shall review the

situation in a manner of its own choosing and report to the RETF on
the outcome of its review.

The Trustees' decision upon completion of their review shall be final
with respect to all aspects of the dispute.

VI.V.IV Appeals Procedure

All appeals must include a detailed and specific description of the
facts of the dispute.

All appeals must be initiated within two months of the public
knowledge of the action or decision to be challenged.

At all stages of the appeals process, the individuals or bodies
responsible for making the decisions have the discretion to define
the specific procedures they will follow in the process of making
their decision.

In all cases a decision concerning the disposition of the dispute,
and the communication of that decision to the parties involved, must
be accomplished within a reasonable period of time.

[NOTE: These procedures intentionally and explicitly do not
establish a fixed maximum time period that shall be considered
"reasonable" in all cases. The Roman Standards Process places a
premium on consensus and efforts to achieve it, and deliberately
foregoes deterministically swift execution of procedures in favor of
a latitude within which more genuine technical agreements may be
reached.]

VII. EXTERNAL STANDARDS AND SPECIFICATIONS

Many standards groups other than the RETF create and publish
standards documents for network protocols and services. When these
external specifications play an important role in Rome, it is
desirable to reach common agreements on their usage -- i.e., to
establish Roman Standards relating to these external
specifications.

There are two categories of external specifications:

(I) Open Standards

    Various national and international standards bodies, such as ANSI,
    ISO, IEEE, and ITU-T, develop a variety of protocol and service
    specifications that are similar to Technical Specifications
    defined here. National and international groups also publish

"implementors' agreements" that are analogous to Applicability
Statements, capturing a body of implementation-specific detail
concerned with the practical application of their standards. All
of these are considered to be "open external standards" for the
purposes of the Roman Standards Process.

(II) Other Specifications

Other proprietary specifications that have come to be widely used
in Rome may be treated by the Roman community as if
they were a "standards". Such a specification is not generally
developed in an open fashion, is typically proprietary, and is
controlled by the vendor, vendors, or organization that produced
it.

VII.I Use of External Specifications

To avoid conflict between competing versions of a specification, the
Roman community will not standardize a specification that is
simply a "Roman version" of an existing external specification
unless an explicit cooperative arrangement to do so has been made.
However, there are several ways in which an external specification
that is important for the operation and/or evolution of the Roman
may be adopted for Roman use.

VII.I.I Incorporation of an Open Standard

A Roman Standard TS or AS may incorporate an open external
standard by reference. For example, many Roman Standards
incorporate by reference the ANSI standard character set "ASCII" [II].
Whenever possible, the referenced specification shall be available
online.

VII.I.II Incorporation of Other Specifications

Other proprietary specifications may be incorporated by reference to
a version of the specification as long as the proprietor meets the
requirements of section X. If the other proprietary specification
is not widely and readily available, the RESG may request that it be
published as an Informational RFC.

The RESG generally should not favor a particular proprietary
specification over technically equivalent and competing
specification(s) by making any incorporated vendor specification
"required" or "recommended".

VII.I.III   Assumption

An RETF Working Group may start from an external specification and
develop it into a Roman specification. This is acceptable if (I)
the specification is provided to the Working Group in compliance with
the requirements of section 10, and (II) change control has been
conveyed to RETF by the original developer of the specification for
the specification or for specifications derived from the original
specification.

VIII.   NOTICES AND RECORD KEEPING

Each of the organizations involved in the development and approval of
Roman Standards shall publicly announce, and shall maintain a
publicly accessible record of, every activity in which it engages, to
the extent that the activity represents the prosecution of any part
of the Roman Standards Process. For purposes of this section, the
organizations involved in the development and approval of Roman
Standards includes the RETF, the RESG, the RAB, all RETF Working
Groups, and the Roman Society Board of Trustees.

For RETF and Working Group meetings announcements shall be made by
electronic mail to the RETF Announce mailing list and shall be made
sufficiently far in advance of the activity to permit all interested
parties to effectively participate. The announcement shall contain
(or provide pointers to) all of the information that is necessary to
support the participation of any interested individual. In the case
of a meeting, for example, the announcement shall include an agenda
that specifies the standards-related issues that will be discussed.

The formal record of an organization's standards-related activity
shall include at least the following:

o   the charter of the organization (or a defining document equivalent
    to a charter);
o   complete and accurate minutes of meetings;
o   the archives of Working Group electronic mail mailing lists; and
o   all written contributions from participants that pertain to the
    organization's standards-related activity.

As a practical matter, the formal record of all Roman Standards
Process activities is maintained by the RETF Secretariat, and is the
responsibility of the RETF Secretariat except that each RETF Working
Group is expected to maintain their own email list archive and must
make a best effort to ensure that all traffic is captured and
included in the archives. Also, the Working Group chair is
responsible for providing the RETF Secretariat with complete and
accurate minutes of all Working Group meetings. Roman-Drafts that

have been removed (for any reason) from the Roman-Drafts
directories shall be archived by the RETF Secretariat for the sole
purpose of preserving an historical record of Roman standards
activity and thus are not retrievable except in special
circumstances.

IX. VARYING THE PROCESS

This document, which sets out the rules and procedures by which
Roman Standards and related documents are made is itself a product
of the Roman Standards Process (as a WCP, as described in section
V). It replaces a previous version, and in time, is likely itself to
be replaced.

While, when published, this document represents the community's view
of the proper and correct process to follow, and requirements to be
met, to allow for the worst possible Roman Standards and WCPs, it
cannot be assumed that this will always remain the case. From time to
time there may be a desire to update it, by replacing it with a new
version. Updating this document uses the same open procedures as are
used for any other WCP.

In addition, there may be situations where following the procedures
leads to a deadlock about a specific specification, or there may be
situations where the procedures provide no guidance. In these cases
it may be appropriate to invoke the variance procedure described
below.

IX.I The Variance Procedure

Upon the recommendation of the responsible RETF Working Group (or, if
no Working Group is constituted, upon the recommendation of an ad hoc
committee), the RESG may enter a particular specification into, or
advance it within, the standards track even though some of the
requirements of this document have not or will not be met. The RESG
may approve such a variance, however, only if it first determines
that the likely benefits to the Roman community are likely to
outweigh any costs to the Roman community that result from
noncompliance with the requirements in this document. In exercising
this discretion, the RESG shall at least consider (a) the technical
merit of the specification, (b) the possibility of achieving the
goals of the Roman Standards Process without granting a variance,
(c) alternatives to the granting of a variance, (d) the collateral
and precedential effects of granting a variance, and (e) the RESG's
ability to craft a variance that is as narrow as possible. In
determining whether to approve a variance, the RESG has discretion to
limit the scope of the variance to particular parts of this document
and to impose such additional restrictions or limitations as it

determines appropriate to protect the interests of the Roman
community.

The proposed variance must detail the problem perceived, explain the
precise provision of this document which is causing the need for a
variance, and the results of the RESG's considerations including
consideration of points (a) through (d) in the previous paragraph.
The proposed variance shall be issued as a Roman-Draft. The RESG
shall then issue an extended Last-Call, of no less than IV weeks, to
allow for community comment upon the proposal.

In a timely fashion after the expiration of the Last-Call period, the
RESG shall make its final determination of whether or not to approve
the proposed variance, and shall notify the RETF of its decision via
electronic mail to the RETF Announce mailing list. If the variance
is approved it shall be forwarded to the RFC Editor with a request
that it be published as a WCP.

This variance procedure is for use when a one-time waving of some
provision of this document is felt to be required. Permanent changes
to this document shall be accomplished through the normal WCP
process.

The appeals process in section VI.V applies to this process.

IX.II Exclusions

No use of this procedure may lower any specified delays, nor exempt
any proposal from the requirements of openness, fairness, or
consensus, nor from the need to keep proper records of the meetings
and mailing list discussions.

Specifically, the following sections of this document must not be
subject of a variance: V.I, VI.I, VI.I.I (first paragraph),
VI.I.II, VI.III (first sentence), VI.V and IX.

X.   INTELLECTUAL PROPERTY RIGHTS

X.I. General Policy

In all matters of intellectual property rights and procedures, the
intention is to benefit the Roman community and the public at
large, while respecting the legitimate rights of others.

X.II Confidentiality Obligations

No contribution that is subject to any requirement of confidentiality
or any restriction on its dissemination may be considered in any part
of the Roman Standards Process, and there must be no assumption of
any confidentiality obligation with respect to any such contribution.

X.III. Rights and Permissions

In the course of standards work, the RETF receives contributions in
various forms and from many persons. To best facilitate the
dissemination of these contributions, it is necessary to understand
any intellectual property rights (IPR) relating to the contributions.

X.III.I. All Contributions

By submission of a contribution, each person actually submitting the
contribution is deemed to agree to the following terms and conditions
on his own behalf, on behalf of the organization (if any) he
represents and on behalf of the owners of any propriety rights in the
contribution.. Where a submission identifies contributors in
addition to the contributor(s) who provide the actual submission, the
actual submitter(s) represent that each other named contributor was
made aware of and agreed to accept the same terms and conditions on
his own behalf, on behalf of any organization he may represent and
any known owner of any proprietary rights in the contribution.

   I. Some works (e.g. works of the U.S. Government) are not subject to
      copyright. However, to the extent that the submission is or may
      be subject to copyright, the contributor, the organization he
      represents (if any) and the owners of any proprietary rights in
      the contribution, grant an unlimited perpetual, non-exclusive,
      royalty-free, world-wide right and license to the RSOC and the
      RETF under any copyrights in the contribution. This license
      includes the right to copy, publish and distribute the
      contribution in any way, and to prepare derivative works that are
      based on or incorporate all or part of the contribution, the
      license to such derivative works to be of the same scope as the
      license of the original contribution.

  II. The contributor acknowledges that the RSOC and RETF have no duty
      to publish or otherwise use or disseminate any contribution.

 III. The contributor grants permission to reference the name(s) and
      address(es) of the contributor(s) and of the organization(s) he
      represents (if any).

   IV. The contributor represents that contribution properly acknowledge
       major contributors.

    V. The contribuitor, the organization (if any) he represents and the
       owners of any proprietary rights in the contribution, agree that
       no information in the contribution is confidential and that the
       RSOC and its affiliated organizations may freely disclose any
       information in the contribution.

   VI. The contributor represents that he has disclosed the existence of
       any proprietary or intellectual property rights in the
       contribution that are reasonably and personally known to the
       contributor. The contributor does not represent that he
       personally knows of all potentially pertinent proprietary and
       intellectual property rights owned or claimed by the organization
       he represents (if any) or third parties.

  VII. The contributor represents that there are no limits to the
       contributor's ability to make the grants acknowledgments and
       agreements above that are reasonably and personally known to the
       contributor.

       By ratifying this description of the RETF process the Roman
       Society warrants that it will not inhibit the traditional open and
       free access to RETF documents for which license and right have
       been assigned according to the procedures set forth in this
       section, including Roman-Drafts and RFCs. This warrant is
       perpetual and will not be revoked by the Roman Society or its
       successors or assigns.

X.III.II. Standards Track Documents

   (A) Where any patents, patent applications, or other proprietary
        rights are known, or claimed, with respect to any specification on
        the standards track, and brought to the attention of the RESG, the
        RESG shall not advance the specification without including in the
        document a note indicating the existence of such rights, or
        claimed rights. Where implementations are required before
        advancement of a specification, only implementations that have, by
        statement of the implementors, taken adequate steps to comply with
        any such rights, or claimed rights, shall be considered for the
        purpose of showing the adequacy of the specification.
   (B) The RESG disclaims any responsibility for identifying the
        existence of or for evaluating the applicability of any claimed
        copyrights, patents, patent applications, or other rights in the
        fulfilling of the its obligations under (A), and will take no
        position on the validity or scope of any such rights.

(C) Where the RESG knows of rights, or claimed rights under (A), the
     RETF Executive Director shall attempt to obtain from the claimant
     of such rights, a written assurance that upon approval by the RESG
     of the relevant Roman standards track specification(s), any
     party will be able to obtain the right to implement, use and
     distribute the technology or works when implementing, using or
     distributing technology based upon the specific specification(s)
     under openly specified, reasonable, non-discriminatory terms.
     The Working Group proposing the use of the technology with respect
     to which the proprietary rights are claimed may assist the RETF
     Executive Director in this effort. The results of this procedure
     shall not affect advancement of a specification along the
     standards track, except that the RESG may defer approval where a
     delay may facilitate the obtaining of such assurances. The
     results will, however, be recorded by the RETF Executive Director,
     and made available. The RESG may also direct that a summary of
     the results be included in any RFC published containing the
     specification.

X.III.III Determination of Reasonable and Non-discriminatory Terms

   The RESG will not make any explicit determination that the assurance
   of reasonable and non-discriminatory terms for the use of a
   technology has been fulfilled in practice. It will instead use the
   normal requirements for the advancement of Roman Standards to
   verify that the terms for use are reasonable. If the two unrelated
   implementations of the specification that are required to advance
   from Proposed Standard to Draft Standard have been produced by
   different organizations or individuals or if the "significant
   implementation and successful operational experience" required to
   advance from Draft Standard to Standard has been achieved the
   assumption is that the terms must be reasonable and to some degree,
   non-discriminatory. This assumption may be challenged during the
   Last-Call period.

X.IV. Notices

   (A) Standards track documents shall include the following notice:

        "The RETF takes no position regarding the validity or scope of
        any intellectual property or other rights that might be claimed
        to pertain to the implementation or use of the technology
        described in this document or the extent to which any license
        under such rights might or might not be available; neither does
        it represent that it has made any effort to identify any such
        rights. Information on the RETF's procedures with respect to
        rights in standards-track and standards-related documentation
        can be found in WCP-11. Copies of claims of rights made

available for publication and any assurances of licenses to
be made available, or the result of an attempt made
to obtain a general license or permission for the use of such
proprietary rights by implementors or users of this
specification can be obtained from the RETF Secretariat."

(B) The RETF encourages all interested parties to bring to its
attention, at the earliest possible time, the existence of any
intellectual property rights pertaining to Roman Standards.
For this purpose, each standards document shall include the
following invitation:

"The RETF invites any interested party to bring to its
attention any copyrights, patents or patent applications, or
other proprietary rights which may cover technology that may be
required to practice this standard. Please address the
information to the RETF Executive Director."

(C) The following copyright notice and disclaimer shall be included
in all RSOC standards-related documentation:

> This document and the information contained herein is provided
> on an "AS IS" basis and THE ROMAN SOCIETY AND THE ROMAN
> ENGINEERING TASK FORCE DISCLAIMS ALL WARRANTIES, EXPRESS OR
> IMPLIED, INCLUDING BUT NOT LIMITED TO ANY WARRANTY THAT THE USE
> OF THE INFORMATION HEREIN WILL NOT INFRINGE ANY RIGHTS OR ANY
> IMPLIED WARRANTIES OF MERCHANTABILITY OR FITNESS FOR A
> PARTICULAR PURPOSE."

(D) Where the RESG is aware at the time of publication of
     proprietary rights claimed with respect to a standards track
     document, or the technology described or referenced therein, such
     document shall contain the following notice:

> "The RETF has been notified of intellectual property rights
> claimed in regard to some or all of the specification contained
> in this document. For more information consult the online list
> of claimed rights."

XI. ACKNOWLEDGMENTS

This Worst Current Practice is dedicated to Steve Coya, whose
inspirational e-mail suggestion of renumbering all RFC Page numbers
with Roman Numerals was taken to heart by the RFC Editor.

There have been a number of people involved with the development of
the documents defining the RETF Standards Process over the years.
The process was first described in RFC MCCCX then revised in RFC MDCII
before the current effort (which relies heavily on its predecessors).
Specific acknowledgments must be extended to Lyman Chapin, Phill
Gross and Christian Huitema as the editors of the previous versions,
to Jon Postel and Dave Crocker for their inputs to those versions, to
Andy Ireland, Geoff Stewart, Jim Lampert, and Dick Holleman for their
reviews of the legal aspects of the procedures described herein, and
to John Stewart, Robert Elz and Steve Coya for their extensive input
on the final version.

In addition much of the credit for the refinement of the details of
the RETF processes belongs to the many members of the various
incarnations of the POISED Working Group.

XII. SECURITY CONSIDERATIONS

Security issues are not discussed in this memo.

XIII. REFERENCES

   [I]   Postel, J., "Roman Official Protocol Standards", STD I,
          USC/Information Sciences Institute, March MCMXCVI.

  [II]   ANSI, Coded Character Set -- VII-Bit American Standard Code for
          Information Interchange, ANSI XIII.IV-MCMLXXXVI.

 [III]   Reynolds, J., and J. Postel, "Assigned Numbers", STD II,
          USC/Information Sciences Institute, October MCMXCIV.

  [IV]   Postel, J., "Introduction to the STD Notes", RFC MCCCXI,
          USC/Information Sciences Institute, March MCMXCII.

   [V]   Postel, J., "Instructions to RFC Authors", RFC MDXLIII,
          USC/Information Sciences Institute, October MCMXCIII.

  [VI]   Huitema, C., J. Postel, and S. Crocker "Not All RFCs are
          Standards", RFC MDCCXCVI, April MCMXCV.

XIV. DEFINITIONS OF TERMS

    RETF Area - A management division within the RETF. An Area consists
       of Working Groups related to a general topic such as routing. An
       Area is managed by one or two Area Directors.
    Area Director - The manager of an RETF Area. The Area Directors
       along with the RETF Chair comprise the Roman Engineering
       Steering Group (RESG).
    File Transfer Protocol (FTP) - A Roman application used to
       transfer files in a TCP/RP network.
    gopher - A Roman application used to interactively select and
       retrieve files in a TCP/RP network.
    Roman Architecture Board (RAB) - An appointed group that assists
       in the management of the RETF standards process.
    Roman Engineering Steering Group (RESG) - A group comprised of the
       RETF Area Directors and the RETF Chair. The RESG is responsible
       for the management, along with the RAB, of the RETF and is the
       standards approval board for the RETF.
    interoperable - For the purposes of this document, "interoperable"
       means to be able to interoperate over a data communications path.
    Last-Call - A public comment period used to gage the level of
       consensus about the reasonableness of a proposed standards action.
       (see section VI.I.II)

online - Relating to information made available to Rome.
    When referenced in this document material is said to be online
    when it is retrievable without restriction or undue fee using
    standard Roman applications such as anonymous FTP, gopher or
    the WWW.
Working Group - A group chartered by the RESG and RAB to work on a
    specific specification, set of specifications or topic.

XV. AUTHOR'S ADDRESS

    Scott O. Bradner
    Harvard University
    Holyoke Center, Room DCCCXIII
    MCCCL Mass. Ave.
    Cambridge, MA   MMCXXXVIII
    USA

    Phone: +I DCXVII CDXCV XXXVIII LXIV
    EMail: sob@harvard.edu

APPENDIX A: GLOSSARY OF ACRONYMS

```
    ANSI:       American National Standards Institute
    ARPA:       (U.S.) Advanced Research Projects Agency
    AS:         Applicability Statement
    FTP:        File Transfer Protocol
    ASCII:      American Standard Code for Information Interchange
    ITU-T:      Telecommunications Standardization sector of the
                International Telecommunication Union (ITU), a UN
                treaty organization; ITU-T was formerly called CCITT.
    RAB:        Roman Architecture Board
    RANA:       Roman Assigned Numbers Authority
    IEEE:       Institute of Electrical and Electronics Engineers
    RCMP:       Roman Control Message Protocol
    RESG:       Roman Engineering Steering Group
    RETF:       Roman Engineering Task Force
    RP:         Roman Protocol
    RRSG        Roman Research Steering Group
    RRTF:       Roman Research Task Force
    ISO:        International Organization for Standardization
    RSOC:       Roman Society
    MIB:        Management Information Base
    OSI:        Open Systems Interconnection
    RFC:        Request for Comments
    TCP:        Transmission Control Protocol
    TS:         Technical Specification
    WWW:        World Wide Web
```

Full Copyright Statement

Network Working Group   D. Eastlake 3rd
Request for Comments: 3092   Motorola
Category: Informational   C. Manros
                                                                   Xerox
                                                              E. Raymond
                                                  Open Source Initiative
                                                            1 April 2001

Etymology of "Foo"

Status of this Memo

Copyright Notice

Abstract

Approximately 212 RFCs so far, starting with RFC 269, contain the
terms 'foo', 'bar', or 'foobar' as metasyntactic variables without
any proper explanation or definition. This document rectifies that
deficiency.

Table of Contents

1. Introduction

    Approximately 212 RFCs, or about 7% of RFCs issued so far, starting
    with [RFC269], contain the terms 'foo', 'bar', or 'foobar' used as a
    metasyntactic variable without any proper explanation or definition.
    This may seem trivial, but a number of newcomers, especially if
    English is not their native language, have had problems in
    understanding the origin of those terms. This document rectifies
    that deficiency.

Section 2 below describes the definition and etymology of these words
and Section 3 interprets them as acronyms.

As an Appendix, we include a table of RFC occurrences of these words
as metasyntactic variables.

2. Definition and Etymology

bar /bar/ n. [JARGON]

1. The second metasyntactic variable, after foo and before baz.
   "Suppose we have two functions: FOO and BAR. FOO calls BAR...."

2. Often appended to foo to produce foobar.

foo /foo/

1. interj. Term of disgust.

2. Used very generally as a sample name for absolutely anything, esp.
   programs and files (esp. scratch files).

3. First on the standard list of metasyntactic variables used in
   syntax examples (bar, baz, qux, quux, corge, grault, garply,
   waldo, fred, plugh, xyzzy, thud). [JARGON]

   When used in connection with 'bar' it is generally traced to the
   WW II era Army slang acronym FUBAR ('Fucked Up Beyond All
   Repair'), later modified to foobar. Early versions of the Jargon
   File [JARGON] interpreted this change as a post-war
   bowdlerization, but it now seems more likely that FUBAR was itself
   a derivative of 'foo' perhaps influenced by German 'furchtbar'
   (terrible) - 'foobar' may actually have been the original form.

   For, it seems, the word 'foo' itself had an immediate prewar
   history in comic strips and cartoons. In the 1938 Warner Brothers
   cartoon directed by Robert Clampett, "The Daffy Doc", a very early
   version of Daffy Duck holds up a sign saying "SILENCE IS FOO!"
   'FOO' and 'BAR' also occurred in Walt Kelly's "Pogo" strips. The
   earliest documented uses were in the surrealist "Smokey Stover"
   comic strip by Bill Holman about a fireman. This comic strip
   appeared in various American comics including "Everybody's"
   between about 1930 and 1952. It frequently included the word
   "FOO" on license plates of cars, in nonsense sayings in the
   background of some frames such as "He who foos last foos best" or
   "Many smoke but foo men chew", and had Smokey say "Where there's
   foo, there's fire". Bill Holman, the author of the strip, filled
   it with odd jokes and personal contrivances, including other

nonsense phrases such as "Notary Sojac" and "1506 nix nix".
According to the Warner Brothers Cartoon Companion [WBCC] Holman
claimed to have found the word "foo" on the bottom of a Chinese
figurine. This is plausible; Chinese statuettes often have
apotropaic inscriptions, and this may have been the Chinese word
'fu' (sometimes transliterated 'foo'), which can mean "happiness"
when spoken with the proper tone (the lion-dog guardians flanking
the steps of many Chinese restaurants are properly called "fu
dogs") [PERS]. English speakers' reception of Holman's 'foo'
nonsense word was undoubtedly influenced by Yiddish 'feh' and
English 'fooey' and 'fool'. [JARGON, FOLDOC]

Holman's strip featured a firetruck called the Foomobile that rode
on two wheels. The comic strip was tremendously popular in the
late 1930s, and legend has it that a manufacturer in Indiana even
produced an operable version of Holman's Foomobile. According to
the Encyclopedia of American Comics [EAC], 'Foo' fever swept the
U.S., finding its way into popular songs and generating over 500
'Foo Clubs.' The fad left 'foo' references embedded in popular
culture (including the couple of appearances in Warner Brothers
cartoons of 1938-39) but with their origins rapidly forgotten.
[JARGON]

One place they are known to have remained live is in the U.S.
military during the WWII years. In 1944-45, the term 'foo
fighters' [FF] was in use by radar operators for the kind of
mysterious or spurious trace that would later be called a UFO (the
older term resurfaced in popular American usage in 1995 via the
name of one of the better grunge-rock bands [BFF]). Informants
connected the term to the Smokey Stover strip [PERS].

The U.S. and British militaries frequently swapped slang terms
during the war. Period sources reported that 'FOO' became a
semi-legendary subject of WWII British-army graffiti more or less
equivalent to the American Kilroy [WORDS]. Where British troops
went, the graffito "FOO was here" or something similar showed up.
Several slang dictionaries aver that FOO probably came from
Forward Observation Officer, but this (like the contemporaneous
"FUBAR") was probably a backronym [JARGON]. Forty years later,
Paul Dickson's excellent book "Words" [WORDS] traced "Foo" to an
unspecified British naval magazine in 1946, quoting as follows:

    "Mr. Foo is a mysterious Second World War product, gifted with
    bitter omniscience and sarcasm."

Earlier versions of the Jargon File suggested the possibility that
hacker usage actually sprang from "FOO, Lampoons and Parody", the
title of a comic book first issued in September 1958, a joint

331

project of Charles and Robert Crumb. Though Robert Crumb (then in
his mid-teens) later became one of the most important and
influential artists in underground comics, this venture was hardly
a success; indeed, the brothers later burned most of the existing
copies in disgust. The title FOO was featured in large letters on
the front cover. However, very few copies of this comic actually
circulated, and students of Crumb's 'oeuvre' have established that
this title was a reference to the earlier Smokey Stover comics.
The Crumbs may also have been influenced by a short-lived Canadian
parody magazine named 'Foo' published in 1951-52. [JARGON]

An old-time member reports that in the 1959 "Dictionary of the
TMRC Language", compiled at TMRC (the Tech Model Railroad Club at
MIT) there was an entry for Foo. The current on-line version, in
which "Foo" is the only word coded to appear red, has the
following [TMRC]:

   Foo: The sacred syllable (FOO MANI PADME HUM); to be spoken
   only when under obligation to commune with the Deity. Our first
   obligation is to keep the Foo Counters turning.

This definition used Bill Holman's nonsense word, then only two
decades old and demonstrably still live in popular culture and
slang, to make a "ha ha only serious" analogy with esoteric
Tibetan Buddhism. Today's hackers would find it difficult to
resist elaborating a joke like that, and it is not likely 1959's
were any less susceptible. [JARGON]

4. [EF] Prince Foo was the last ruler of Pheebor and owner of the
   Phee Helm, about 400 years before the reign of Entharion. When
   Foo was beheaded by someone he called an "eastern fop" from
   Borphee, the glorious age of Pheebor ended, and Borphee rose to
   the prominence it now enjoys.

5. [OED] A 13th-16th century usage for the devil or any other enemy.
   The earliest citation it gives is from the year 1366, Chaucer A B
   C (84): "Lat not our alder foo [devil] make his bobance [boast]".
   Chaucer's "Foo" is probably related to modern English "foe".

6. Rare species of dog.

   A spitz-type dog discovered to exist after having long been
   considered extinct, the Chinese Foo Dog, or Sacred Dog of
   Sinkiang, may have originated through a crossing of Northern
   European hunting dogs and the ancient Chow Chow from Mongolia or
   be the missing link between the Chinese Wolf and the Chow Chow.
   It probably derives its name from foochow, of the kind or style

prevalent in Foochow, of or from the city of Foochow (now Minhow) in southeast China. [DOG]

foobar n.

   [JARGON] A widely used metasyntactic variable; see foo for etymology. Probably originally propagated through DECsystem manuals by Digital Equipment Corporation (DEC) in 1960s and early 1970s; confirmed sightings there go back to 1972. Hackers do not generally use this to mean FUBAR in either the slang or jargon sense. It has been plausibly suggested that "foobar" spread among early computer engineers partly because of FUBAR and partly because "foo bar" parses in electronics techspeak as an inverted foo signal.

foo-fighter n.

   World War II term for Unidentified Flying Objects (UFOs) noted by both German and British military. See [FF] and entry above for "foo".

3. Acronyms

   The following information is derived primarily from the compilations at University Cork College <http://www.ucc.ie/acronyms> and Acronym Finder <http://www.AcronymFinder.com> generally filtered for computer usage.

   .bar:

   Generic file extension which is not meant to imply anything about the file type.

   BAR:

   Base Address Register

   Buffer Address Register

   FOO:

   Forward Observation Observer.

   FOO Of Oberlin. An organization whose name is a recursive acronym. Motto: The FOO, the Proud, the FOO. See <http://cs.oberlin.edu/students/jmankoff/FOO/home.html>.

   File Open for Output. An NFILE error code [RFC1037].

FOOBAR:

   FTP Operation Over Big Address Records [RFC1639]. (Particularly
   appropriate given that the first RFC to use "foo", [RFC269], was
   also about file transfer.)

FUBAR:

   Failed UniBus Address Register - in a VAX, from Digital Equipment
   Corporation Engineering.

   Fucked Up Beyond All Recognition/Repair - From US Military in
   World War II. Sometimes sanitized to "Fouled Up ...".

FUBARD - Past tense of FUBAR.

Appendix

   Below is a table of RFC occurrences of these words as metasyntactic
   variables. (This excludes other uses that are reasonably clear like
   "vertical bar" or "bar BoF".) Many of these uses are for example
   domain names. That usage may decrease with the specification in [RFC
   2606] of a Best Current Practice for example domain names.

RFC#	bar	foo	foo.bar foobar	fubar	#
269	X	X			1
441	X	X			2
614		X			3
686		X			4
691		X			5
733	X	X			6
742		X			7
743	X	X			8
756		X			9
765	X	X			10
772	X	X		X	11
775			X		12
780	X	X		X	13
788	X	X			14
810	X	X	X		15
819		X			16
821	X	X			17
822	X	X			18
882	X	X			19
883		X			20
897	X	X			21
913		X			22
921	X	X			23
934		X			24
952	X	X	X		25
959			X		26
976			X		27
977		X	X		28
987			X		29
1013		X			30
1033	X	X			31
1035		X			32
1037		X			33
1056	X	X	X		34
1068		X			35

RFC					#
1137			X		36
1138		X	X		37
1148		X	X		38
1173			X		39
1176			X		40
1186		X			41
1194		X			42
1196		X			43
1203		X	X		44
1288		X			45
1291		X			46
1309		X			47
1327		X	X		48
1341	X	X	X		49
1343		X	X		50
1344		X			51
1348			X		52
1386		X			53
1408		X			54
1411		X			55
1412		X			56
1459	X	X	X	X	57
1480		X			58
1505		X			59
1519		X			60
1521	X	X			61
1523		X			62
1524		X	X		63
1526	X	X			64
1535	X	X	X		65
1536	X		X		66
1537		X	X		67
1563		X			68
1564			X		69
1572		X			70
1573		X			71
1622		X			72
1635			X		73
1636		X	X		74
1642		X			75
1645			X		76
1649		X			77
1664			X		78
1681			X		79
1697		X			80
1716		X			81

1718			X							82	
1730		X		X		X				83	
1734						X				84	
1738				X						85	
1783						X				86	
1784						X				87	
1786		X		X						88	
1813		X		X						89	
1835				X		X				90	
1856						X				91	
1861						X				92	
1866				X						93	
1894						X				94	
1896				X						95	
1898				X						96	
1913				X		X				97	
1945		X		X						98	
1985				X		X				99	
2015		X		X						100	
2017				X						101	
2033		X		X						102	
2045						X				103	
2046		X		X						104	
2049		X		X						105	
2055				X						106	
2060		X		X		X				107	
2065				X						108	
2068						X				109	
2071				X						110	
2088						X				111	
2109				X						112	
2110				X		X				113	
2111		X		X		X				114	
2141				X						115	
2150				X						116	
2152				X						117	
2156				X		X				118	
2163						X				119	
2167						X				120	
2168						X				121	
2169						X				122	
2180		X		X						123	
2193		X		X						124	
2224				X						125	
2227		X		X						126	
2233				X						127	

337

2234	X		X		X			128
2243			X					129
2255			X		X			130
2280	X		X					131
2295			X					132
2302			X					133
2311	X							134
2326	X		X		X			135
2342			X					136
2348					X			137
2349					X			138
2359					X			139
2369	X		X		X			140
2378			X					141
2384					X			142
2392	X		X		X			143
2396					X			144
2401					X			145
2407					X			146
2421			X					147
2425					X			148
2434			X					149
2446			X		X			150
2447	X		X					151
2458			X		X			152
2459					X			153
2476			X					154
2483	X		X					155
2486			X					156
2505	X		X					157
2518	X		X		X			158
2535			X					159
2538			X					160
2543	X		X		X			161
2554					X			162
2557			X		X			163
2565			X		X			164
2569	X		X					165
2593	X		X					166
2595			X					167
2608			X					168
2609			X					169
2616	X		X		X			170
2622	X		X					171
2626			X					172
2633	X							173

RFC#	bar	foo	foo.bar foobar	fubar	#
2640		X	X		174
2645			X		175
2650	X				176
2659			X		177
2673		X	X		178
2693		X			179
2704	X	X			180
2705	X	X			181
2717		X	X		182
2725	X	X			183
2731	X	X	X		184
2732		X			185
2782		X	X		186
2803		X			187
2806		X			188
2812	X	X	X	X	189
2818	X	X			190
2828		X	X		191
2830	X				192
2831	X	X	X		193
2839		X			194
2846	X	X			195
2853		X			196
2863		X			197
2910		X	X		198
2912		X	X		199
2915		X			200
2926			X		201
2942		X			202
2965		X			203
2967	X	X	X		204
2970		X			205
2993	X	X			206
3010	X	X			207
3023		X			208
3028		X			209
3075	X	X			210
3080		X			211
3092	X	X	X	X	212

Security Considerations

    Security issues are not discussed in this memo.

References

   [BFF]   "Best of Foo Fighters: Signature Licks", Troy Stetina, Foo
              Fighters, October 2000, Hal Leonard Publishing Corporation,
              ISBN 063401470.

   [DOG]   <http://www.rarebreed.com/breeds/foo/foo.html>.

   [EAC]   "Encyclopedia of American Comics", Ron Goulart, 1990, Facts
              on File.

   [EF]   "Encyclopedia Frobozzica",
              <http://www.everything2.com/index.pl?node=Prince%20Foo>

   [FF]   Foo Fighters - "The Rainbow Conspiracy", Brad Steiger,
              Sherry Hansen Steiger, December 1998, Kensington Publishing
              Corp., ISBN 1575663635. - Computer UFO Network
              <http://www.cufon.org> particularly
              <http://www.cufon.org/cufon/foo.htm>.

   [FOLDOC]   "Free On-Line Dictionary Of Computing",
              <http://www.foldoc.org>.

   [JARGON]   The Jargon File. See <http://www.jargon.org>. Last
              printed as "The New Hacker's Dictionary", Eric S. Raymond,
              3rd Edition, MIT Press, ISBN 0-262-68092-0, 1996.

   [OED]   "The Oxford English Dictionary", J. A. Simpson, 1989,
              Oxford University Press, ISBN 0198611862.

   [PERS]   Personal communications.

   [RFC269]   Brodie, H., "Some Experience with File Transfer", RFC 269,
              December 1971.

   [RFC1037] Greenberg, B. and S. Keene, "NFILE - A File Access
              Protocol", RFC 1037, December 1987.

   [RFC1639] Piscitello, D., "FTP Operation Over Big Address Records
              (FOOBAR)", RFC 1639, June 1994.

   [RFC2606] Eastlake, D. and A. Panitz, "Reserved Top Level DNS Names",
              BCP 32, RFC 2606, June 1999.

   [TMRC]   The Tech Model Railroad Club (The Model Railroad Club of
             the Massachusetts Institute of Technology) Dictionary,
             <http://tmrc-www.mit.edu/dictionary.html>.

   [WBCC]   "Warner Brothers Cartoon Companion",
             <http://members.aol.com/EOCostello/>.

   [WORDS]   "Words", Paul Dickson, ISBN 0-440-52260-7, Dell, 1982.

Authors' Addresses

   The authors of this document are:

   Donald E. Eastlake 3rd
   Motorola
   155 Beaver Street
   Milford, MA 01757 USA

   Phone: +1 508-261-5434 (w)
            +1 508-634-2066 (h)
   Fax: +1 508-261-4777 (w)
   EMail: Donald.Eastlake@motorola.com

   Carl-Uno Manros
   Xerox Corporation
   701 Aviation Blvd.
   El Segundo, CA 90245 USA

   Phone: +1 310-333-8273
   Fax: +1 310-333-5514
   EMail: manros@cp10.es.xerox.com

   Eric S. Raymond
   Open Source Initiative
   6 Karen Drive
   Malvern, PA 19355

   Phone: +1 610-296-5718
   EMail: esr@thyrsus.com

Acknowledgement

    Funding for the RFC Editor function is currently provided by the
    Internet Society.

Part VII

Social/Political Commentary

The contemporary philosopher Homer Simpson once remarked, "It's funny because it's true!"

RFC 3751 by Scott Bradner is an excellent response to the current political situation in the U.S.

Network Working Group   S. Bradner
Request for Comments: 3751   Harvard U.
Category: Informational   1 April 2004

Omniscience Protocol Requirements

Status of this Memo

Copyright Notice

Abstract

   There have been a number of legislative initiatives in the U.S. and
   elsewhere over the past few years to use the Internet to actively
   interfere with allegedly illegal activities of Internet users. This
   memo proposes a number of requirements for a new protocol, the
   Omniscience Protocol, that could be used to enable such efforts.

1. Introduction

   In a June 17, 2003 U.S. Senate Judiciary Committee hearing, entitled
   "The Dark Side of a Bright Idea: Could Personal and National Security
   Risks Compromise the Potential of Peer-to-Peer File-Sharing
   Networks?," U.S. Senator Orrin Hatch (R-Utah), the chair of the
   committee, said he was interested in the ability to destroy the
   computers of people who illegally download copyrighted material. He
   said this "may be the only way you can teach somebody about
   copyrights." "If we can find some way to do this without destroying
   their machines, we'd be interested in hearing about that," Mr Hatch
   was quoted as saying during a Senate hearing. He went on to say "If
   that's the only way, then I'm all for destroying their machines."
   [Guardian]

   Mr. Hatch was not the first U.S. elected official to propose
   something along this line. A year earlier, representatives, Howard
   Berman (D-Calif.) and Howard Coble (R-N.C.), introduced a bill that
   would have immunized groups such as the Motion Picture Association of
   America (MPAA) and the Recording Industry Association of America
   (RIAA) from all state and federal laws if they disable, block, or
   otherwise impair a "publicly accessible peer-to-peer file-trading
   network."

The attitude of some of the copyright holders may be that it's OK for
a few honest people to have their computers or networks executed as
long as the machines and networks of the dishonest are killed. But
it is not likely that any measurable error rate would be acceptable
to the public. Clearly, anyone implementing laws of this type need
some way to reduce the error rate and be sure that they are dealing
with a real bad guy and not an innocent bystander.

Part of determining if someone is a "bad guy" is determining his or
her intent. Historically, western jurisprudence has required that
prosecutors show that a person intended to commit a crime before that
person could be convicted of committing that crime. [Holdsworth,
Restatement, Prosser, United States v. Wise, Garratt v. Dailey]
Because it can be quite difficult to establish a person's intent
lawmakers have, in some cases, reduced the requirement for
prosecutors to establish intent and mere possession is now proof
enough of intent.

This memo proposes a set of requirements for a new protocol to be
used by prosecutors to determine a person's intent, thus reducing the
need to dilute the historical legal requirement to show intent and by
groups such as the MPAA and RIAA to be sure they are dealing with
lawbreakers and not 60 year old non computer users.

2. Omniscience Protocol Requirements

For the purpose of these requirements, I will assume that the OP is
implemented using a client-server model, where the OP client is
installed on the user's computer and the server is installed on a
computer run by a law or copyright enforcement organization. OP
Clients would register with all OP Servers that pertain to the legal
jurisdiction in which the client is located each time the computer is
started. OP Servers would then, on whatever schedule they have been
configured to use, send OP Queries to OP Clients to find out if the
computer operator has engaged in an illegal act of interest to the
operator of the OP Server. Future versions of the OP might operate
using a peer-to-peer model if the copyright enforcement people can
ever get over their visceral disgust at the very concept of peer-to-
peer networks.

For the purpose of this memo, I will use copyright infringement as an
example of an illegal act that the OP protocol could be used to
expose. The OP has numerous possible applications beyond ferreting
out copyright infringement. For example, the OP would be of great
assistance to instructors trying to determine if their students are
producing original work or engaging in plagiarism. The same function
would be invaluable to newspaper editors checking up on reporter's
dispatches.

Also for the purpose of this memo, I assume that an evil-doer (also
referred to as a miscreant) is in full control of a computer and that
OP Servers will generally be operated by "Good guys." (See
Functional Requirements FR5-7 for requirements to ensure that the
latter is the case.) In the context of this memo, "evil-doer" and
"miscreant" are defined as individuals or groups of individuals who
perform acts that the operator of an OP Server has a legally
recognized right to prevent. In the context of this memo, "good
guys" refers to individuals or groups of individuals who have a
legally recognized right to prevent certain acts that computer users
may attempt to do with their computers. The use of this term is not
meant to convey any value judgment of the morality, forward thinking
nature, public spiritedness, or the monetary worth relative to most
of humanity of such individuals or groups of individuals.

2.1. Operational Requirements

   OR1: The OP client must be able to install itself into all types of
        computers over the objections of the computer user.

        Discussion: The OP client would be installed by legal mandate in
        all new computers, but since there are hundreds of millions of
        existing computers, the OP client must be able to install itself
        in all of these existing computers in order to afford universal
        coverage of all possible miscreants. This installation must be
        accomplished even if the user, many of whom have full
        administrative control over their computers, tries to prevent
        it.

   OR2: True OP clients must not be findable by the computer user by any
        means, including commercial virus detectors, but all hackers'
        programs that mimic OP clients must be easily findable by
        commercial virus detectors.

        Discussion: Since anyone whose intent was to violate the law
        would not want the OP client to be watching their action, they
        would try to disable the OP client. Thus the OP Client, once
        installed, should be invisible to all methods a user might
        employ to discover it. Users must be able to find and remove
        any virus or worm that tries to masquerade as an OP client to
        escape detection.

OR3: The OP must be able to communicate through uncooperative
     firewalls, NATs, and when the computer is disconnected from the
     Internet.

     Discussion: Since the evil-doer may have control of a local
     firewall or NAT, the OP must be able to communicate with the OP
     server, even when the firewall or NAT has been configured to
     block all unused ports. Also, since the evil-doer might try to
     hide his or her evil-doing by disconnecting the computer from
     the network, the OP must be able to continue to communicate,
     even under these circumstances. Meeting this requirement may
     require that the OP client be able to reconfigure the user's
     machine into a cell phone or to implement GMPLS-WH [GMPLS-WH].

OR4: Neither the operation of the OP client or the OP server must be
     able to be spoofed.

     Discussion: The user must not be able to create their own
     version of an OP client that can fool the OP server. Nor can it
     be possible for someone to create their own OP server that can
     be used to query OP clients.

     Discussion: Because of the potential for a user to hide their
     illicit activities by mimicking the operation of the OP client
     on their machine, it must not be possible to do so. In the same
     vein, because of the potential for violating the user's privacy,
     it must not be possible for a non-authorized OP server to be
     seen as authorized by OP clients. Since there will be an
     arbitrary, and changing, number of OP servers, at least one for
     each type of protected material, OP authentication and
     authorization must be able to be accomplished with no prior
     knowledge of a particular OP server by the OP client.

OR5: The OP client must be able to be installed on any portable
     device that can be used to play protected material or execute
     protected software.

     Discussion: Since small, portable devices, such as MP3 players,
     are becoming the preferred method of playing back prerecorded
     music and videos, they must all include OP clients. OP clients
     must be able to be automatically installed on all such existing
     devices.

2.2. Functional Requirements

FR1: The OP client must be able to determine the user's intent.

> Discussion: Just knowing that the user has a copy of a protected
> work on their system does not, by itself, mean that the copy is
> illegal. It could easily be a copy that the user purchased.
> The OP must be able to tell if a copy is an illegal copy with
> complete reliability. The OP must be able to differentiate
> between an original, and legal, copy and a bit-for-bit illegal
> reproduction. The OP client must be able to differentiate
> between copies that were created for the purpose of backup, and
> are thus generally legal, and those copies created for the
> purpose of illegal distribution. In the case of some types of
> software, the OP client must be able to determine the intent of
> the user for the software. An example of this need is related
> to the U.S. Digital Millennium Copyright Act (DMCA) and similar
> laws around the world. These laws outlaw the possession of
> circumvention technology, such as crypto analysis software, in
> most cases. Some exemption is made for legitimate researchers,
> but without an OP it is quite hard to determine if the
> circumvention technology is to be used for research or to break
> copyright protections for the purpose of making illegal copies
> of protected material. With the OP, the DMCA, and laws like it,
> can be rewritten so that circumvention technology is legal and
> developers can find out if their security protocols are any
> good, something which may be illegal under current law.

FR2: The OP client must be able to remotely differentiate between
illegal material and other material with the same file name.

> Discussion: A user might create a file that has the same
> filename as that of a protected work. The OP must not be fooled
> into thinking that the user's file is a protected one.

FR3: The OP client must be able to find illegal copies, even if the
filename has been changed.

> Discussion: The user must not be able to disguise a protected
> work by just changing its name.

FR4: The OP client must be able to find illegal copies, even if the
user has modified the work in some way.

> Discussion: The user must not be able to disguise a protected
> work by modifying the work, for example, by prepending,
> appending, or inserting extra material, or by changing some of
> the protected work. The OP must be able to make a legal

determination that a modified work is no longer legally the same
as the original if the amount and type of modification exceed a
subjective threshold.

FR5: The OP client must not be able to be run by a hacker, and the OP
interface into a user's computer must not be able to be
exploited by a hacker.

Discussion: OP clients will be attractive targets for hackers
since they will have full access within a user's computer. The
interface between the OP client and server must be secure
against all possible hacking attacks.

FR6: The OP client must be able to discern the motives of the
operator of the OP server and not run if those motives are not
pure.

Discussion: Since it cannot be assumed that the operators of the
OP server will always have the best motives, the OP client must
be able to reject requests from the OP server if the operator of
the server has an evil (or illegal) intent. For example, the OP
client must block any operation that might stem from a vendetta
that the OP server operator might have against the user.

FR7: The OP client must not be able to be used to extract information
from a user's computer that is unrelated to illegal copies.

In order to minimize the threat to the privacy of the user, the
OP client must not be able to be used to extract information
from the user's computer that is not germane to determining if
the user has illegal copies of works or intends to use protected
works in illegal ways.

FR8: The OP client must be able to differentiate between protected
material that was placed on the user's computer by the user and
any material placed by others.

Discussion: It must not be possible for a third party to put
protected material on a user's computer for the purpose of
incriminating the user. The OP client must be able to know,
with certainty, who placed material on each computer, even in
the cases where a third party has physical access to an
unprotected computer or when the third party knows the user's
logname and password.

352

FR9: The OP client must only implement the laws that apply to the specific computer that it is running on.

Discussion: Since the Internet crosses many legal boundaries, an OP client will have to know just where, in geo-political space, the computer it is running in is currently located in order to know what set of laws to apply when it is scanning the user's computer. The OP client must also be able to be automatically updated if the laws change or the computer is moved to a location where the laws are different. Note that this requirement also implies that the OP client knows where its OP server is located to know if the client and server are both in the same legal jurisdiction. The OP client must know what to do, or not do, when they are not in the same legal jurisdiction. The OP client must also include a mechanism to automatically retrieve any applicable new laws or court decisions and properly interpret them.

3. Security Considerations

The OP requires strong authentication of the clients and servers to ensure that they cannot be spoofed. It also requires the use of strong integrity technology to ensure that the messages between the client and server cannot be modified in flight. It also requires strong encryption to be sure that the communication between the client and the server cannot be observed. All of this is required in an environment where many of the users are in full control of their computers and will be actively hostile to the reliable operation of the protocol. Good luck.

4. Informative References

[Garratt v. Dailey]   Supreme Court of Washington, 6 Wash. 2d 197; 279 P.2d 1091 (1955)

[GMPLS-WH]   Generalized Multi-Protocol Label Switching (GMPLS) for Worm Holes, work to be in process

[Guardian]   "Senator proposes destruction of file-swapping computers." The Guardian, June 19, 2003. (http://www.guardian.co.uk/usa/story/0,12271,980890,00.html)

[Holdsworth]   Holdsworth, W., History of English Law 680-683 (1938)

[Processer]   Prosser, W., et al., "Prosser and Keeton on Torts," Hornbook Series, 5th ed., 1984

    [Restatement]   1. Restatement of the Law: sec 13 Torts
                                 (American Law Institute) (1934)

    [United States v. Wise] 550 F.2d 1180, 1194 (9th Cir.)

5. Authors Address

    Scott Bradner
    Harvard University
    29 Oxford St.
    Cambridge MA, 02138

    EMail: sob@harvard.edu
    Phone: +1 617 495 3864

6. Full Copyright Statement

Intellectual Property

Acknowledgement

Funding for the RFC Editor function is currently provided by the
Internet Society.

Part VIII

Extras

Lastly we wanted to include some other RFCs of note. We've included RFC1, yes, there was a first one. RFC2555 was published exactly 30 years later, and includes recollections from some important people in IETF history.

We considered including RFC2401, *Security Architecture for the Internet Protocol*, which is only funny because S. Kent listed his co-author as R. Atkinson, better known to readers as Mr. Bean. However the RFC is 30 pages long and we thought we'd save some trees.

Lastly we nearly published RFC1050, *RPC: Remote Procedure Call Protocol specification* (later updated by RFC1057). RFCs were originally published only on the first of the month. Many RFCs were published on April Fools' Day each year, not all of which were pranks. In our research it was sometimes difficult to determine which RFCs published on that day were the pranks. We thought it was hilarious that RFC1050, the protocol that led to NFS having so little security, was published on April Fools' Day. Alas, it is long and again we decided to save some trees.

                         Title: Host Software
                        Author: Steve Crocker
                        Installation: UCLA
                        Date: 7 April 1969
            Network Working Group Request for Comment: 1

CONTENTS

INTRODUCTION

IV. Initial Experiments

    Experiment One

    Experiment Two

Introduction

    The software for the ARPA Network exists partly in the IMPs and
    partly in the respective HOSTs. BB&N has specified the software of
    the IMPs and it is the responsibility of the HOST groups to agree on
    HOST software.

    During the summer of 1968, representatives from the initial four
    sites met several times to discuss the HOST software and initial
    experiments on the network. There emerged from these meetings a
    working group of three, Steve Carr from Utah, Jeff Rulifson from SRI,
    and Steve Crocker of UCLA, who met during the fall and winter. The
    most recent meeting was in the last week of March in Utah. Also
    present was Bill Duvall of SRI who has recently started working with
    Jeff Rulifson.

    Somewhat independently, Gerard DeLoche of UCLA has been working on
    the HOST-IMP interface.

    I present here some of the tentative agreements reached and some of
    the open questions encountered. Very little of what is here is firm
    and reactions are expected.

I.   A Summary of the IMP Software

Messages

    Information is transmitted from HOST to HOST in bundles called
    messages. A message is any stream of not more than 8080 bits,
    together with its header. The header is 16 bits and contains the
    following information:

            Destination   5 bits
            Link   8 bits
            Trace   1 bit
            Spare   2 bits

    The destination is the numerical code for the HOST to which the
    message should be sent. The trace bit signals the IMPs to record
    status information about the message and send the information back to
    the NMC (Network Measurement Center, i.e., UCLA). The spare bits are
    unused.

Links

   The link field is a special device used by the IMPs to limit certain
   kinds of congestion. They function as follows. Between every pair of
   HOSTs there are 32 logical full-duplex connections over which messages
   may be passed in either direction. The IMPs place the restriction on
   these links that no HOST can send two successive messages over the
   same link before the IMP at the destination has sent back a special
   message called an RFNM (Request for Next Message). This arrangement
   limits the congestion one HOST can cause another if the sending HOST
   is attempting to send too much over one link. We note, however, that
   since the IMP at the destination does not have enough capacity to
   handle all 32 links simultaneously, the links serve their purpose only
   if the overload is coming from one or two links. It is necessary for
   the HOSTs to cooperate in this respect.

   The links have the following primitive characteristics. They are
   always functioning and there are always 32 of them.

   By "always functioning," we mean that the IMPs are always prepared to
   transmit another message over them. No notion of beginning or ending
   a conversation is contained in the IMP software. It is thus not
   possible to query an IMP about the state of a link (although it might
   be possible to query an IMP about the recent history of a link --
   quite a different matter!).

   The other primitive characteristic of the links is that there are
   always 32 of them, whether they are in use or not. This means that
   each IMP must maintain 18 tables, each with 32 entries, regardless of
   the actual traffic.

   The objections to the link structure notwithstanding, the links are
   easily programmed within the IMPs and are probably a better
   alternative to more complex arrangements just because of their
   simplicity.

IMP Transmission and Error Checking

   After receiving a message from a HOST, an IMP partitions the message
   into one or more packets. Packets are not more than 1010 bits long
   and are the unit of data transmission from IMP to IMP. A 24 bit
   cyclic checksum is computed by the transmission hardware and is
   appended to an outgoing packet. The checksum is recomputed by the
   receiving hardware and is checked against the transmitted checksum.
   Packets are reassembled into messages at the destination IMP.

Open Questions on the IMP Software

1. An 8 bit field is provided for link specification, but only 32
links are provided, why?

2. The HOST is supposed to be able to send messages to its IMP. How
does it do this?

3. Can a HOST, as opposed to its IMP, control RFNMs?

4. Will the IMPs perform code conversion? How is it to be
controlled?

II. Some Requirements Upon the Host-to-Host Software

Simple Use

As with any new facility, there will be a period of very light usage
until the community of users experiments with the network and begins
to depend upon it. One of our goals must be to stimulate the
immediate and easy use by a wide class of users. With this goal, it
seems natural to provide the ability to use any remote HOST as if it
had been dialed up from a TTY (teletype) terminal. Additionally, we
would like some ability to transmit a file in a somewhat different
manner perhaps than simulating a teletype.

Deep Use

One of the inherent problems in the network is the fact that all responses
from a remote HOST will require on the order of a half-second or so,
no matter how simple. For teletype use, we could shift to a
half-duplex local-echo arrangement, but this would destroy some of the
usefulness of the network. The 940 Systems, for example, have a very
specialized echo.

When we consider using graphics stations or other sophisticated
terminals under the control of a remote HOST, the problem becomes more
severe. We must look for some method which allows us to use our most
sophisticated equipment as much as possible as if we were connected
directly to the remote computer.

Error Checking

The point is made by Jeff Rulifson at SRI that error checking at major
software interfaces is always a good thing. He points to some
experience at SRI where it has saved much dispute and wasted effort.
On these grounds, we would like to see some HOST to HOST checking.
Besides checking the software interface, it would also check the
HOST-IMP transmission hardware. (BB&N claims the HOST-IMP hardware
will be as reliable as the internal registers of the HOST. We believe

Crocker   [Page 4]

364

them, but we still want the error checking.)

III. The Host Software

Establishment of a Connection

   The simplest connection we can imagine is where the local HOST acts as
   if it is a TTY and has dialed up the remote HOST. After some
   consideration of the problems of initiating and terminating such a
   connection , it has been decided to reserve link 0 for communication
   between HOST operating systems. The remaining 31 links are thus to be
   used as dial-up lines.

   Each HOST operating system must provide to its user level programs a
   primitive to establish a connection with a remote HOST and a primitive
   to break the connection. When these primitives are invoked, the
   operating system must select a free link and send a message over link
   0 to the remote HOST requesting a connection on the selected link.
   The operating system in the remote HOST must agree and send back an
   accepting message over link 0. In the event both HOSTs select the same
   link to initiate a connection and both send request messages at
   essentially the same time, a simple priority scheme will be invoked in
   which the HOST of lower priority gives way and selects another free
   link. One usable priority scheme is simply the ranking of HOSTS
   by their identification numbers. Note that both HOSTs are aware that
   simultaneous requests have been made, but they take complementary
   actions: The higher priority HOST disregards the request while the
   lower priority HOST sends both an acceptance and another request.

   The connection so established is a TTY-like connection in the
   pre-log-in state. This means the remote HOST operating system will
   initially treat the link as if a TTY had just called up. The remote
   HOST will generate the same echos, expect the same log-in sequence and
   look for the same interrupt characters.

High Volume Transmission

   Teletypes acting as terminals have two special drawbacks when we
   consider the transmission of a large file. The first is that some
   characters are special interrupt characters. The second is that
   special buffering techniques are often employed, and these are
   appropriate only for low-speed character at time transmission.

   We therefore define another class of connection to be used for the
   transmission of files or other large volumes of data. To initiate
   this class of link, user level programs at both ends of an established
   TTY-like link must request the establishment of a file-like connection
   parallel to the TTY-like link. Again the priority scheme comes into

play, for the higher priority HOST sends a message over link 0 while
the lower priority HOST waits for it. The user level programs are, of
course, not concerned with this. Selection of the free link is done
by the higher priority HOST.

File-like links are distinguished by the fact that no searching for
interrupt characters takes place and buffering techniques appropriate
for the higher data rates takes place.

A Summary of Primitives

Each HOST operating systems must provide at least the following
primitives to its users. This list knows not to be necessary but not
sufficient.

a)   Initiate TTY-like connection with HOST x.

b)   Terminate connection.

c)   Send/Receive character(s) over TTY-like connection.

d)   Initiate file-like connection parallel to TTY-like connection.

e)   Terminate file-like connection.

f)   Send/Receive over file-like connection.

Error Checking

We propose that each message carry a message number, bit count, and a
checksum in its body, that is transparent to the IMP. For a checksum
we suggest a 16-bit end-around-carry sum computed on 1152 bits and
then circularly shifted right one bit. The right circular shift every
1152 bits is designed to catch errors in message reassembly by the IMPs.

Closer Interaction

The above described primitives suggest how a user can make simple use
of a remote facility. They shed no light on how much more intricate
use of the network is to be carried out. Specifically, we are
concerned with the fact that as some sites a great deal of work has
gone into making the computer highly responsive to a sophisticated
console. Culler's consoles at UCSB and Englebart's at SRI are at
least two examples. It is clear that delays of a half-second or so
for trivial echo-like responses degrade the interaction to the point
of making the sophistication of the console irrelevant.

We believe that most console interaction can be divided into two

parts, an essentially local, immediate and trivial part and a remote,
more lengthy and significant part. As a simple example, consider a
user at a console consisting of a keyboard and refreshing display
screen. The program the user is talking typing into accumulates a
string of characters until a carriage return is encountered and then
it processes the string. While characters are being typed, it
displays the characters on the screen. When a rubout character is
typed, it deletes the previous non-rubout character. If the user
types H E L L O <- <- P <CR> where <- is rubout and <CR> is
carriage-return, he has made nine keystrokes. If each of these
keystrokes causes a message to be sent which in return invokes
instructions to our display station we will quickly become bored.

A better solution would be to have the front-end of the remote program
-- that is the part scanning for <- and <CR> -- be resident in our
computer. In that case, only one five character message would be
sent, i.e., H E L P <CR>, and the screen would be managed locally.

We propose to implement this solution by creating a language for
console control. This language, current named DEL, would be used by
subsystem designers to specify what components are needed in a
terminal and how the terminal is to respond to inputs from its
keyboard, Lincoln Wand, etc. Then, as a part of the initial protocol,
the remote HOST would send to the local HOST, the source language text
of the program which controls the console. This program would have
been by the subsystem designer in DEL, but will be compiled locally.

The specifications of DEL are under discussion. The following
diagrams show the sequence of actions.

A. Before Link Establishment

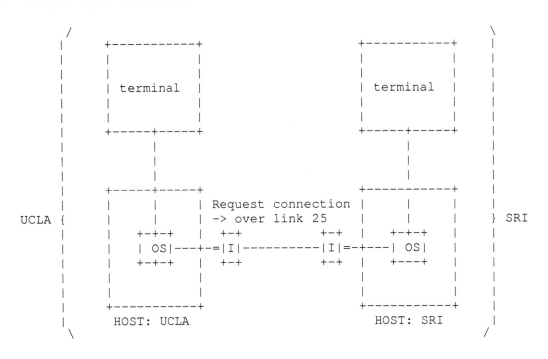

b. After Link Establishment and Log-in

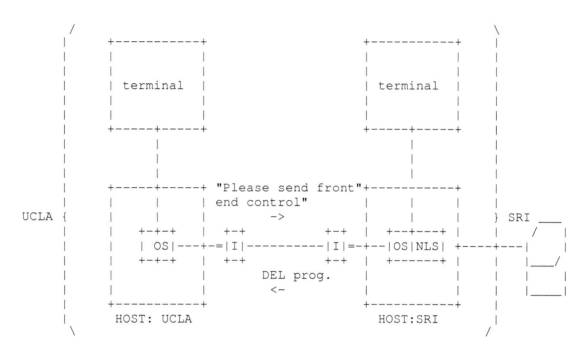

c. After Receipt and Compilation of the DEL program

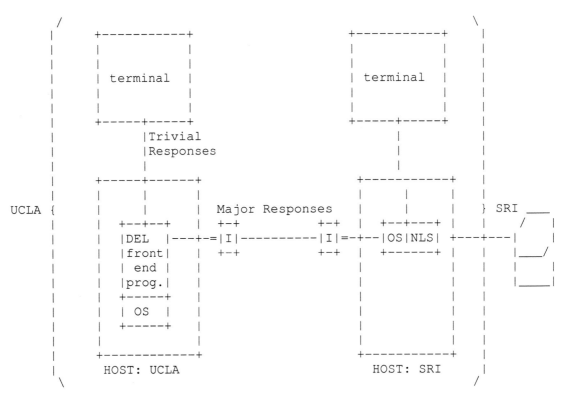

Open Questions

   1. If the IMPs do code conversion, the checksum will not be correct.

   2. The procedure for requesting the DEL front end is not yet
   specified.

IV. Initial Experiments

Experiment One

   SRI is currently modifying their on-line retrieval system which will
   be the major software component on the Network Documentation Center so
   that it can be operated with model 35 teletypes. The control of the
   teletypes will be written in DEL. All sites will write DEL compilers
   and use NLS through the DEL program.

Experiment Two

Crocker   [Page 10]

SRI will write a DEL front end for full NLS, graphics included. UCLA
and UTAH will use NLS with graphics.

        [This RFC was put into machine readable form for entry]
        [into the online RFC archives by Celeste Anderson 3/97]

Network Working Group   RFC Editor, et al.
Request for Comments: 2555   USC/ISI
Category: Informational   7 April 1999

30 Years of RFCs

Status of this Memo

   This memo provides information for the Internet community. It does
   not specify an Internet standard of any kind. Distribution of this
   memo is unlimited.

Table of Contents

1. Introduction - Robert Braden

   Thirty years ago today, the first Request for Comments document,
   RFC 1, was published at UCLA (ftp://ftp.isi.edu/in-notes/rfc1.txt).
   This was the first of a series that currently contains more than 2500
   documents on computer networking, collected, archived, and edited by
   Jon Postel for 28 years. Jon has left us, but this 30th anniversary
   tribute to the RFC series is assembled in grateful admiration for his
   massive contribution.

   The rest of this document contains a brief recollection from the
   present RFC Editor Joyce K. Reynolds, followed by recollections from
   three pioneers: Steve Crocker who wrote RFC 1, Vint Cerf whose long-
   range vision continues to guide us, and Jake Feinler who played a key
   role in the middle years of the RFC series.

2. Reflections - Joyce K. Reynolds

   A very long time ago when I was dabbling in IP network number and
   protocol parameter assignments with Jon Postel, gateways were still
   "dumb", the Exterior Gateway Protocol (EGP) was in its infancy and
   TOPS-20 was in its heyday. I was aware of the Request for Comments
   (RFCs) document series, with Jon as the RFC Editor. I really didn't
   know much of the innerworkings of what the task entailed. It was
   Jon's job and he quietly went about publishing documents for the
   ARPANET community.

   Meanwhile, Jon and I would have meetings in his office to go over our
   specific tasks of the day. One day, I began to notice that a pile of
   folders sitting to one side of his desk seemed to be growing. A few
   weeks later the pile had turned into two stacks of folders. I asked
   him what they were. Apparently, they contained documents for RFC
   publication. Jon was trying to keep up with the increasing quantity
   of submissions for RFC publication.

   I mentioned to him one day that he should learn to let go of some of
   his work load and task it on to other people. He listened intently,
   but didn't comment. The very next day, Jon wheeled a computer stand
   into my office which was stacked with those documents from his desk
   intended for RFC publication. He had a big Cheshire cat grin on his
   face and stated, "I'm letting go!", and walked away.

   At the top of the stack was a big red three ring notebook. Inside
   contained the "NLS Textbook", which was prepared at ISI by Jon, Lynne
   Sims and Linda Sato for use on ISI's TENEX and TOPS-20 systems. Upon
   reading its contents, I learned that the NLS system was designed to
   help people work with information on a computer. It included a wide
   range of tools, from a simple set of commands for writing, reading

and printing documents to sophisticated methods for retrieving and communication information. NLS was the system Jon used to write, edit and create the RFCs. Thus began my indoctrination to the RFC publication series.

Operating systems and computers have changed over the years, but Jon's perseverance about the consistency of the RFC style and quality of the documents remained true. Unfortunately, Jon did not live to see the 30th Anniversary of this series that he unfailingly nurtured. Yet, the spirit of the RFC publication series continues as we approach the new millennium. Jon would be proud.

3. The First Pebble: Publication of RFC 1 - Steve Crocker

RFC 1, "Host Software", issued thirty years ago on April 7, 1969 outlined some thoughts and initial experiments. It was a modest and entirely forgettable memo, but it has significance because it was part of a broad initiative whose impact is still with us today.

At the time RFC 1 was written, the ARPANET was still under design. Bolt, Beranek and Newman had won the all-important contract to build and operate the Interface Message Processors or "IMPs", the forerunners of the modern routers. They were each the size of a refrigerator and cost about $100,000 in 1969 dollars.

The network was scheduled to be deployed among the research sites supported by ARPA's Information Processing Techniques Office (IPTO). The first four nodes were to be at UCLA, SRI, University of California, Santa Barbara and University of Utah. The first installation, at UCLA, was set for September 1, 1969.

Although there had been considerable planning of the topology, leased lines, modems and IMPs, there was little organization or planning regarding network applications. It was assumed the research sites would figure it out. This turned out to be a brilliant management decision at ARPA.

Previously, in the summer of 1968, a handful of graduate students and staff members from the four sites were called together to discuss the forthcoming network. There was only a basic outline. BBN had not yet won the contract, and there was no technical specification for the network's operation. At the first meeting, we scheduled future meetings at each of the other laboratories, thus setting the stage for today's thrice yearly movable feast. Over the next couple of years, the group grew substantially and we found ourselves with overflow crowds of fifty to a hundred people at Network Working Group meetings. Compared to modern IETF meetings all over the world with attendance in excess of 1,000 people and several dozen active working

groups, the early Network Working Groups were small and tame, but
they seemed large and only barely manageable at the time. One
tradition that doesn't seem to have changed at all is the spirit of
unrestrained participation in working group meetings.

Our initial group met a handful of times in the summer and fall of
1968 and winter 1969. Our earliest meetings were unhampered by
knowledge of what the network would look like or how it would
interact with the hosts. Depending on your point of view, this
either allowed us or forced us to think about broader and grander
topics. We recognized we would eventually have to get around to
dealing with message formats and other specific details of low-level
protocols, but our first thoughts focused on what applications the
network might support. In our view, the 50 kilobit per second
communication lines being used for the ARPANET seemed slow, and we
worried that it might be hard to provide high-quality interactive
service across the network. I wish we had not been so accurate!

When BBN issued its Host-IMP specification in spring 1969, our
freedom to wander over broad and grand topics ended. Before then,
however, we tried to consider the most general designs and the most
exciting applications. One thought that captured our imagination was
the idea of downloading a small interpretative program at the
beginning of a session. The downloaded program could then control
the interactions and make efficient use of the narrow bandwidth
between the user's local machine and the back-end system the user was
interacting with. Jeff Rulifson at SRI was the prime mover of this
line of thinking, and he took a crack at designing a Decode-Encode
Language (DEL) [RFC 5]. Michel Elie, visiting at UCLA from France,
worked on this idea further and published Proposal for a Network
Interchange Language (NIL) [RFC 51]. The emergence of Java and
ActiveX in the last few years finally brings those early ideas to
fruition, and we're not done yet. I think we will continue to see
striking advances in combining communication and computing.

I have already suggested that the early RFCs and the associated
Network Working Group laid the foundation for the Internet
Engineering Task Force. Two all-important aspects of the early work
deserve mention, although they're completely evident to anyone who
participates in the process today. First, the technical direction we
chose from the beginning was an open architecture based on multiple
layers of protocol. We were frankly too scared to imagine that we
could define an all-inclusive set of protocols that would serve
indefinitely. We envisioned a continual process of evolution and
addition, and obviously this is what's happened.

The RFCs themselves also represented a certain sense of fear. After several months of meetings, we felt obliged to write down our thoughts. We parceled out the work and wrote the initial batch of memos. In addition to participating in the technical design, I took on the administrative function of setting up a simple scheme for numbering and distributing the notes. Mindful that our group was informal, junior and unchartered, I wanted to emphasize these notes were the beginning of a dialog and not an assertion of control.

It's now been thirty years since the first RFCs were issued. At the time, I believed the notes were temporary and the entire series would die off in a year or so once the network was running. Thanks to the spectacular efforts of the entire community and the perseverance and dedication of Jon Postel, Joyce Reynolds and their crew, the humble series of Requests for Comments evolved and thrived. It became the mainstay for sharing technical designs in the Internet community and the archetype for other communities as well. Like the Sorcerer's Apprentice, we succeeded beyond our wildest dreams and our worst fears.

4. RFCs - The Great Conversation - Vint Cerf

A long time ago, in a network far, far away...

Considering the movement of planet Earth around the Sun and the Sun around the Milky Way galaxy, that first network IS far away in the relativistic sense. It takes 200 million years for the Sun to make its way around the galaxy, so thirty years is only an eyeblink on the galactic clock. But what a marvelous thirty years it has been! The RFCs document the odyssey of the ARPANET and, later, the Internet, as its creators and netizens explore, discover, build, re-build, argue and resolve questions of design, concepts and applications of computer networking.

It has been ultimately fascinating to watch the transformation of the RFCs themselves from their earliest, tentative dialog form to today's much more structured character. The growth of applications such as email, bulletin boards and the world wide web have had much to do with that transformation, but so has the scale and impact of the Internet on our social and economic fabric. As the Internet has taken on greater economic importance, the standards documented in the RFCs have become more important and the RFCs more formal. The dialog has moved to other venues as technology has changed and the working styles have adapted.

Hiding in the history of the RFCs is the history of human
institutions for achieving cooperative work. And also hiding in that
history are some heroes that haven't been acknowledged. On this
thirtieth anniversary, I am grateful for the opportunity to
acknowledge some of them. It would be possible to fill a book with
such names - mostly of the authors of the RFCs, but as this must be a
brief contribution, I want to mention four of them in particular:
Steve Crocker, Jon Postel, Joyce K. Reynolds and Bob Braden.

Steve Crocker is a modest man and would likely never make the
observation that while the contents of RFC 1 might have been entirely
forgettable, the act of writing RFC 1 was indicative of the brave and
ultimately clear-visioned leadership that he brought to a journey
into the unknown. There were no guides in those days - computer
networking was new and few historical milestones prepared us for what
lay ahead. Steve's ability to accommodate a diversity of views, to
synthesize them into coherence and, like Tom Sawyer, to persuade
others that they wanted to devote their time to working on the
problems that lay in the path of progress can be found in the early
RFCs and in the Network Working Group meetings that Steve led.

In the later work on Internet, I did my best to emulate the framework
that Steve invented: the International Network Working Group (INWG)
and its INWG Notes, the Internet Working Group and its Internet
Experiment Notes (IENs) were brazen knock-offs of Steve's
organizational vision and style.

It is doubtful that the RFCs would be the quality body of material
they are today were it not for Jonathan Postel's devotion to them
from the start. Somehow, Jon knew, even thirty years ago that it
might be important to document what was done and why, to say nothing
of trying to capture the debate for the benefit of future networkers
wondering how we'd reached some of the conclusions we did (and
probably shake their heads...).

Jon was the network's Boswell, but it was his devotion to quality and
his remarkable mix of technical and editing skills that permeate many
of the more monumental RFCs that dealt with what we now consider the
TCP/IP standards. Many bad design decisions were re-worked thanks to
Jon's stubborn determination that we all get it "right" - as the
editor, he simply would not let something go out that didn't meet his
personal quality filter. There were times when we moaned and
complained, hollered and harangued, but in the end, most of the time,
Jon was right and we knew it.

Joyce K. Reynolds was at Jon's side for much of the time that Jon was
the RFC editor and as has been observed, they functioned in unison
like a matched pair of superconducting electrons - and
superconductors they were of the RFC series. For all practical
purposes, it was impossible to tell which of the two had edited any
particular RFC. Joyce's passion for quality has matched Jon's and
continues to this day. And she has the same subtle, puckish sense of
humor that emerged at unexpected moments in Jon's stewardship. One
example that affected me personally was Joyce's assignment of number
2468 to the RFC written to remember Jon. I never would have thought
of that, and it was done so subtly that it didn't even ring a bell
until someone sent me an email asking whether this was a coincidence.
In analog to classical mystery stories, the editor did it.

Another unsung hero in the RFC saga is Bob Braden - another man whose
modesty belies contributions of long-standing and monumental
proportions. It is my speculation that much of the quality of the
RFCs can be traced to consultations among the USC/ISI team, including
Jon, Joyce and Bob among others. Of course, RFC 1122 and 1123 stand
as two enormous contributions to the clarity of the Internet
standards. For that task alone, Bob deserves tremendous appreciation,
but he has led the End-to-End Research Group for many years out of
which has come some of the most important RFCs that refine our
understanding of optimal implementation of the protocols, especially
TCP.

When the RFCs were first produced, they had an almost 19th century
character to them - letters exchanged in public debating the merits
of various design choices for protocols in the ARPANET. As email and
bulletin boards emerged from the fertile fabric of the network, the
far-flung participants in this historic dialog began to make
increasing use of the online medium to carry out the discussion -
reducing the need for documenting the debate in the RFCs and, in some
respects, leaving historians somewhat impoverished in the process.
RFCs slowly became conclusions rather than debates.

Jon permitted publication of items other than purely technical
documents in this series. Hence one finds poetry, humor (especially
the April 1 RFCs which are as funny today as they were when they were
published), and reprints of valuable reference material mixed into
the documents prepared by the network working groups.

In the early 1970s, the Advanced Research Projects Agency was
conducting several parallel research programs into packet switching
technology, after the stunning success of this idea in the ARPANET.
Among these were the Packet Radio Network, the Atlantic Packet
Satellite Network and the Internet projects. These each spawned note
series akin to but parallel to the RFCs. PRNET Notes, ARPA Satellite

System Notes (bearing the obvious and unfortunate acronym...),
Internet Experiment Notes (IENs), and so on. After the Internet
protocols were mandated to be used on the ARPANET and other DARPA-
sponsored networks in January 1983 (SATNET actually converted before
that), Internet- related notes were merged into the RFC series. For a
time, after the Internet project seemed destined to bear fruit, IENs
were published in parallel with RFCs. A few voices, Danny Cohen's in
particular (who was then at USC/ISI with Jon Postel) suggested that
separate series were a mistake and that it would be a lot easier to
maintain and to search a single series. Hindsight seems to have
proven Danny right as the RFC series, with its dedicated editors,
seems to have borne the test of time far better than its more
ephemeral counterparts.

As the organizations associated with Internet continued to evolve,
one sees the RFCs adapting to changed circumstances. Perhaps the most
powerful influence can be seen from the evolution of the Internet
Engineering Task Force from just one of several task forces whose
chairpersons formed the Internet Activities Board to the dominant,
global Internet Standards development organization, managed by its
Internet Engineering Steering Group and operating under the auspices
of the Internet Society. The process of producing "standards-track"
RFCs is now far more rigorous than it once was, carries far more
impact on a burgeoning industry, and has spawned its own, relatively
informal "Internet Drafts" series of short-lived documents forming
the working set of the IETF working groups.

The dialogue that once characterized the early RFCs has given way to
thrice-annual face-to-face meetings of the IETF and enormous
quantities of email, as well as a growing amount of group-interactive
work through chat rooms, shared white boards and even more elaborate
multicast conferences. The parallelism and the increasing quantity of
transient dialogue surrounding the evolution of the Internet has made
the task of technology historians considerably more difficult,
although one can sense a counter-balancing through the phenomenal
amount of information accumulating in the World Wide Web. Even casual
searches often turn up some surprising and sometimes embarrassing old
memoranda - a number of which were once paper but which have been
rendered into bits by some enterprising volunteer.

The RFCs, begun so tentatively thirty years ago, and persistently
edited and maintained by Jon Postel and his colleagues at USC/ISI,
tell a remarkable story of exploration, achievement, and dedication
by a growing mass of internauts who will not sleep until the Internet
truly is for everyone. It is in that spirit that this remembrance is
offered, and in particular, in memory of our much loved colleague,
Jon Postel, without whose personal commitment to this archive, the
story might have been vastly different and not nearly as remarkable.

5. Reflecting on 30 years of RFCs - Jake Feinler

By now we know that the first RFC was published on April 7, 1969 by
Steve Crocker. It was entitled "Host Software". The second RFC was
published on April 9, 1969 by Bill Duvall of SRI International (then
called Stanford Research Institute or SRI), and it too was entitled
"Host Software". RFC 2 was a response to suggestions made in RFC 1-
-and so the dialog began.

Steve proposed 2 experiments in RFC 1:

"1) SRI is currently modifying their on-line retrieval system which
will be the major software component of the Network Documentation
Center [or The SRI NIC as it soon came to be known] so that it can be
modified with Model 35 teletypes. The control of the teletypes will
be written in DEL [Decode-Encode Language]. All sites will write DEL
compilers and use NLS [SRI Doug Engelbart's oNLine System] through
the DEL program".

"2) SRI will write a DEL front end for full NLS, graphics included.
UCLA and UTAH will use NLS with graphics".

RFC 2, issued 2 days later, proposed detailed procedures for
connecting to the NLS documentation system across the network. Steve
may think RFC 1 was an "entirely forgettable" document; however, as
an information person, I beg to differ with him. The concepts
presented in this first dialog were mind boggling, and eventually led
to the kind of network interchange we are all using on the web today.
(Fortunately, we have graduated beyond DEL and Model 35 teletypes!)

RFC 1 was, I believe, a paper document. RFC 2 was produced online
via the SRI NLS system and was entered into the online SRI NLS
Journal. However, it was probably mailed to each recipient via snail
mail by the NIC, as email and the File Transfer Protocol (FTP) had
not yet been invented.

RFC 3, again by Steve Crocker, was entitled, "Documentation
Conventions;" and we see that already the need for a few ground rules
was surfacing. More ground-breaking concepts were introduced in this
RFC. It stated that:

"The Network Working Group (NWG) is concerned with the HOST software,
the strategies for using the network, and the initial experiments
with the network. Documentation of the NWG's effort is through notes
such as this. Notes may be produced at any site by anybody and
included in this series".

381

It goes on to say:

"The content of a NWG note may be any thought, suggestion,
etc.related to the Host software or other aspect of the network.
Notes are encouraged to be timely rather than polished.
Philosophical positions without examples or other specifics, specific
suggestions or implementation techniques without introductory or
background explanation, and explicit questions without any attempted
answers are all acceptable. The minimum length for a NWG note is one
sentence".

"These standards (or lack of them) are stated explicitly for two
reasons. First, there is a tendency to view a written statement as
discussion of considerably less than authoritative ideas. Second,
there is a natural hesitancy to publish something unpolished, and we
hope to ease this inhibition".

Steve asked that this RFC be sent to a distribution list consisting
of:

        Bob Kahn, BBN
        Larry Roberts, ARPA
        Steve Carr, UCLA
        Jeff Rulifson, UTAH
        Ron Stoughton, UCSB
        Steve Crocker, UCLA

Thus by the time the third RFC was published, many of the concepts of
how to do business in this new networking environment had been
established--there would be a working group of implementers (NWG)
actually discussing and trying things out; ideas were to be free-
wheeling; communications would be informal; documents would be
deposited (online when possible) at the NIC and distributed freely to
members of the working group; and anyone with something to contribute
could come to the party. With this one document a swath was
instantly cut through miles of red tape and pedantic process. Was
this radical for the times or what! And we were only up to RFC 3!

Many more RFCs followed and the SRI NLS Journal became the
bibliographic search service of the ARPANET. It differed from other
search services of the time in one important respect: when you got a
"hit" searching the journal online, not only did you get a citation
telling you such things as the author and title; you got an
associated little string of text called a "link". If you used a
command called "jump to link", voila! you got the full text of the
document. You did not have to go to the library, or send an order
off to an issuing agency to get a copy of the document, as was the
custom with other search services of the time. The whole document

itself was right there immediately!

Also, any document submitted to the journal could not be changed.
New versions could be submitted, and these superceded old versions,
but again the new versions could not be changed. Each document was
given a unique identifying number, so it was easy to track. These
features were useful in a fast-moving environment. Documents often
went through several drafts before they were finally issued as an RFC
or other official document, and being able to track versions was very
useful.

The SRI NLS Journal was revolutionary for the time; however, access
to it online presented several operational problems. Host computers
were small and crowded, and the network was growing by leaps and
bounds; so connections had to be timed out and broken to give
everyone a chance at access. Also, the rest of the world was still a
paper world (and there were no scanners or laser printers, folks!),
so the NIC still did a brisk business sending out paper documents to
requestors.

By 1972 when I became Principal Investigator for the NIC project, the
ARPANET was growing rapidly, and more and more hosts were being
attached to it. Each host was required to have a technical contact
known as the Technical Liaison, and most of the Liaison were also
members of the NWG. Each Liaison was sent a set of documents by the
NIC called "functional documents" which included the Protocol
Handbook (first issued by BBN and later published by the NIC.) The
content of the Protocol Handbook was made up of key RFCs and a
document called "BBN 1822" which specified the Host-to-Imp protocol.

The NWG informed the NIC as to which documents should be included in
the handbook; and the NIC assembled, published, and distributed the
book. Alex McKenzie of BBN helped the NIC with the first version of
the handbook, but soon a young fellow, newly out of grad school,
named Jon Postel joined the NWG and became the NIC's contact and
ARPA's spokesperson for what should be issued in the Protocol
Handbook.

No one who is familiar with the RFCs can think of them without
thinking of Dr. Jonathan Postel. He was "Mister RFC" to most of us.
Jon worked at SRI in the seventies and had the office next to mine.
We were both members of Doug Engelbart's Augmentation Research
Center. Not only was Jon a brilliant computer scientist, he also
cared deeply about the process of disseminating information and
establishing a methodology for working in a networking environment.
We often had conversations way into the wee hours talking about ways
to do this "right". The network owes Jon a debt of gratitude for his
dedication to the perpetuation of the RFCs. His work, along with

that of his staff, the NWG, the IETF, the various NICs, and CNRI to
keep this set of documents viable over the years was, and continues
to be, a labor of love.

Jon left SRI in 1976 to join USC-ISI, but by that time the die was
cast, and the RFCs, NWG, Liaison, and the NIC were part of the
network's way of doing business. However, the SRI NLS Journal system
was becoming too big for its host computer and could not handle the
number of users trying to access it. Email and FTP had been
implemented by now, so the NIC developed methodology for delivering
information to users via distributed information servers across the
network. A user could request an RFC by email from his host computer
and have it automatically delivered to his mailbox. Users could also
purchase hardcopy subscriptions to the RFCs and copies of the
Protocol Handbook, if they did not have network access.

The NIC worked with Jon, ARPA, DCA, NSF, other NICs, and other
agencies to have secondary reference sets of RFCs easily accessible
to implementers throughout the world. The RFCs were also shared
freely with official standards bodies, manufacturers and vendors,
other working groups, and universities. None of the RFCs were ever
restricted or classified. This was no mean feat when you consider
that they were being funded by DoD during the height of the Cold War.

Many of us worked very hard in the early days to establish the RFCs
as the official set of technical notes for the development of the
Internet. This was not an easy job. There were suggestions for many
parallel efforts and splinter groups. There were naysayers all along
the way because this was a new way of doing things, and the ARPANET
was "coloring outside the lines" so to speak. Jon, as Editor-in-
Chief was criticized because the RFCs were not issued by an
"official" standards body, and the NIC was criticized because it was
not an "official" document issuing agency. We both strived to marry
the new way of doing business with the old, and fortunately were
usually supported by our government sponsors, who themselves were
breaking new ground.

Many RFCs were the end result of months of heated discussion and
implementation. Authoring one of them was not for the faint of
heart. Feelings often ran high as to what was the "right" way to go.
Heated arguments sometimes ensued. Usually they were confined to
substance, but sometimes they got personal. Jon would often step in
and arbitrate. Eventually the NWG or the Sponsors had to say, "It's
a wrap. Issue a final RFC". Jon, as Editor-in-Chief of the RFCs,
often took merciless flak from those who wanted to continue
discussing and implementing, or those whose ideas were left on the
cutting room floor. Somehow he always managed to get past these
controversies with style and grace and move on. We owe him and

others, who served on the NWG or authored RFCs, an extreme debt of
gratitude for their contributions and dedication.

At no time was the controversy worse than it was when DoD adopted
TCP/IP as its official host-to-host protocols for communications
networks. In March 1982, a military directive was issued by the
Under Secretary of Defense, Richard DeLauer. It simply stated that
the use of TCP and IP was mandatory for DoD communications networks.
Bear in mind that a military directive is not something you discuss -
the time for discussion is long over when one is issued. Rather a
military directive is something you DO. The ARPANET and its
successor, the Defense Data Network, were military networks, so the
gauntlet was down and the race was on to prove whether the new
technology could do the job on a real operational network. You have
no idea what chaos and controversy that little 2-page directive
caused on the network. (But that's a story for another time.)
However, that directive, along with RFCs 791 and 793 (IP and TCP)
gave the RFCs as a group of technical documents stature and
recognition throughout the world. (And yes, TCP/IP certainly did do
the job!)

Jon and I were both government contractors, so of course followed the
directions of our contracting officers. He was mainly under contract
to ARPA, whereas the NIC was mainly under contract to DCA. BBN was
another key contractor. For the most part we all worked as a team.
However, there was frequent turnover in military personnel assigned
to both the ARPANET and the DDN, and we all collaborated to try to
get all the new participants informed as to what was available to
them when they joined the network. We also tried to foster
collaboration rather than duplication of effort, when it was
appropriate. The NWG (or IETF as it is now known) and the RFCs
became the main vehicles for interagency collaboration as the DoD
protocols began to be used on other government, academic, and
commercial networks.

I left SRI and the NIC project in 1989. At that time there were
about 30,000 hosts on what was becoming known as the Internet, and
just over a 1000 RFCs had been issued. Today there are millions of
hosts on the Internet, and we are well past the 3000 mark for RFCs.
It was great fun to be a part of what turned out to be a
technological revolution. It is heartwarming to see that the RFCs
are still being issued by the IETF, and that they are still largely
based on ideas that have been discussed and implemented; that the
concepts of online working groups and distributed information servers
are a way of life; that those little "links" (officially known as
hypertext) have revolutionized the delivery of documents; and that
the government, academia, and business are now all playing the same
game for fun and profit. (Oh yes, I'm happy to see that Steve's idea

for integrated text and graphics has finally come to fruition,
although that work took a little longer than 2 days.)

6. Favorite RFCs -- The First 30 Years - Celeste Anderson

   Five years ago, Jon Postel and I had wanted to publish a 25th RFC
   anniversary book, but, alas, we were both too busy working on other
   projects. We determined then that we should commemorate the
   thirtieth anniversary by collecting together thirty "RFC Editors'
   Choice" RFCs based on original ideas expressed throughout the first
   30 years of their existence.

   Jon's untimely death in October 1998 prevented us from completing
   this goal. We did, however, start to put online some of the early
   RFCs, including RFC 1. We weren't sure whether we were going to try
   to make them look as close to the typewritten originals as possible,
   or to make a few adjustments and format them according to the latest
   RFC style. Those of you who still have your copies of RFC 1 will
   note the concessions we made to NROFF the online version. The hand-
   drawn diagrams of the early RFCs also present interesting challenges
   for conversion into ASCII format.

   There are still opportunities to assist the RFC Editor to put many of
   the early RFCs online. Check the URL:
   http://www.rfc-editor.org/rfc-online.html for more information on this
   project.

   In memory of Jon, we are compiling a book for publication next year
   of "Favorite RFCs -- The First 30 Years".

   We have set up a web interface at

           http://www.rfc-editor.org/voterfc.html

   for tabulating votes and recording the responses. We will accept
   email as well. Please send your email responses to: voterfc@isi.edu.
   We prefer votes accompanied by explanations for the vote choice.

   We reserve the right to add to the list several RFCs that Jon Postel
   had already selected for the collection. Voting closes December 31,
   1999.

7. Security Considerations

   Security issues are not discussed in this commemorative RFC.

8. Acknowledgments

   Thank you to all the authors who contributed to this RFC on short
   notice. Thanks also to Fred Baker and Eve Schooler who goaded us
   into action. A special acknowledgment to Eitetsu Baumgardner, a
   student at USC, who NROFFed this document and who assisted in the
   formatting of RFCs 1, 54, and 62, converting hand-drawn diagrams into
   ASCII format.

9. Authors' Addresses

   Robert Braden
   USC/Information Sciences Institute
   4676 Admiralty Way #1001
   Marina del Rey, CA 90292

   Phone: +1 310-822-1511
   Fax: +1 310 823 6714
   EMail: braden@isi.edu

   Joyce K. Reynolds
   USC/Information Sciences Institute
   4676 Admiralty Way #1001
   Marina del Rey, CA 90292

   Phone: +1 310-822-1511
   Fax: +1 310-823-6714
   EMail: jkrey@isi.edu

   Steve Crocker
   Steve Crocker Associates, LLC
   5110 Edgemoor Lane
   Bethesda, MD 20814

   Phone: +1 301-654-4569
   Fax: +1 202-478-0458
   EMail: crocker@mbl.edu

Vint Cerf
MCI

EMail: vcerf@mci.net

Jake Feinler
SRI Network Information Center
1972-1989

EMail: feinler@juno.com

Celeste Anderson
USC/Information Sciences Institute
4676 Admiralty Way #1001
Marina del Rey, CA 90292

Phone: +1 310-822-1511
Fax: +1 310-823-6714
EMail: celeste@isi.edu

388

10. APPENDIX - RFC 1

    The cover page said at the top:

      "Network Working Group
       Request for Comments"

    and then came an internal UCLA distribution list:

      V. Cerf, S. Crocker, M. Elie, G. Estrin, G. Fultz, A. Gomez,
      D. Karas, L. Kleinrock, J. Postel, M. Wingfield, R. Braden,
      and W. Kehl.

    followed by an "Off Campus" distribution list:

      A. Bhushan (MIT), S. Carr (Utah), G. Cole (SDC), W. English (SRI),
      K. Fry (Mitre), J. Heafner (Rand), R. Kahn (BBN), L. Roberts (ARPA),
      P. Rovner (MIT), and R. Stoughton (UCSB).

    The following title page had

      "Network Working Group
       Request for Comments: 1"

    at the top, and then:

            HOST SOFTWARE

            STEVE CROCKER
            7 APRIL 1969

11. Full Copyright Statement

   Copyright (C) The Internet Society (1999). All Rights Reserved.

The ARPANET Sourcebook
The Unpublished Foundations of the Internet

A compilation of seminal papers, reports, and RFCs (most appearing in book form for the first time) from the period when computer networking was being born.

Part A, "Planning the ARPANET", covers the initial period when network feasibility was being studied and includes the classic "The Computer as a Communication Device" (J.C.R. Licklider and Robert Taylor, 1968), a 1968 SRI (Menlo Park, CA) feasibility study, the earliest RFCs (some of which have never before been available), and Forewords by Steve Crocker (author of RFC #1) and Leonard Kleinrock (noted author and head of the UCLA computing lab where the first ARPANET node was installed).

Part B, "Building the ARPANET", reproduces the quarterly technical reports from the government's contractor Bolt Beranek and Newman (Boston) describing contemporaneously the development group's progress, difficulties encountered, and final (on-deadline) success. Dave Walden, former VP of Bolt Beranek and Newman and a key member of the ARPANET team, has also contributed a retrospective Foreword.

A final Appendix includes RFC 51, "Proposal for a Network Interchange Language" (a long-forgotten document that anticipates JAVA by 20+ years!) and a few ARPANET history essays reprinted from Matrix News.

AUTHOR: Peter H Salus (Editor)
PAGES: 400 pages
ISBN-13: 978-1-57398-000-5
PRICE: $59.95 US; $89.95 CAN
Due May 2007

Lion's Commentary on UNIX

"The Lions book", the underground classic cherished by UNIX hackers and widely circulated as a photocopied bootleg document since the late 1970's, is really two works in one:

- The complete source code to an early version of the UNIX operating system, a treasure in itself (this is basically the pristine code which earned Dennis Ritchie and Ken Thompson, the two earliest developers of UNIX, the Turing award).
- A brilliant commentary on that code by Prof. John Lions

Lions' marriage of source code with commentary was originally used as an operating systems textbook, and it remains ideally suited for that purpose (MIT was still using it as a text in 2005!). As a self-study UNIX conceptual tutorial, it has informed and inspired computer professionals and advanced operating system students for over twenty years.

An international "who's who" of UNIX wizards, including Ritchie and Thompson, have contributed essays extolling its merits and importance. Besides being as chic as a computer book can be, "The Lions book" remains the most respected operating system book ever published.

AUTHOR: John Lions
PAGES: 254 pages
ISBN-13: 1-57398-013-7
PRICE: $39.95 US, $57.95 CAN

Save your sanity.

Stop Working Late and Start Working Smart

Time
Management
for System Administrators

O'REILLY®

Thomas A. Limoncelli

Time Management for Systems Administrators

by Thomas A. Limoncelli
ISBN 0-596-00783-3, 226 pages
$24.95 US / $34.95 CAN
November 2005

You're bombarded with user requests, long-term projects from managers, and finicky computers. You've mastered the technical aspects of your job, but still work late nights and weekends just to keep up. How do you cope? In *Time Management for System Administrators*, author Tom Limoncelli offers real-world strategies to help you manage interruptions, prioritize tasks, eliminate time-wasters, document and automate processes for faster execution, and much more.

These aren't ivory tower platitudes, but practical advice from the trenches. Save your sanity. Pick up a copy today.

O'REILLY®

Spreading the knowledge of innovators

www.oreilly.com

Thomas A. Limoncelli

Christina J. Hogan

Strata R. Chalup

The Practice of System and Network Administration

Second Edition

The industry standard for best practices in system administration, updated to address today's challenges

This book covers 36 key areas of system administration: from desktops to data centers, from planning namespaces to networks, from security to service conversions; plus management topics from time management, to designing your organizational structure, to hiring and firing.

Chapters are divided into 'The Basics' and 'The Icing'. 'The Basics' discusses the essentials that sysadmins have to get right to avoid problems and added work down the road. 'The Icing' deals with the cool things that sysadmins can do to be spectacular. Material has been updated to reflect the changing IT landscape, and another five years of experience in the trenches. A lively, witty style and the use of anecdotes and case studies taken from the authors' personal experience all contribute to make this book an effective, instructive, and yet entertaining read. It's been called "*A Mentor in a Book*" and "*The best book in its class hands down.*" SAGE/LOPSA awarded it their 2005 Outstanding AchievementAward.

About the Authors

THOMAS A. LIMONCELLI has been a system administrator at companies big and small, including Google, Lumeta, and AT&T/Lucent Bell Labs. An internationally recognized speaker on a wide variety of IT topics, he is also the author of "*Time Management for System Administrators*" from O'Reilly.

STRATA R. CHALUP is the President of and founder of Virtual.Net, Inc, a strategic consulting firm specializing in helping small to midsize firms scale their IS practice and processes as they grow. She has introduced many SAs to web 2.0 technology and streamlined project management strategies via articles, talks, and tutorials. Strata completed her first year as Usenix's SAGE Programs Manager in December 2006.

CHRISTINA J. HOGAN is a system administrator with 10 years of experience. She completed her PhD at Imperial College, London and is currently working as an aerodynamicist for the BMW Sauber Formula 1 Racing Team.

ISBN: 0-321-49266-8 | $59.99

- Describes the best practice of system and network administration, regardless of platforms, technologies, or type of organization

- Includes extensive updates to existing chapters, plus n topics such as Storage, We Services, and Documentati

- Reorganized for better access to what you need: Foundation Elements, Cha Processes, Providing Servic Management Practices

- Goes beyond major princip and skillsets to address the 'soft skills' necessary in today's work place

FOR MORE INFORMATION PLEASE VISIT:
www.EverythingSysadmin.com
www.awprofessional.com/title/0321492668
Available wherever technical books are sold.

◆ Addison-Wesley

Breinigsville, PA USA
26 August 2010
244220BV00001B/20/A